FATHER ARSENY
A CLOUD OF WITNESSES

Also available from
ST VLADIMIR'S SEMINARY PRESS:

Father Arseny, 1893–1973:
Priest, Prisoner, Spiritual Father

FATHER ARSENY

A Cloud of Witnesses

Translated from the Russian by
VERA BOUTENEFF

ST VLADIMIR'S SEMINARY PRESS
CRESTWOOD, NEW YORK
2001

*The benefactors who have made this publication possible
wish to dedicate it in thanksgiving for their children,
Michael, David, King, Olivia, Karl and Sophia*

Library of Congress Cataloging-in-Publication Data

Otets Arsenii, Part 5. English
    Father Arseny : a cloud of witnesses / translated from the Russian by Vera Bouteneff.
      p.   cm.
    "First published in Russian as the 5th part of Otets Arsenii, fourth expanded
edition"—T.p. verso.
    ISBN 0-88141-232-5
    1. Arsenii, otets.   2. Russkaia pravoslavnaia tserkov'—Soviet Union—Clergy—
Biography.   3. Orthodox Eastern Church—Soviet Union—Clergy—Biography.
4. Persecution—Soviet Union.   I. Bouteneff, Vera.   II. Title.
    BX597.A74 O7413 2001
    281.9'092—dc21
    [B]

2001048510

FATHER ARSENY
A Cloud of Witnesses

Copyright © 2001 by Vera Bouteneff

ST VLADIMIR'S SEMINARY PRESS
575 Scarsdale Road, Crestwood, NY 10707
1-800-204-2665

First published in Russian as the 5th part of *Otets Arsenii*,
fourth expanded edition, St Tikhon's Orthodox Theological Institute Press,
Brotherhood of the All Merciful Savior, Moscow, 2000

ISBN 0-88141-232-5

Contents

Introduction

AFTER THE FIRST VOLUME appeared, several people wrote to me with different reactions and several of them asked where they could find a copy of the Russian text. I always answered that the only place I knew it to exist was in Russia. A young couple decided to go to Russia; they went to Rostov (not knowing this was the town where Father Arseny lived after he left the camp) and purchased two copies of the book: one for themselves and one for me. I was amazed to find that in this later edition there was a part that had been unknown when I started the first volume. Of course, I immediately started working on its translation.

The introduction to that latest edition mentioned that Father Arseny had been buried in Rostov, that there was a granite stone with his name, "Father Arseny," and his dates on it. Later it was mentioned that this stone had been stolen and that the exact place where he reposes is unknown, because his spiritual children are dead . . .

This made a strong impression on me and, after a short while, I decided that I wanted to erect a monument to Father Arseny so that people would know where to come and pray for him, or to him. After some research, it became clear to me that I should ask Father Vladimir Vorobiev (he was responsible for the book's publication in Russia; a very motivated, energetic and devoted man) to help me. We decided on the cost, and they started working . . .

My feeling was that I was not going to tell them what I wanted the monument to look like. The monument is in Russia, for the Russian people, they have to like it and it has to be close to their hearts. I was promised that it would be ready in May.

In May of 2001, I went to Russia with my eldest grandson, Eugene Sokoloff, and we found that the monument was indeed ready and was going to be installed on the 25th of May.

We left Moscow early that morning. It was drizzling, we were excited and moved . . .

As we approached Rostov, the clouds disappeared, the sun shone in a blue sky (just as in so many of Father Arseny's stories where the weather expresses the circumstances). We arrived at the cemetery right after the van in which Father Vladimir and the members of his parish had arrived. Some 75 to 100 people were there, among whom were many priests who had come from villages all around Rostov. When we arrived, five priests started vesting—white paschal garments. Tears of joy were rolling down my cheeks.

I saw the monument—simple, beautiful, sober, placed on a small platform just at the entrance to the cemetery, with big trees and green grass around it. A path led into the woods right behind the monument. My joy had no bounds.

First the priest blessed the monument, then a *panikhida* (memorial prayer service) was served, beautifully sung by the members of the parish of Father Vladimir. I was so happy to have my grandson with me to share in all this and to support me.

Many priests thanked me, saying that now they would know where to bring pilgrimages, that this monument would unite them in prayer. Thanks be to God!

A meal awaited us in the beautiful Rostov Kremlin, a jewel of the 11th to 14th centuries, which has already been almost completely restored. We visited the cathedral and then, as a gift, we were to hear the famous Rostov bells. They are the most famous bells in all Russia and are played only for great feasts—our Father Arseny well deserved to have them rung for him. A completely unforgettable experience.

It makes me so happy to share these blessings with you all, our readers!

The monument to Father Arseny in Rostov

Father Arseny

Some information about the life of Father Arseny
Translated from the third edition of the book (1998)

FATHER ARSENY WAS BORN in Moscow in 1894. In 1911 he finished secondary school and went to study in the Historical Philological Faculty of the Imperial University of Moscow. An eight-month-long illness in 1916 delayed his graduation from the university to 1917. During his time at university he wrote his first treatises on art with a focus on early Russian architecture. He then went to the Optina Pustyn Monastery where, after spending some time in spiritual search, he received the blessing to become a monk. It is possible that he also was tonsured a monk there. In 1919 he was ordained a priest (hieromonk) and took the position of third priest in one of the Moscow churches. (For this he had to obtain special permission from Patriarch Tikhon, since monks were generally not permitted to serve in parishes.)

At the beginning of 1921 Father Arseny became the second priest in the same church, and by the end of 1921, when the rector, Father Paul, was transferred (and then arrested), Father Arseny became the main priest of the parish. In the first eight years of his work he gathered together a community of respectable size and became their beloved pastor and confessor.

In 1927 Father Arseny was arrested for the first time and sent to the "northern regions." Two years later he returned, but was forbidden to live closer to Moscow than a hundred kilometers. In 1929 he again became a parish priest, though obviously not in Moscow. In 1931 he was arrested again and banished to the Vologda region for five years. Subsequently he was arrested for the third time, spent a year in prison and was again exiled.

After six years in a prison camp he received permission to live in the Vologda, Arkhangelsk and Vladimir regions. He was not allowed to serve in a church, so he held services at home. During this period he traveled in secret to Moscow several times. There he would meet with Bishop Afanassy (Sakharov) and would on occasion ask him to ordain to the priesthood several of his spiritual children. Father Arseny stayed secretly in touch with his spiritual flock.

In 1939 he was again sent to Siberia, then to the Ural. At the end of 1940 he was interned in the Ural Prison Camp. In March 1941 he was transferred to a Labor Camp. Here almost all correspondence and visits with his spiritual children ceased. In 1941 he was transferred to a "special camp" (one of strictest regime), where *all* correspondence and visits were strictly forbidden.

Father Arseny was freed from this camp only in 1958, whereupon he went to live in the town of Rostov the Great, in the house of Nadezhda Petrovna.

Father Arseny died in 1975 and was buried in the cemetery of Rostov. On his grave, a granite stone carries the simple inscription:

Father Arseny
1894–1975

❧ Love Your Neighbor ❧

A Talk

---·•·---

January 19, 1964

TALKS AFTER EVENING TEA were rather rare. Usually a few people would have come and Father Arseny would have had to talk with each one of them, listen to them, hear their confessions—and that took all his time. When he was ready to go to bed he would be truly exhausted, though before going to sleep he would still pray for a long time.

On normal days, there were rarely less than five people in Nadezhda Petrovna's house. On days off or on federal holidays, ten or twelve people would come! At such times Nadezhda Petrovna would get uneasy, since she well knew that if the local police decided to come and check, Father Arseny might be arrested.[1] But, thank God, during all the time he lived in this town that never happened—and he lived there seventeen years.

Every now and then, though rarely, everyone would sit quietly in the dining room and a talk would emerge naturally. It might emerge from a question asked by someone; or Father Arseny might ask one of the guests to share what he or she had lived through—something good, something that had brought him or her to God; then again, sometimes Father Arseny himself might tell about people he had met, events he had lived through, or his own thoughts. This is how all the memoirs that were later gathered came to be. Some of the memoirs were transcribed from the words of the narrator, others were written down by the narrator after Father Arseny had asked him or her to do so. Sometimes we had to wait a year or more to see the written text.

Everything that was written down was gathered together by A.B. and by Elizaveta Alexandrovna and was given for safekeeping to trustworthy people. These memoirs were the repository of the long lives of

---

[1] The Communist Party forbade gatherings of any sort because it feared conspiracy—so ten or twelve people could be considered "dangerous." —Trans.

our brothers and sisters, the spiritual children of Father Arseny; new ones also came after 1958.[2]

When Father Arseny asked his spiritual children to write their memoirs about the labor camp, he always requested them not to write in "camp lingo"; that is, no jargon, no slang. "Write without all this dirt, write in a cultured Russian style." I succeeded in writing down several of the talks that Father Arseny led: interesting and spiritually useful memoirs.

That day only eight friends were gathered around the table. People were talking about faith in God and love for one's neighbor. No one was arguing about anything, but people were simply talking: what is more important, deep faith or complete surrender of oneself to helping others?

Father Arseny was sitting in an armchair, slowly sipping his tea and stirring it occasionally with a little spoon. He listened to it all, then smiled and said: "Let us remember the words of our Lord Jesus Christ when the Pharisee asked him which was the most important commandment. Jesus told him, 'You shall love the Lord your God with all your heart, and with all your soul, and with all your mind. This is the greatest and first commandment. And a second is like it: You shall love your neighbor as yourself. On these two commandments hand all the law and the prophets' (Mt 22:36–40).

"The words of the Savior are so clear and definite about the love for God and for the neighbor that he does not deem we add anything. Still the Apostle James says: 'What good is it, my brothers and sisters, if you say you have faith but do not have works? Can faith save you?' (Jas 2:14).

"And later Paul says to the Corinthians, 'If I speak in tongues of mortals and of angels, but do not have love, I am a noisy gong or a clanging cymbal.' And then, 'If I have all faith, so as to remove mountains, but do not have love, I am nothing. If I give away all my posses-

---

[2]The year Father Arseny was freed from labor camp and came to live in Rostov.

sions, and if I hand over my body to be burned, but do not have love, I gain nothing' (Cor 13:1–3).

"Deep faith in God and love for your brother are inseparable," Father Arseny continued, "and if a man does good deeds, loves people, perhaps even gives his life for others but does not love God, does not believe in God, then, in spite of his goodness he is spiritually dead because he does not want to know God. I happen to have met such people. They may be good, warm-hearted, ready to give away their last piece of bread, but they are indifferent to God, not accepting of Him— they may even be God's enemies. And, you know, in spite of all their 'goodness' I could see something missing in their behavior, their character, their outlook on life: they had made a religion out of their own goodness, and for them that had replaced God."

And Father Arseny added: "I do not want to judge those who do good deeds but do not believe in God. I am only a hieromonk, I am not a learned theologian, I am only telling you what the Holy Fathers say . . ."

⊰ 2 ⊱

Father Ilarion

———•+•———

"IN THE COURSE OF my life as a pastor," said Father Arseny, "I happened to meet people who, by the grace of God, had the gift of insight and foresight. They were able to read in other people's souls everything they had done, and even see their future.

"In labor camp and in exile I saw the miraculous healing of totally hopeless, dying patients through the prayers of bishops, priests and monks. I saw hopeless cases, people who had lost all will, all physical strength, who were weakened by the loss of all desire to live. After the priest Valentin had prayed with them they changed completely, were healed, regained their will to live and left the camp before I did (and now they—already old—come and visit me). Father Valentin was a priest in one of the churches in Moscow and was shot on November 21, 1942. For a while I was with him in the same camp and the same barracks. He had a very strong prayer life and he helped other people.

"By the way, I was also condemned to be shot that November 21, the feast day of the Archangel Michael. In the morning, after the roll call, the convoy took me to the watch (the gate used to enter and leave the camp). They gathered together about twenty-five people, mostly priests and deacons, and one bishop. It was cold, the convoy was impatient, we were cold, but we started singing, 'It is meet to bless Thee, O Theotokos' and 'Holy God.' The guards said nothing: they knew that these would be our last words before dying. We knew they were going to take us to be shot in the big Voroni Ditch, which was where they used to shoot prisoners.

"About an hour went by while we were singing quietly. Suddenly a soldier ran in and ordered certain prisoners to come out, he shouted their numbers. He called my number. He called out five people in all and said, 'Quick! Go back to your barracks.' The others were led out, and in about fifteen minutes we heard the sound of machine guns. Why did they pull me out of this group of condemned prisoners? I do not know. This was God's will.

"Two more times while I was in labor camp they called me out to be shot with no notice, but each time, after long hours of waiting, they sent me back to my barracks or to work. God's ways are inscrutable!

"So they called me on January 19, 1943, the day of Epiphany, the Baptism of Christ, and then again on August 19, 1943, the day of Transfiguration. Of course this was all God's plan. He spared me from death, and here I am, sitting with you: this is God's gift to me, a sinner!

"Executions were called 'cleansings' by the administration, and they usually happened on the eve of Soviet feasts. People were brought together from different parts of the camp, there was no judging, people were simply gathered into a group, led out of the camp, and shot.

"On August 19, 1943, when they had gathered together a group of prisoners, we waited around for about two hours, and then suddenly a prisoner started laughing. At first he laughed quietly, then louder and louder. His laugh was resounding and happy. Those who were standing close to him tried to stop him, but without success. His laugh was contagious: two or three people joined him. The others, me included, prayed. You know," said Father Arseny, looking at us, "I was scared, but my soul hurt for these people who were going to die in a few minutes and who were spending their last minutes laughing. I prayed, crossing myself and blessing them with the sign of the cross; the others did the same. I heard that in our group there were two bishops, whom I did not know, they had been brought in from a faraway camp. Again they called my name to send me back to the barracks: why did they take me three times to be shot and then return me to the barracks? I do not know. To scare me? But the living conditions in the camp were almost the equivalent of being shot."

"I was a witness to miracles performed by highly spiritual people who had led a long life of prayer, helping others and serving as pastors. Living near them, receiving grace through them, I learned to pray and tried to be like them at least a little bit!

"I remember, as if he were now in front of my eyes, a country priest, Father Ilarion, whose monastic name was Ioan. He was small in stature, with a good face, lively eyes and a long white beard. I lived in exile almost two years in a village near Arkhangelsk, (a city on the White Sea, far to the north). The village was large, and you could see an old wooden church on top of a hill. It was amazingly beautiful, built in the old tradition of piety, with one flame-shaped-dome on top of the church and another one on the bell tower. These cupolas were covered with aspen shingles and, depending on the sun's light, were golden or silver-gray. The church was ancient, but still solid. When you entered you were amazed by the number of icons hanging on the walls. The icons had darkened with age but you could still see the faces of the saints very well. Though several oil lamps were always burning, it was rather dark, but when you entered you found yourself engulfed in prayer and you felt far away from the world with its vain bustle. The inside of the church was impeccably clean and candles would be burning, beeswax candles because other candles were not delivered from the big city— these were made by a young parishioner who loved coming to church. The choir had five or six women, and it was serious and prayerful. It was impossible not to pray when you entered this church. There were about fifty or sixty parishioners, both old and young.[3]

"Father Ilarion served exactly according to the rule, but he served in such a way that he completely captured the attention of the faithful and made them participants in the service. The creed, the 'Our Father' were sung by all with great joy. On Sundays and on feast days, after an unhurried confession, twelve to fifteen people would take communion. For a village church, that was a lot. They had no wine, so Father Ilarion used to prepare juice from raspberries, cranberries and honey but worried, 'Lord, you said to use the grape, and what am I doing? Will God forgive me?'

"In the beginning, I could not understand why all the parishioners listened so attentively to the service. I had served in many Moscow cathedrals with priests of great spirituality, but I had never seen such attention. But once I got caught up in Father Ilarion's serving, I understood, I comprehended—he was serving together with the people, he

---

[3]Everything Father Arseny describes seems "normal" to us. But it was an exception in Soviet Russia where such active parishes were usually shut down. It is a credit to Father Ilarion, who was risking his life to serve the way he felt he had to serve. —Trans.

was one of the people, he was not separate from them, he was with them, in them; and this is why a very special grace blessed and united them. For about sixty years after the Arkhangelsk seminary, Father Ilarion had served the liturgy daily in this same church of the Holy Trinity; he also gave short sermons with moral advice (even though in those days it was strictly forbidden to give sermons[4])—sixty years of uninterrupted daily contact with his parishioners. They all came to him for advice and instruction, and not only from this village, but also from neighboring ones.

"In the village Father Ilarion was deeply beloved, and people helped him and the church as best they could. Father Ilarion was poor. An old woman—Babushka Olga—looked after him. His house was spotlessly clean, icons hung on the walls, old ones, very beautiful ones. They were very primitive, such as you almost never see nowadays. The smell of dried flowers and herbs filled the house with a special aroma that mixed with the smell of wax candles. There were very few books on the shelves. Father Ilarion's wife had died about twenty years before, I believe it was in 1918. Five years after her death, with the permission of his bishop, he became a monk and took the name Ioan. He was tonsured in secret, so the parishioners kept on calling him Father Ilarion. He himself only told me of it a year after I arrived. He had two children: a son, Boris, killed in World War I, and a daughter who died in 1925. Only one granddaughter was left: she had become a doctor and was married to a doctor. Once a year she would come to visit Father Ilarion, look after him; she was always trying to convince him to go live with her in Yaroslavl (near Moscow). She said it was time for him to retire. I happened to be present at one of these conversations. Father Ilarion made the same answer every time: 'God called me to serve here, this is where I want to end my days, in the church of the Holy Trinity. The parishioners are tied to my soul; I will not leave them.'

"When I came to Arkhangelsk Father Ilarion was eighty years old, but he was very active and energetic, quick to undertake anything. He liked working as a carpenter and he raised bees for honey. On rare occa-

---

[4]The authorities were hoping to kill Orthodoxy by depriving it of the oxygen of learning. —Trans.

sions he would have to go to neighboring villages to serve *panihidas* or *molebens*[5]—and he would be sad because he would be unable to serve the liturgy on those days.

"I talk in such detail about Father Ilarion because I saw him serving and I saw his relationship with his parishioners. He was entirely absorbed in a deep faith in God and a love for people. He was a true *starets*[6] whom God had rewarded with the gift of insight and of the healing of mental and physical illnesses. I had been a spiritual child of priests from Optina (the elders Nektary and Anatoly), I had met the elders Father Alexei Mechev, Bishop Bartholomew (Remov)[7] and many others famous for their spirituality, and I sincerely believe that simple Father Ilarion was at least as spiritual as they were. It was clear for me to see how far I was from their strength of faith and their spirituality!

"I was surprised that in such a remote village, in a small country church, that in some sixty years of constant work on himself he had managed to achieve such high spiritual perfection. I thank God that He permitted me to see this man, that He permitted me to walk with him for at least a little while and be taught by him to relate to people. That has helped me the rest of my days to help my brothers around me.

"After a while, the authorities forbade me to enter the church, but I managed to serve several liturgies in secret with him; in the evening we would also pray together in secret, in his house. Several times I witnessed him healing people—people with advanced cancer, infectious pneumonia, heart attack and other serious illnesses. People would be cured, get up and go back to work.

"In the church there was a miracle-working icon of the Mother of God of the Sign.[8] Father Ilarion would come to the ailing person, place the icon on him or her and pray intensely while anointing him with Holy Chrism. He would then sprinkle Holy Water on him and put his hand on him. He called for the intercession of the Mother of God and of the Saint whose name the patient bore.

---

[5]A memorial service for the dead; a thanksgiving service. —Trans.

[6]An elder. —Trans.

[7]All of these were and still are very famous for their spirituality and ability to perform miracles. —Trans.

[8]Remembered in the church on December 10th. —Trans.

"It was strange to see that neither the one healed nor his relatives would realize that they had just seen a miracle, a real and pure miracle. They figured that that was just the way things were—'he was a priest after all.' But I, the priest Arseny, felt spiritual joy at what I had seen!"

"Here is another example of a miracle which happened in my presence and made a bigger impression on the local people than any miracle of healing:

"A peasant with a heavily laden cart was walking along the road that passed through the village. The road was muddy after the melting of the snow. Mud was knee deep! The horse could barely pull its load and was exhausted. Suddenly the wheels plunged into a deep hole and the cart stopped. The man started beating the horse on its back, tried to push the cart; several men tried to help, but they could not budge the cart. The owner got beastly angry and started to whip the horse on its stomach, leaving a bloody welt after each hit. The people around him started begging him to take pity on the horse—the horse was trembling and tears were running from its eyes; but the man kept on beating it. The horse tried to pull, but was unable to move the cart. The local people tried to take the whip from the man's hands, but then he took an ax and started walking toward the people, seized the whip again and kept on striking the horse. I myself tried to take the whip from him, but he hit me in the chest and I fell into the mud. The people helped me up . . . The man shouted, 'This is my horse, I can beat it if I want!' Everyone realized that he was going to destroy the horse, which was ready to fall.

"Just at this moment, nobody knows from where, Father Ilarion appeared. He took the whip from the man and hit him in the face with its stock and, without looking at him, went over to the horse. The peasant grabbed his ax and raised it to strike Father Ilarion on the head, but . . . the ax fell out of his hands, flew over the cart and fell into the mud. Turning to the man, Father Ilarion said, 'So, your snout hurts from the whip?'

" 'Why did you hit me on the snout? That hurt.'

" 'You hurt? And what do you think the horse feels?'

"He walked over to the horse, gently patted it on the back and, pulling out his handkerchief, swabbed the bloody welts. Then he told a woman who was standing near by, 'Aksinia, please fetch me some linseed oil.' She did and, after wiping away the blood, Father Ilarion poured some oil onto his hand and anointed the welts. The horse calmed down and the tears stopped running from its eyes. Father Ilarion took hold of the bridle and told the peasant, 'You there, push the cart just a little!' He blessed himself with the sign of the cross several times, pulled lightly on the bridle and the loaded cart came easily out of the deep muddy hole and moved onto the road.

"Father Ilarion walked over to the peasant and said, 'You know, Vassily, forgive me for hitting you so hard, but I could not stop you any other way! Go in peace and with the help of God. When you get home, put some more oil on the horse's welts and give it two days' rest. And don't let this happen again! Understand?' And, having blessed everyone, he left.

"The peasant went over to his horse, patted her on the back and, turning to the onlookers said, 'Brothers, who was that?'

"That was our priest, Father Ilarion, all the villages around here know him. But who are you? You are not from around here?'

" 'No,' he said and continued, 'How is that I wanted to hit a priest with an ax? What a sin!' "

"I have to say again that the life Father Ilarion led was a constant spiritual exercise, always caring for others, never for himself. He never served his own self, but constantly prayed and served the other. Carefully observing his life and the way people looked at him I saw that all of his deeds were seen to be natural to his vocation as a priest. Everyone felt that that's the way it should be! But what happened with the horse was exceptional and stunned those simple people. There was a lot of talk about it: 'Hey! Papa-Larion, perhaps he's a saint, not afraid of nothing. A miracle, the horse went with the cart!'

"I loved Father Ilarion; we were friends. I considered him my teacher and tried to learn from him. And what I was able to learn, by the grace of God, helped me survive in the camp and find the right way to be around prisoners and spiritual children.

"Performing miracles is a gift of God granted to those who have achieved the fullness of faith and have followed the commandment of loving one's brother.

"Father Ilarion lived according to both these laws and God gave him the power of healing and of insight—the ability to read other people's souls. Again and again do I thank God for His generosity in letting me meet the elder Nectary, the monk Mihail, and the simple country priest Father Ilarion. And how many of these saints have died: they were shot, or beaten to death, or buried alive, or slowly destroyed in camps or exile! But never will their spiritual efforts be forgotten, never will their spilled blood have been spilled in vain. On them and on their prayers will the Russian Orthodox Church live, and will the Mother of God keep and protect the Church and the Russian land."

Father Arseny arose, crossed himself, and blessed us all in silence. We saw that tears were running down his face. Holding our breath, we heard Father Arseny's words and recognized that, in remembering the past, he was reliving his life in his mind. The faces of those he loved were appearing in front of his eyes.

Written down by Xenia Galitski
(From the notes that were kept by V. V. Bykov until 1998)

⊰ 3 ⊱

Time Past – Today
Father Ilarion

———◦———

THE NEXT EVENING we gathered around the table again. What we had heard yesterday interested us all. Olga Sergeevna asked, "Father Arseny, tell us—what ever happened to Father Ilarion?"

"To my shame, I don't know. One morning very early we served a liturgy, in secret, inside the church, and I left for home. At one o'clock in the afternoon men from the NKVD[9] came; they took five people away and I was one of them. They took us to their office. That was in May 1941. I wasn't able to say good-bye to anyone, and that was the beginning of my sojourns in labor camps—till the beginning of 1958.

"I would like to ask Alexander Sergeevich to go to Arkhangelsk and find out what happened there." Turning to Alexander Sergeevich, he said, "You are on leave from work and you are the youngest of us all. This was a long time ago, twenty-four years ago, but do find out about Father Ilarion, find out whatever you can. When you return, tell us about it. This trip is not dangerous, nature is beautiful there, and perhaps you would even be able to rest a little."

Alexander Sergeevich was one of the people sitting around the table. He was about twenty-eight years of age, energetic and handsome. I was seeing him for the first time, but the others called him Sasha, so they probably knew him.[10]

On February 20, 1965, I heard the story of Alexander Sergeevich's trip. So I decided to write down his report, and this is what he said:

"I arrived at the Arkhangelsk railroad station by train, then I traveled by bus and by truck, paying with bottles of vodka (nobody was interested in money, vodka was the only currency!). I made it to Pet-

---

[9]The secret police. —Trans.

[10]Sasha is a very common diminutive of the name Alexander. —Trans.

rovski and wanted to make my way to Troitskoie,[11] where Father Arseny had lived in exile, but nobody remembered such a village. I asked one driver, two drivers, a third one, but they all answered, 'We don't know!' Suddenly an older driver said, 'Oh, yes, I know the village Troitskoie, there is an enormous collective farm there now, called Illitch; the name Troitskoie has been forgotten! You can get there only by car; it is about 90 to 110 kilometers away, so you cannot get there for less than two bottles. Go to the barbershop: there are always lots of people there. Their hair grows at home and they go there to have it cut.'

"So I bought four bottles of vodka, put them in my bag and started looking for a car, and in fact at the barbershop I found a guy who was working on the Ilitch collective farm. We came to an agreement: he just had to load his truck and then we would go. He wanted three bottles, then he thought for a minute and said, 'All right, I will take you there for two.' We climbed into the truck and were off. From time to time I prayed for a successful outcome to this trip. We traveled for three hours; the ride was so bumpy because of the bad road that I hurt all over. We arrived. I got off the truck and could barely walk because I was so shaken up. It was already about six o'clock in the evening, so I needed to find a place to stay. I asked my driver and he said, 'Go to any house and they will let you in, but better talk to the woman, not to the man. She will take money, but he will want vodka. The women cannot manage when their men are drunk.'

"I walked into the village. The houses were large, tall and beautiful. I saw one that I liked and knocked at the door. A woman came out who was about twenty years old. She looked at me and asked, 'What do you need?'

"I answered, 'I need a place to stay for about five days.'

"'All right, come on in,' and she named a price. The weather was very hot, so she said, 'I will put you up in a cool room on a straw mattress.'

"I entered the house, washed up, and saw to my surprise that there

---

[11] *Troitsa* means "Trinity" in Russian, so the village had been named after the church. — Trans.

was an icon in the 'red corner.'[12] I made the sign of the cross and went into the cool room. The woman's name was Lyuba. After she had seen me make the sign of the cross she looked at me with some interest and said, "Alexander, you are probably hungry; come, sit down and I will fix you something to eat.' I started to refuse, since I felt embarrassed. After she laid the table, I stood up, said the 'Our Father' and then sat back down to eat. She put some milk on the table, cheese cakes, mushrooms and cabbage soup. She served in a welcoming way, asked me about myself and told me about her family.

"I told her why I had come, asked her where the church and cemetery were. Lyuba had heard about Father Ilarion. The cemetery still existed, but the church had been burned down. She had heard about Father Ilarion from her mother and grandmother. 'They said he was a good priest, that people loved him. I will take you to my mother's, my daughter is there now; you can talk to her and find out what you want to know.'

"I looked at Lyuba and her true Russian feminine beauty stunned me and charmed me. Lyuba suddenly blushed and said, 'What are you looking at? Haven't you seen a woman before? Go get some sleep; I will wake you up for dinner,' and she left.

"I went, lay down on the straw mattress and fell asleep. I woke up with someone pushing at me and saying, 'Hey, mister, wake up. It's time for dinner. Mama has it all fixed!" I found next to me a little girl probably no older than two, who was pushing at my shoulder with her little fist. Amazed, I stared at her; then, remembering where I was, I got up and went to eat. In the room I found only Lyuba and her daughter, Nina. 'Where is your husband?' I asked. Lyuba waved away my question and said, 'Did you come here to ask me questions? Just sit and eat.'

"In the morning she went with me to the cemetery in the churchyard. Like all country cemeteries it was covered with tall grass, the mounds had been flattened by rain, crosses had fallen over. Some graves were still surrounded by a low fence; some had crosses with roofs and were painted blue. I walked around for a very long time reading all the

---

[12]The "red corner" is the corner that faces you when you enter a room. It was traditional to place an icon in that corner of each room. —Trans.

markers, but could not find Father Ilarion's grave. I probably walked for
some four hours, after which I was hot and tired and decided to go back.
The house was empty so I picked up a book that was on the shelf, sat
down on the porch, and began to read. Suddenly I heard Lyuba saying,
'Let me into the house. You are blocking the door and I can't get by.'

"I looked at Lyuba and was once again amazed by her beauty. She
probably read my thoughts, because she walked way around me to get
into the house. We sat at the table, just the two of us and I was too
embarrassed to eat anything. Lyuba noticed this and said, 'You are not
in Moscow now, so forget being shy and simply eat!'

" 'Lyuba, where is your husband?' I asked.

" 'Since this is the second time you ask, I will answer. He was trying
to make a fortune and went to Iakutia to look for diamonds. Instead he
found another woman and wrote me that he won't be coming back. So
here I am alone with Nina. I work on the collective farm while my
mother watches my little girl for me. I was silly, I was so young, I had
just finished high school and there he was! I got married and . . . he left
me, but there was never any real love. Why I am telling you all this, I do
not know. You just came into my house, you made the sign of the cross,
you believe in God and here I am, not even baptized. I believe in God
and pray every day; my mother and my grandmother are believers and
they remember Father Ilarion, they learned a lot from him. I will take
you to them tomorrow: perhaps they will be able to tell you something.'

"She took the plates away, washed them and went off to work. The
next day she took me to her mother's and to her grandmother's. The
mother was about forty years old, the grandmother perhaps sixty. They
were happy to hear that I had come to find out about Father Ilarion.
The grandmother even remembered Father Arseny—he had lived three
houses down from her on her street twenty-five years earlier!

"I carefully wrote down everything they said and I will tell you it
all. They spoke of Father Ilarion with great respect, they remembered
the influence he had on his neighbors, and they remembered his death
and the closing of the church.

"Father Ilarion served in his church until September 1941. By that
time only twenty or thirty people were coming on Sundays and only
five to eight were taking communion. He continued to serve in his

church even though on weekdays only four or five old people were able to come because the collective farm required that everyone else work on it. It was threatened that if people were found inside the church it would be closed down.

"In September 1941 the women could not remember the exact date, on a Sunday, Father Ilarion was celebrating the liturgy and getting ready to give communion. Four agents of the secret police walked into the church and did not take their hats off. They pushed the parishioners aside, went to the ambo and tried to tear the chalice with its consecrated gifts away from Father Ilarion. One of them went in through the Royal Doors and was just about to seize the chalice. Father Ilarion pushed him aside and consumed the gifts; they snatched the empty chalice from his hands and smashed it onto the altar. Another one stood in the Royal Doors and shouted, 'Citizens, go home: the church is closed, the priest is under arrest, he is an enemy of the people.'

"The four of them entered the sanctuary and approached Father Ilarion. He stood there calmly and tried to set right the empty chalice that was laying on the altar table. He made the sign of the cross, blessed everyone and slowly fell to the floor. The police tried to raise him up, but he was dead. After consulting among themselves they swore filthily and said, 'Your priest is dead. Bury him, we don't need him now,' and they left, leaving the church unlocked . . .

" 'The old women washed Father Ilarion's body and buried him without a church service since there was no one to do the service. They put up a big oak cross and people still visit his grave. He left good memories; people still tell stories about him. The church stayed open and the parishioners quickly took away the icons and hid them in their houses. Aunt Mavrusha also took away the antimens, the chalice, the paten and the Gospel, and put them away in her house. We still have these icons, my grandmother rescued them. A week later the police came again but they found nothing left inside the church. When they asked where everything was they only got the answer, "We don't know!" They became angry and burned the church down. It used to stand near the cemetery. More than twenty years have passed but people still remember Father Ilarion. Tomorrow you will go and find his grave and you will pray for the repose of his soul.' I said that I had looked but could not find it. 'Well, tomorrow night, when I come back from the collective farm, I will show you. The granddaughter of Father Ilarion came to venerate the grave after the war; she still corresponds with Babushka Glaphira and recently sent us some money to put up a new cross. Well, now we told you everything we know.'

"The next morning I went to the cemetery again, but could not find the grave. I walked and walked, suddenly I heard, 'Who are you looking for?'

"I turned around and saw a woman sitting next to a brand-new cross. I walked over to her and told her that I was looking for the grave of Father Ilarion. 'Are you blind? The grave is right here, you are standing right next to it!'

"I lifted my head and saw a new cross with an inscription reading, 'FATHER ILARION.' I knelt and started praying. I felt calm and illumined. I remembered his martyr's death, the way he consumed the Gifts which were about to be desecrated. I remembered that he had been buried without a church service and I saw in front of me the image of a great, righteous man.

"The woman who was sitting next to the cross talked with me, but she could not tell me anything new. 'I was a girl of twelve. I do remember Father Ilarion. My mother took me to him for confession and communion. I felt good, I felt happy in that church. On our collective farm, when someone is sad or depressed, or has a problem, he or she goes to Father Ilarion's grave. You ask me if I remember Father Arseny: no, I don't. At that time more than twenty people had been sent here in exile.'

"I stopped by Babushka Mavrusha's and told her why I had come. She handed the antimens, the chalice and the paten over to me, and gave me an icon of the Mother of God of Smolensk, amazingly beautiful. She asked me to pray for Father Ilarion.

"Though it was time for me to leave, I did not really want to go. I asked Lyuba, 'May I stay another week?'

"She answered, 'I won't chase you away; do stay.' During those five days we had become good friends and Nina loved to play with me. There was a rare purity and goodness in Lyuba's soul, thoughts and upbringing . . . Well, I will just tell you: I fell in love with this abandoned woman and her little girl, Nina. Her beauty and inner charm subjugated me. Could I have expected that I, a Muscovite, would meet and fall in love with a woman way out in the boondocks that are Arkhangelsk's collective farm? But this was God's will.

"Lyuba, who was a woman with a perceptive and pure soul, soon noticed how I felt and became more careful with me. The day of my departure came: I went to pray at Father Ilarion's grave and asked him to help me in my relationship with Lyuba. I went to bid farewell to the old women, and at noontime I was ready to leave. As she was saying good-bye to me, Lyuba's mother said, 'Let God arrange your life, Alexander' and then she blessed me. That evening, on the eve of my departure, Lyuba and I were sitting down to dinner. We were both silent and sad. Suddenly I said, 'Lyuba, come to Moscow this winter.'

" 'Who would I go to? I don't know anybody there, so what for?'

" 'Come to visit me; I will show you Moscow,' I said (it sounded so silly!).

" 'To you?' asked Lyuba, surprised. 'what for?'

" 'Come with Nina, I will meet you!'

"And most likely she detected something in my voice, for she answered, 'You are not afraid? I will come this winter, so you better not have any regrets!' She would not take any money for my stay."

Father Arseny listened to Alexander Sergeevich in spite of the fact that he had already heard it all one time before at Alexander's arrival. Father Arseny celebrated the funeral service for the monk Ioan-Father Ilarion: he put away the chalice, antimens and paten carefully and used them on special days. Father Arseny said: "Alexander Sergeevich! Your story is not complete, please tell us everything."

"Well, since you ask me, I will tell you everything," answered Alexander Sergeevich.

"I could not forget Lyuba. I told Father Arseny about her and corresponded with her. In December, having received Father Arseny's blessing, I went back to the Illitch collective farm without notifying Lyuba. It was freezing, but I managed to get there. When I went to Lyuba's house I found that it was locked, that no one was living in it. I went to Maria Timofevna, Lyuba's mother. I could not open the gate because the dogs were barking ferociously; but I knocked hard on it. Babushka Tatiana came out, calmed the dog and asked, 'Who are you looking for and why?'

"I told her who I was and she recognized me, saying, 'Do come in and tell us all.' As I was taking my coat off, Maria Timofevna walked in and asked, 'What did you come back for?'

"And I just blurted out, 'To fetch Lyuba!'

" 'I was expecting something like this, my heart was telling me about this, but she is the only one who can make that decision. But don't you forget that she has Nina, who is almost three years old and that it is not easy to raise somebody else's child. Nor does she know anything of your Moscow. I know that you have written her many letters, but letters are one thing, real life quite another. Think it over! Measure seven times, cut once.[13] I would worry about Lyuba.'

"I did not have time to answer before Lyuba came in. I ran to her and said, 'Lyuba, I have come to fetch you.' She looked at me for a long time and then suddenly blossomed, lit up. Her serious look disappeared and she started laughing and said, 'And did you ask me? We have known each other no time at all.'

" 'I am here to ask, will you come to me with Nina and will you be my wife?' Again I saw a light in her eyes and she answered, 'I will marry you and I will bring Nina.'

"I hugged her, her babushka Tatiana, Nina and Maria Timofevna and I stayed for a week. The whole of the collective farm was surprised by the news and came to look over this guy who had come from Moscow to fetch a woman with a child. And I did leave there with Lyuba and Nina.

"In the beginning she lived at my cousin's and on the third day we went to visit Father Arseny. He spoke to her for a long time and five days later Lyuba and Nina were baptized by Father Sergei in the church of the Protection of the Mother of God in Akulovo near Moscow.[14] He also married us. And that's all!"

---

[13]This is a common Russian proverb. —Trans.

[14]Father Sergei Orlov served in the Church of Protection in Akulovo from 1946 to 1975.

A little abrasive, not always very tactful, Anna Fedorovna said, "She sure was daring to come away with an unmarried man, but she found an easy way to get herself to Moscow.[15] I sure would like to have a look at her."

Alexander Sergeevich blushed and did not know what to answer, but was visibly hurt. Father Arseny smiled and, turning to Anna Fedorovna, said, "Turn around, Lyubov Andreevna is sitting right next to you." We all looked around; of course we had seen this woman constantly, but no one had realized that she was Alexander's wife. Anna Fedorovna, embarrassed, began to apologize. Lyuba was amazingly beautiful, as well as nice and pleasant in her demeanor. Smiling, she said, "Anna Fedorovna, you are right. It *was* easy, if surprising, for me to find myself in Moscow, but there was one very good reason for this: Sasha and I loved each other and we love each other now and that is all there is to it!"

Cutting off the talk, Father Arseny arose and said, "Let us pray for the repose of the soul of Father Ilarion and let us thank the Lord God for his generosity which has united Alexander and Lyubov." We went into his room and found a cross on the table, and three oil lamps lighting the faces on the icons. A feeling of quiet and prayer entered into our souls.

Well, in 1972, as I was looking over my notes about Father Arseny, I decided to add a few words. I ended up becoming very good friends with Lyuba: she is a rare person, full of goodness, tact and forgiveness! They are still a united family and they often come to visit Father Arseny, and I have noticed that he is especially attentive to Lyuba.

How inscrutable are God's ways!

From the notes of Xenia Galitski
From the archive of Bykov (received in 1999)

---

[15]Moscow was considered a very desirable place to live because goods arrived there long before they ever reached the provinces. —Trans.

❧ 4 ❧

The Psychiatrist

THE RENOWNED PSYCHIATRIST, professor and medical doctor Dmitri Evgenievich Melikov (trained by Ganushkin) was my friend for many years. He used to be the spiritual child of Father Alexei Mechev, then of his son Father Sergei Mechov. In 1964, he asked me to take him to Father Arseny in Rostov. He had met him in the 1930s. Mitia[16] was having serious problems in his private and professional lives. Besides that, he had also had a serious operation in 1956 or '57: his stomach had had to be removed and he had many consecutive illnesses. His diet had become a difficult challenge.

He was tall, handsome and strong, an extremely good person who was very busy with his work but who was still always ready to help any friend who sought his medical advice—or, not only medical, but financial as well! His private life was always full of complications and at such times he would withdraw into himself. In his youth, from 1924 to 1930, he had created a Christian student study group; he was arrested and imprisoned. Throughout his life he was often called in to the Lyubianka prison for interrogation. He was under constant surveillance by the secret police.

I don't know what was bothering Dmitri, but he said he needed the help of a good priest as soon as possible, and he knew that I often went to see Father Arseny, who had been freed from a labor camp in 1958. Dmitri was a strong believer and had visited many excellent priests up to 1941. During one of my visits to Father Arseny I asked his permission to bring Dmitri along on my next visit.

I do not know what they talked about, but we were unable to leave that same evening since the next train was only at two o'clock the next afternoon. Knowing of Dmitri's complicated diet, Nadezhda Petrovna had prepared something bland. That evening Father Arseny talked with

---

[16]Mitia is a common diminutive of Dmitri. —Trans.

Dmitri for more than three hours. In the morning all the visitors went
to confession and then took communion. At two that afternoon, we left
for Moscow on a train that was almost empty: in our section we were
all alone.

While we had been traveling to Father Arseny, Mitia had been
depressed, but on the way back things were entirely different: he was
alight, joyous, full of energy. We talked almost the entire time or, to be
more precise, he talked. I already knew something of him, I knew his
last wife, knew of his life, but as we were traveling he seemed to want
to tell me everything about himself, to show me the dark side of his
deeds, to talk about the fact that he had been married more than once.
He was not really telling all this to me, but to himself: he was analyzing himself and I was but a silent witness; it is quite possible that he
even forgot I was there!

"I am so extremely happy," said Dmitri, "that I saw Father Arseny
twice. In the course of my life I have met with many priests. I loved and
respected them, and tried to listen to and follow their advice, but yesterday and today I received more than I have ever received before. I
started telling Father Arseny about my family life, about my problems
at work, and I named a few people who did not understand me. Father
Arseny blessed himself with the sign of the cross, stopped me and
started talking, quietly. He entered into my inner self, into my spiritual
life and read the layers that had accumulated within my soul. I listened
and saw myself, saw the innumerable mistakes I had made, mistakes I
had not corrected but had let invade my whole being. He spoke about
people with whom a mutual understanding had never been established:
they misunderstood me and I misunderstood them. He mentioned
them by name and spoke for them; he showed me how they looked at
things and, as if he knew them, gave me their view of how the situations had evolved.

" 'Why is it so difficult for all of you? Because each person sees only
himself and does not want to see another's position even for a minute.'
He was right in everything he said. After a lengthy and cathartic talk
and confession, the profound heaviness of my sins and emotions was
lifted, I understood what I had to do and I return home a different man.

"Do understand," said Mitia. "One might have thought that his was the talk of an experienced psychoanalyst, perhaps a psychiatrist with years and years of experience. He asked me no leading questions. Every now and then he would bless himself. He opened up before me all my inner world, and not only mine, but also that of the people with whom I was having difficulties. What amazed me was that he knew and understood these people without ever having seen them or heard anything about them."

In fact, Father Arseny was not an experienced psychiatrist, psychologist or psychoanalyst; however, he simply had an all-encompassing love for human beings which was united with his love for God, his immense spiritual experience, and his God-given gift of entering into the human soul with perspicacity and intuition.

"I am a professor, a medical doctor, a psychiatrist who has seen thousands of people both sick and healthy. I have an enormous experience of work, I have written many books and reviews about psychiatry, but I felt like a mere student in front of him, a student who had just started taking a required course. If I, a psychiatrist, could only know the psychology and the inner world of my patients as Father Arseny does, I think that all my patients would be cured by now. But to become a person like Father Arseny, there has to be constant prayer to God and an all-consuming love for mankind: the combination of these two creates an ascetic, a man of prayer, a true elder."

We came to visit Father Arseny twice more together; later Dmitri came by himself. On his second visit, we had was a very interesting talk which I wrote down as soon as I returned to Moscow.

When we arrived, there were already a couple of people there from Moscow, Voronez and Vladimir. In the evening we were in the dining room. Antonina Sergevna, knowing that Dmitri Evgenievich was a psychiatrist, asked him a question: "Tell me something. Jesus Christ healed possessed people. Were they mentally ill?"

Dmitri answered, "A person can be mentally ill or can be spiritually ill—these are distinct illnesses. People who are spiritually ill are possessed. They are possessed by a thirst to kill, an uncontrollable desire to do evil, to torture people, to make them suffer. All their spiritual essence is imbued with evil: they venerate evil and venerate demonic powers. Remember the two demoniacs who lived in the tombs (Mt 8:23): they were possessed. Think of the NKVD investigators: the ones who interrogate people and torture them and, with a shrewd understanding of human weaknesses, verbally abuse and use people and demean women. These investigators are seriously spiritually ill; the power of evil, demonism, has seized their souls, but many of them are not mentally ill at all. I have met such spiritually ill people more than once. Psychiatry can do nothing for them: they are possessed.

"Healing from a spiritual illness can occur by the grace of God only with the help of a spiritual ascetic, one who is immersed entirely in prayer, in the love of God and of mankind. It is not just any priest who can heal such a possessed person. Jesus Christ Himself said, 'This kind can come out only through prayer and fasting' (Mk 9:29).

"Mental illness can be treated in psychiatric hospitals or at home by medication, physiotherapy, work, psychoanalysis. Many priests believe that psychoanalysis is sinful because the analyst forces himself into the patient's soul, thus replacing confession; they think that only in confession should one open one's innermost treasure. But, as a doctor of psychiatry, I have seen more than once that psychoanalysis by an experienced psychoanalyst has entirely healed a patient.

"It can also happen that a patient can be the victim of both mental and spiritual illnesses. It is extremely difficult to treat such people. In my practice I have not once seen such a patient be cured. Besides, in seeing a spiritual illness, a doctor might not distinguish it from a mental illness; even if he does, he cannot say, 'Go see a priest!'[17] It is also important to note that a person who has a spiritual illness—a demoniac—would never want to be healed by a priest, he would not want to be exorcised.

"People who have suffered mental illness at certain times in their lives have created works worthy of a genius (Vrubel, Garshin and others). Sometimes when they came into the Church, they became deeply believing people and were cured. They could be helped by spiritual

---

[17]Not only would medical training certainly never suggest that a doctor of psychology send a patient to a priest, but also in communist times if a doctor did give such advice he could be sent to prison. Religion was considered the opiate of the people. —Trans.

guidance, by prayer and by the whole spirit of the Orthodox Church. Sometimes spiritual guides of some communes have sent me their spiritual children for consultation. Many of these people later became excellent priests, monks, nuns, painters. Their illness was cured by faith in God."

A question was asked: "Do truly healthy people exist?"

Dmitri answered, "What a strange question! Of course they exist, and they are the majority, but many have peculiarities, even idiosyncrasies, but that is not mental illness. Sometimes people have minor distortions which one might call 'psychological colds.' These sometimes occur as result of stress, shock, or upset. They can become serious if not addressed in time. Some strangeness in people can be due to their upbringing, to the society around them, to a difficult childhood, to the bad influence of evil people. The influence of faith and of the Church are very beneficial in such cases: they can free a person from his less serious aberrations or quirks. More stubborn ailments, not necessarily serious, but personally disturbing character traits, can be quickly helped by psychoanalysis."

"I agree with much of what you say," said Father Arseny, "but I want to add that spiritual illness is frightening because under the influence of dark powers it is contagious and can spread like an epidemic. Look at our 'Leaders': they were spiritually ill people, dark powers possessed their souls, evil filled their being, and they contaminated millions of people, and as a result we saw the creation of the gulag. Millions of people were destroyed in camps, either shot, starved or fiercely tortured and humiliated. The destruction of churches, the mass elimination of bishops, priests, deacons and believers could have happened only because the 'germ' of dark evil was introduced into the masses by the 'leaders.'

"Their faith in demonic powers knew no limit: millions of people contaminated by their evil supported the 'cult of the personality,'[18] participated in repressions, denunciations, the creation of the gulag and

---

[18]The "personality" implied in this expression was Stalin: he was idealized, his personality was blown up until his adulation became a cult. —Trans.

worked in the camps. Many did not understand the purpose of making people suffer and die. Perhaps, in fact, some of them did understand— they knew they had to denounce, kill and destroy as demanded by the authorities. So they saw it as necessary and useful. Only when they found themselves interrogated, tortured, or sent to the gulag did they begin to understand and only then were they cured of their previous illness—but not all of them were cured even then. Some of them kept on thinking that they had rightly sent people to their deaths, rightly destroyed peasants' ownership by sending them to death by starvation, and rightly denounced innocent people, and they would have continued to do such things if they had not themselves been caught and sent to labor camps 'by mistake.' These people were suffering incurably from the illness of evil—they were possessed.

"I happen to have met in camp inmates who had once held very high positions: they had been denouncers, investigators—contaminated by evil. By caring, by a kind word, by helping them, it was possible to save their souls, to help them realize the sinfulness of their previous actions and to bring them to God. It was a hard path for them, and a hard one for those who helped them. If they broke with evil and came to God, the Faith and the Church, nothing could force them to turn off their newly chosen path.

"Among the imprisoned criminals there was a group of people known as the 'camp rabble' who hovered around the big criminals: they served them, lived by petty theft and on small gifts from those who were most cruel and preyed on the weak. These members of the 'camp rabble' had no conscience, demonic evil was their life: it was impossible to eliminate that from them. The serious recidivist (one who had been caught more than once) was as a rule intelligent, but had taken the path of evil; you could talk to these people, prove something to them and they rather often turned to the Faith; I had a chance to hear the confession of such people, their confession was deep and sincere, with a true desire to make peace with God.

"Demonic evil spreads like an epidemic with the help of books, newspapers, magazines, radio programs, but mostly with the rapidly spreading influence of television. All this enters the home of people and poisons the soul of a child, a youngster or an adult."

✛

During our third visit to Father Arseny we had an interesting talk about Christian student study groups. Both Dmitri and I had been members of such groups.

"Such Christian student study groups came to exist in the years 1916–1918," said Mitia, "in many of the universities in Moscow, Leningrad, Kiev, Samara and other cities. Their reason for being was the study of the Gospel and of the Old Testament. Each group had fifteen to twenty members, mostly students, but some were older. The members were very diverse: Orthodox, Catholics, Baptists, Protestants, evangelicals. The variety of faiths represented gave a special flavor to these meetings. The members were always very friendly with each other. In my opinion these group were very useful in bringing students into Christianity, helping them study the Scriptures, understand them, comment on them. Such an exchange of opinions made it easier to remember and absorb what one had read.

"Usually a member of the group would choose a text from the Holy Scriptures, work on it at home, and make a presentation during the next meeting. Sometimes an organizer would ask two members to work on the same text and give a presentation during the next meeting. After the presentation there would be discussion. It was interesting to figure out who had the best and most correct explanation."

Mitia told about the work of the group and gave us examples of different texts which had been studied: the parable of the prodigal son, and one of the beatitude "Blessed are the poor in spirit."

"At this time there are few who know about these Christian groups," said Father Arseny, "but I knew many people who were members of such groups. Many priests in Moscow did not like these groups and some priests would not allow their members to come to confession, which was of course a big mistake, especially as it happens that many members of these groups became priests, or secretly took monastic vows; and two even became bishops. Hundreds of them joined the Orthodox church, and became its faithful members and died in labor camps or in exile. On the other hand, several Orthodox members of these groups became Protestants, Baptists, and some of them even became theosophists and anthroposophists; it is true that the majority left those teachings and later returned to the Church. I knew the Martinovski who started these groups: he was a good person, not fanatical, but with a Protestant's clear mind. It is quite true that in their time these groups brought good things to many, but some of the members became confused by of the diversity of beliefs in the group.

"You said that Father Sergei Mechev, whose spiritual son you were, considered these groups to be useful, since they attracted young people to God and to the study of the Bible. Perhaps it is so, but I believe that in the terrible years from 1917 to 1928 the best possible place for students was the Russian Orthodox Church itself, its parishes, services, confession and communion."

I saw by Dmitri's face that he did not entirely agree. Father Arseny noticed the same thing and after a short silence continued, "Dmitri Evgenievich, I had, and I still have, several spiritual children who were members of these Christian study groups. I noticed that they, having joined the Church, looked at everything intellectually, especially in the beginning. I don't want to say that they were critical, but they were cautious. Most of them did not have that childlike faith that accepts God, the Mother of God, and the saints with their whole heart, their whole mind and their whole soul. You say a word and they analyze it, filtering it somehow; but after a while this attitude left. Apparently the independent study of the Holy Scriptures and the independent explanation of it left their souls in the habit of filtering everything through their mind. I myself was not involved in these groups: something else complicated and difficult was absorbing me.

"By the way, Dmitri Evgenievich, we have here, among us, a person who was once a member of one of these groups."

"Who is it?" asked Mitia.

A sixty-five-year-old woman stood up. She was Anna Vladimirovna, a good friend of mine. She said, "Dmitri Evgenievich, Mitia, have you forgotten? Don't you recognize me?"

Mitia jumped up, saying, "Anya, Anya!" and he ran over to hug her.

We traveled back to Moscow together, the three of us. Mitia and Anya completely forgot my existence, so I lay on the top bunk reading a book. I did not go to Father Arseny's with Mitia any more. He knew the way and went without me.

These last years I almost never see Dmitri; this is how life goes . . .

Written by Alexander V.
Received by V.V. Bykov in 1999

I Meet Daniil Matveevich

———•—•———

ON JUNE 23, 1963 a terrible thing happened. My daughter Anya, my son Igor, my mother and I were on the way by car to the countryside near Pushkino. My husband, an experienced driver, was at the wheel; he had been driving us back and forth from Moscow to the country for three years. We passed Pushkino. There were very few cars on the road and we were not going fast when suddenly an enormous truck appeared on our lane—it was trying to pass the car ahead of it. The driver lost control of his truck and slammed into our car, and our car rolled over several times. I came to on the road. I could not understand where I was and kept screaming, "Anya, Igor!" but got no answer. I tried to stand up, but fell back in acute pain. Ambulances arrived and people were put into them and I found myself in one.

My husband, Nikolai, and my son, Igor, died; my ten-year-old daughter survived; my mother was very seriously injured and so was I. I had to stay in the hospital for three months. I had several operations and came out almost fine, though for a while I had to stay at home or in a sanitarium for rehabilitation.

I am unable to talk or write about my pain. I was unable to work for three months even after my health was reestablished. I probably appeared to many to have lost my mind. I cried all the time and I hated life, hated my fate and hated anyone who tried to console me. I had not even been able to go to the funeral of my husband and son because I was in the hospital. People around me, my relatives, friends and colleagues were amazingly nice to me. They tried to help me, but were unable to relieve my pain. I was angry at everybody and everything, I felt that everyone else was happy and that God—I did believe in God—had sent me this ineradicable pain. I was furious at God: "Why? Why had He sent me such pain, what for?" I kept on repeating this question like a crazy woman. "Why? Why did my innocent Nikolai, my little Igor, my mother, Natalia, now an invalid, and myself have to suffer? Why?" I could find no answer within myself or from the people around me.

I had a best friend, a real friend—Lena. We grew up together and went to school together. She was a person of deep faith and a very kind person, a person of prayer. We loved each other very much: my husband had sometimes even been jealous of our friendship. I knew that Lena and her husband, Yuri, had been going to see a priest somewhere out of town. I knew that this priest had led a community before the war, had been sent to labor camps for a whole lifetime, and had finally been freed in 1958. He was now living in R. (later I found out that it was Rostov the Great). Lena and Yuri had two children.[19]

I used to visit them almost every day and mostly talked to Yuri. I was probably repeating the same thing every one of those days! He would listen to me in silence, put his arm around my shoulders, and take away some of the pain for at least that evening. Lena kept talking about God, His mercy and His will, and kept asking me to come to church with her. I could not bear such talk: how could God and the Church relieve me when I was overwhelmed by such grief? Talking to Lena irritated me and I avoided her. I could only repeat the same thing over and over: Why? Why?

One day Lena told me that she was going to see the priest Father Arseny. I had heard this name from her before. A few days earlier I had behaved in an awful way to her by shouting hysterically in front of her husband and children, "It is easy for you to talk: yours are all alive and well, and all I have left is pain." The next day I was ashamed of the way I had acted and, to iron out the effect of it, agreed to go with her, although I was sure that it was useless. That was in 1964.

The train was moving slowly, the weather was gray and rainy, the day was gloomy—just like my state of mind. We were silent. I looked through the window and saw stark trees and telephone poles; Lena was reading a book. When I no longer wanted to look outside, I sat angrily in one corner of our compartment and stared at the corner opposite and hated myself for my lack of character, my lack of will. Why had I agreed to go visit some Pops who was unknown to me? What could he do to

---

[19]The story "Lena" in volume I is about the way Yuri and Lena met.

help? Could he return my family to me? It was stupid; I had already heard far too many words of consolation.

The train stopped at the station. We walked to a house and pulled the bell handle. An elderly woman opened the door and said in a welcoming voice, "You have arrived just in time for lunch, do come in. Father Arseny told me you were coming." How absurd: how could he know we were coming?

I got even more angry and, to add to my temper, a large cat kept rubbing itself against my legs. We took our coats off, washed our hands and went into the dining room. It was a big room which contained a long table with chairs around it and pushed against the walls. No one else was there. Lena kissed the woman and called her Nadezhda Petrovna, and for some reason left the room. People unknown to me started to come into the room; Lena finally returned and introduced me to them. I was boiling with rage. I was furious at myself and at Lena. What was I here for? To eat a meal in a strange house? To see some priest I had never met before? Talk to him? What for? My enormous pain would stay with me no matter what.

We sat down to eat. I was told to sit next to a man about my age; he told me his name was Georgy.

A priest walked in. He was tall and thin with a kind and tired face. He greeted us, said the prayer before the meal and blessed the food; I did not make the sign of the cross. I paid no attention to what we were talking about; that disgusting cat kept on rubbing my legs and irritated me so that I wanted to kick it! The meal ended, we said a prayer, and people left. I ended up alone with Father Arseny. He got up from his chair, came to me and said: "Let's go!"

I moved as though I were sleepwalking. He sat me down on the sofa and said, "Tell me why you came to see this unknown priest."

I almost exploded. I started talking, almost shouting with rage, hatred and almost the desire to offend. He sat there, silent. I talked and talked and kept on repeating, "Why? What for?" I wore myself out and finally ran down. I looked at the priest in surprise. Where were his consoling words, where was the spiritual help Lena had promised?

Father Arseny got up, tended his oil lamps and lit several candles. He then walked over to me and said, "Please kneel." Obediently, I got up and knelt. He put his hand on my head and started to pray, mentioning my daughter, Anya, and my mother, Natalia, several times and then he knelt and started praying a petition to the Mother of God[20]: "O You, my blessed Queen, my hope, O Mother of God, protector of orphans and of the estranged, patron of those who have been offended, savior of those who are sinking, consolation of all those who suffer, You see my pain, You see my grief and my despondency. Help me, I am helpless, strengthen me in my pain. You know what I have lived through, help me, place Your hand over my head because I have no one to place my hope in. You are my only protector, You are my protector and my intercessor before God. I have sinned, I have sinned before You and before my brothers. O my Mother, be my comforter, be my helper, and save me, drive from me my grief, pain and despair. Help me, O Mother of my God." Then he said the troparion to the icon of the Mother of God called "Unexpected Joy": "Today we, Your faithful people, rejoice in spirit and glorify You, the Protector of us Christians. Coming to Your pure image we proclaim: O merciful Mother of God, give us an unexpected joy for, although we are burdened by many sins and sorrows, cleanse us from all evil. Pray to Your son, Jesus Christ, our God asking Him to save our souls."

He spoke the words of the prayer clearly. The warmth and depth of Father Arseny's voice brought to the inner depth of my soul, for the first time in my life, the mystery and warmth of the prayer to the Mother of God, protector and defender of us sinners.

"Morning, afternoon or evening—you choose the time, be it at home, at work, or on the way to work—pray these prayers and She, the Mother of our God, is sure to help you. Go often to a church where you can find the 'Unexpected Joy' icon of the Mother of God and read the akathist. You need no consoling words or discussion of your grief from me: your whole earthly sorrow is expressed in these prayers. Pray them and come back to visit me with Lena." He gently put his hand on my shoulder and, having blessed me, led me to the door.

Early the next morning I went to confession and took Communion. During confession Father Arseny said, "Your grief is enormous,

---

[20]The words of the prayer are those Father Arseny pronounced.

one cannot measure it or compare it to anything. You are the mother and the wife of ones who have died. But neither you nor I know the will of God. Your pain is enormous and I, the priest Arseny, understand that. But I bow down before the will of God. He is the only one, yes, the only one who knows the path of each. The Fathers of the Church said that God calls a man to Himself in the best moments of his life. Pray for those who died, pray the prayers to the Mother of God, and keep in mind the two main commandments: 'You shall love the Lord your God with all your heart and with all your soul and with all your mind. This is the greatest and first commandment. And a second is like it: You shall love your neighbor as yourself. On these two commandments hang all the law and the prophets' (Mt 22:37–40). When you enter the dining room, look at the people there. Many of them carry the weight of a heavy sorrow, but they are at ease, because they believe in God. Last night you sat next to Georgy Alexeevich; he has lived through a colossal pain. His daughter and wife were murdered after they had been done violence to—but look, he can endure it all: he may be in heavy grief, but he is in prayer."

This was an unusual confession. I had never confessed in such a way. I would start telling something, and by using two or three half questions he would open something deeply secret from within me, something I might have been hiding even from myself and tried never to recall—and now I was telling such things to a priest. I just could not avoid telling them, but I could see and understand that Father Arseny knew what was on my conscience; I could tell that if I did not say everything I felt that my repentance would not be complete, and I would go back to what I might have omitted.

I saw my relationship with my husband and with my mother in a new way; I saw what my mistakes had been; even the deaths of my son and husband appeared to me in a new light. The confession with Father Arseny seemed to have taken away the curtain that existed between my soul and my faith, I had to rethink many things and reevaluate them spiritually. I was immeasurably thankful to Lena for having brought me here. Our friendship became even more solid: I had new interests and new topics of conversation to share with both Yuri and Lena.

A meal came again and we all gathered around the table. The con-

versation was about church news, about the health of some Natalia
Petrovna, who was unknown to me, and about the way you could treat
her with herbs. Father Arseny took part in these conversations, ate very
little, wanted to drink two cups of some kind of juice, but one of the
guests, a doctor whose name was Lyuda took the second cup away from
him saying, "Father Arseny, you may be my spiritual father, but you are
trying to fool me and drink more than is allowed. More than one cup
is not good for your edema." Everyone smiled. The big cat which had
been so irritating to me before jumped on everybody's laps, jumped on
mine and licked my cheek.

Suddenly the bell rang very loudly. Nadezhda Petrovna, worried, ran to
open the door. We heard a noise in the hall, the door to the dining room
banged opened wide, and an enormous man did not just enter, but fell
in, carrying two bags, a knapsack on his back and a package under one
arm. He threw it all down on the floor and, cupping his hands to receive
a blessing, he walked directly to Father Arseny. "Your blessing, Father,"
he said. Then he hugged Father Arseny, seized him in his arms and kissed
him. We could all see that the faces of this noisy giant and of Father
Arseny were wet with tears. Their joy in meeting was obvious. Then this
giant went over to Nadezhda Petrovna (the hostess of the house), picked
her up by the shoulders, repeated, "Petrovna! Petrovna!" and kissed her
warmly. He then walked around the table saying something to each, lifting some, just hugging others. When he came to me, he picked me up,
kissed me and said for no reason, "Masha is a good person, but she is not
one of us. Don't be sad, Masha, you will soon find your niche!" He sat
me back on my chair and continued to walk around the table.

He was so enormous, so noisy and so good-humored that it was
impossible to be hurt by anything he did. Everybody was made happy
by his visit, though I found out later that only Father Arseny, the doctor Julia and Nadezhda Petrovna had known him before. "So, now I will
give you your gifts. I have been fishing for two weeks in the waters of
Astrakhan." Unwrapping a long package, he pulled out a giant sturgeon
and gave it to Father Arseny and said, "Before I smoked it, it was this
big," and spread his arms almost out to the next wall.

"Daniil Matveevich, you will have to shorten your arms! You will break these walls with your fish," said Father Arseny, smiling.

"But I am a fisherman and we fishermen may catch a fish that is a foot long, but will say it was a yard long. Fishermen only catch big fish!" We all laughed.

"Well, now I have a present for each one of you. First, Nadezhda Petrovna: for you I got three liters of the best caviar. I caught the fish, I cleaned it and salted the caviar myself. You will be licking your fingers. But I know you, you will feed it to your guests and to Father Arseny."

Walking around the table, he gave each person a large piece of sturgeon or a jar of red or black caviar. He came up to me, looked at me attentively and said loudly, "This is your first visit?"

"Yes, yes," I answered.

"I see you have a great sorrow. Unwrap this package when you get home. Give this jar to your sick mother and this one to your daughter." He lifted me up again from my chair and kissed me three times. "Don't be sad, my dear. God is merciful: pray to Him."

Nobody had ever spoken this way to me before, but it was impossible to mind this man's behavior: he was too spontaneous. But how did he know about my grief, about my mother or my daughter? It seemed to me that Father Arseny was also surprised by this.

Nadezhda Petrovna fed Daniil Matveevich. The evening tea was finished, the conversations did not last long, and people started to discuss which trains to take back to Moscow and how to meet there. It was late. Everyone was tired and Nadezhda Petrovna started telling each one where he or she would sleep. Father Arseny said, "Daniil will sleep in my room. Go get yourself a mattress."

One of the doctors who was taking care of Father Arseny said, "I ask you both not to talk all night: you are both tired and both sick."

Daniil Matveevich laughed and said, "My dear, doctors have given me no more than one month to live, and Father Arseny will live much longer than I will!" and he hugged the doctor. Daniil Matveevich was obviously happy that he would be sleeping in Father Arseny's room.

We each went our way. I slept with Lena and three other women on straw mattresses. We rose early and prayed. My mood was good. We went to liturgy in Father Arseny's room and took communion. I did not know why, but Father Arseny asked Lena and me to stay on for another day. Lena and I visited some museums during the day and joined the others in the evening. We finished dinner. The conversation was general and interesting to all. Father Arseny was sitting in his armchair and praying silently with his prayer rope. Daniil Matveevich's powerful voice sounded like thunder; in this atmosphere I felt surprisingly well and cozy.

One of the guests asked Daniil Matveevich to tell us about his life and how he had met Father Arseny. He resisted for a while, obviously unhappy with this request, but after a silence he gathered his thoughts and started to talk.

"Everything I am about to tell you has to do with my path to God.

"Professionally, I am a geologist, a doctor of sciences. I have received recognition from the government for the discovery of precious ores, and I have traveled all over Siberia and the Far East. I have worked successfully on geological expeditions. My colleagues were also good people and friendly, and in our line of work that is perhaps the most important thing.

"In 1951 a new organizer was assigned to our group who was a member of the Communist Party. He was an unexceptional little man with an ugly face; he was also arrogant and rude and had a poor knowledge of geology, but was extremely sure of himself—he felt himself to be more important than the chief geologist of the region. He saw us just as human material he had to train or retrain and so on. Many of us were upset: here was someone who knew nothing and yet he was trying to teach us. They talked about it, and I was one of them. I told you in the beginning something about my education and experience so that you can understand that I knew something about geology; I had also written several books on the subject. All right, so I told him, 'You are ignorant and untalented, you know nothing about our work and here you are trying to give orders to me, who am a doctor of sciences and a laureate.'

"Soon after this Seryogin was arrested, then other three colleagues; I was arrested in Iakutia and taken to Moscow to the Lyubianka prison. I will not speak about the interrogations, torture, beatings. I will only tell that they always put handcuffs on me when they interrogated me because they were afraid of my strength. I survived three interrogations which lasted seventy-two hours each; it took six interrogators to question me without stopping. I spent a great deal of time in various kinds of prison cells but I never signed an admission of guilt. They said I was a spy, a saboteur who had sold information to foreign countries about the location of precious ores. They condemned me to death: I was to be shot, they took away my medals and titles, but then they sent me to die in a labor camp of strictest regime. They never canceled my condemnation to be shot, so every time there was a 'cleansing' in the camp, I could be the one to be shot. The same thing happened to Father Arseny.

"I was raised in a believing family. My mother, Irina Leonidovna, believed deeply and prayed much. She instilled faith in God in me. But, little by little I let go of my faith during my travels in Siberia and the Far East, though some sparks of faith still remained within me. While I was in prison I recalled almost all the prayers I knew, and while they were torturing me I prayed the 'Our Father' unceasingly through clenched teeth. But what really irritated my interrogators was that no punishment cells, no torture could change my appearance: I still looked healthy, enormous and strong.

"They sent me to the 'Special Labor Camp.' I remember they brought us to it on foot. It was freezing; we were wet and tired when we entered the barracks. The criminals leaped on us to take away our things, anything they could. The others were so exhausted that they gave away everything they had in silence. When they came to me, I said, 'Don't you touch me!' They still tried. So, I hit several of them: I hit one in the mouth so hard that he lost his teeth, I broke somebody else's arm and so on. They came onto me with their *shivs*.[21] I hit them all. They started to give me some respect, and they stopped trying to take anything away from me. They did try to kill me twice on the field with axes, but I was on guard and so several of them ended up crippled . . . No one reported me to the authorities. It was a 'special camp,' so there were no 'little people' and the real professional criminals have their own code

---

[21]As in other prison situations, the camp criminals would fashion knives from files, pieces of metal and the like. —Trans.

of ethics about reporting and 'honor.' Sometimes somebody did squeal, but then one of 'his own' would kill him.

"They sent me to cut down trees: they needed men to fell trees, men to lop off the branches, men to saw the trunks, men to load the logs. My boss ordered me to fell trees and Father Arseny was to work with me. We became friends. I found out that he was a priest, a monk, and we had some interesting talks, and I started to think about God. The faith my mother had instilled lived on in my soul.

"Once in the winter our group was felling trees. We had to walk three kilometers from the camp to the place of work. The walk itself was tiring since we had to walk through deep snow. We arrived exhausted and drenched with sweat in spite of the freezing temperatures (–20°c). Our guards were also tired and angry. First we had to make a campfire to warm them up, and then we started work. It is a fine kind of work, a jeweler's task—your only tools are your ax and a two-handled saw (we had no power saws). The forest was beautiful, the trees were tall, worthy for masts, the bark on trunks was beautiful. Sometimes you saw away and are sorry—the tree is a living being.

"We felled three or four trees, then started work on a fifth. We sawed and chopped where needed, deciding where the tree should fall. We shouted to the others to step aside. The last bit of sawing, a last bit of ax work, and we waited, we waited for the tree to fall. But a strong wind blew up, and the tree started falling, not where we wanted it to, but in our direction. I ran to one side, but I tripped on an old stump and fell down. I could see that the tree was going to pin me and I could see Father Arseny standing nearby. I shouted, 'Run!' I knew it was the end for me.

"Perhaps you know how a tree falls. First you hear a cracking sound as the trunk is being torn away from the remaining stump and you hear a sound like crying. Then as it is falling, its branches catch the branches of neighboring trees, the trunk creaks menacingly and, after it crashes onto the ground, it emits a deep sigh—and the butt end of the tree hits the ground, smashing everything that is in its path.

"I knew good and well that this was the end for me. The butt end was about to come down on my head. Father Arseny made the sign of the cross and pushed it to one side with his hands. The branches of the pine tree were still breaking, but the butt end suddenly lay two meters away from me. I stood up a believing man. I had witnessed a miracle, a real miracle.[22] I saw God and followed Father Arseny and never looked back. I recalled in detail my mother's teachings. This is how I found God.

"The miracle was such an obvious one that all who had been near the falling tree were amazed. How could a man push aside a tree that must have weighed several tons? One of the *zeks*[23] made the sign of the cross.

"I can bring to mind yet another occurrence (although I believe nothing happens 'by chance,' but is the will of God). Well, the criminals were stealing rations—their thin soup and kasha—from the political prisoners, the 'enemies of the people.' Once or twice I noticed that while food was being handed out they were stealing Father Arseny's ration. So I decided to teach those criminal prisoners a lesson. I started keeping an eye on Father Arseny when it was getting close to his turn for food. First I saw the criminal Holodov—a crude, cruel man—with Father Arseny right behind him. When Holodov got his ration he did not walk away but waited for Father Arseny to get his. Then he snatched his cup and his food and was about to pour it into his own. I was just about to catch the criminal—but then I froze. Father Arseny was calmly moving his hand away and then, looking into Holodov's eyes, said, 'Leave it alone, go with God, don't do it again.' Cruel, crude Holodov who feared no one in our barracks, cringed and tamely went away. My help was unneeded. I then understood that Father Arseny was not defenseless, that God was with him and was watching over him and protecting him."

Daniil Matveevich brought his memoirs to a close. I was watching him and it seemed to me that the face of this large, energetic man was constantly changing. At times he was smiling, joyous, lively; at other times, when he was silent, you could see in his face a cloud of sadness and deep suffering, a cloud that disappeared when somebody would

---

[22]Those who have felled trees can vouch that pushing aside a falling tree with your hands is as impossible as pushing a moving locomotive off its rails.

[23]Prisoners. —Trans.

talk to him. It was obvious that deep grief and pain lived in his soul.

Father Arseny sat looking at Daniil Matveevich with love and concern. I felt that something was worrying him—you could feel a deep caring and a desire to help him.

When I wrote this memoir, Daniil Matveevich had already died. He foretold the month and day of his own death—September 12, 1966. It was the feast day of Saint Daniel of Moscow, in whose honor he had been named.

Daniil Matveevich was a cheerful, kind, life-loving man. He lived not for himself but for others; he gave his all to all of them: the money he earned, his strength, his kindness of heart. He was always ready to support the ailing with a warm word, to give him or her hope and a certitude that things would improve.

I thought that my meeting with Daniil Matveevich was a thing of the moment, but God and my future spiritual father Arseny decided otherwise.

After that long talk, confession, liturgy and communion I realized that my life would be taking a completely new course under Father Arseny's direction. That evening Father Arseny called me by myself into his room and said, "Maria Adrianovna, I want to ask you to do something. I know that you are grieving, but you have seen Daniil Matveevich— he is terminally ill with cancer of the liver and will not live longer than eighteen months. Would you be able to take it upon yourself to care for him, to look after him till the end?

"I can see you are surprised. You have a sick mother and a daughter, and this is the first time you have seen me, the hieromonk Arseny, or Daniil Matveevich, and here I am suddenly making such a request of you. Believe me, God will help you through it all and your immeasurable grief will melt in kindness. Daniil Matveevich is not of this world: he will give joy and peace to your family."

I stopped to think. The request was unusual and beyond my strength. I did not know Daniil Matveevich; how would my mother and daughter, Anya, take this? What would it mean to look after him?

I began to protest: "But . . ." Father Arseny did not let me finish. "But," he said, "Daniil Matveevich will drop by your place with a package from me, and that will be the beginning of your family's getting to know him." He said it as though the decision had been made, but he also added, "I will ask Lena, Yuri, and Georgy Alexeevich to help you as much as they can—and by the way, Georgy Alexeevich is an excellent surgeon."

And, as promised by Father Arseny, some ten days later Daniil Matveevich stopped by my place and gave me a large prosphora.[24] I had never seen one before.

From that day on, Daniil Matveevich began to stop by. Mama, who had trouble walking, and my daughter, Anya, were glad to see him. It must be said that my mother is a very intelligent person, a fifth-generation intellectual, and proud of it; she wouldn't talk to just anybody. She is a very authoritative person. She spoke to Daniil Matveevich gladly for hours, and when he did not come, I could see that she was watching for him. Before the accident, my mother had worked in an institute for the study of the effects of radium. She had loved her work, was a doctor of physical sciences, and suffered bitterly at being an invalid. Daniil Matveevich became a regular and desired guest in our house. He had a bad habit of bringing expensive gifts. He brought flowers because he knew I loved them; sometimes he would suddenly appear with an ice cream cake. I would get upset and ask, "What is that for?" but Anya would eat it in delight while Mama smiled and said nothing. Several times Daniil Matveevich brought Georgy Alexeevich, who examined my mother and said he would find her a bed in the best hospital: they would operate on her and she would be able to walk much better. Georgy Alexeevich worked as a surgeon in that same hospital.

Daniil Matveevich's health was deteriorating. The pain in his liver became stronger, he lost weight and easily grew tired. When he had to go into the hospital, we all visited him: Anya, Lena, Yulia, Olga, Irina and of course myself and many others. He came out of the hospital in

---

[24]Bread used for the commemoration of the living and the dead during the preparation for liturgy. —Trans.

better shape and gained some weight but you could still see that he was very seriously ill.

I remember that one day many of our friends stopped by. It was not a holiday, so I was surprised to see them, but happy that they were all Father Arseny's spiritual children. I was surprised that each of the guests had brought a gift. Daniil Matveevich appeared with a large ice-cream cake, somebody else had a bottle of champagne. I later found out that they had all agreed to do that in order to psychologically attack me!

Daniil Matveevich stood up and said, "Masha! (he always called me that) I have no more than six or seven months left to live. I have a three-room apartment in which I have a collection of minerals. I will die and all that will be lost. I want your daughter, Anya, to have it. All of us here know about this, including your mother. You must come with me to the Town Hall and register as my wife, and sign for the ownership of the apartment. It is only a formality. Father Arseny will talk it over with you. He wants you to come visit him next Saturday or Sunday, with Lena, Yuri and Georgy Alexeevich."

I exploded. I said many unpleasant things and refused absolutely, unconditionally to all this. I could not understand why our guests did not get upset, but smiled and continued eating and drinking. I got angry with Daniil Matveevich: he was sick, he was dreaming up crazy things, he had organized this reception. I absolutely did not need his apartment or its museum of minerals. "I have my own three-room apartment, and most of all, I am not a pawn you can move around at a whim."

I said all this and I was surprised when my mother said, "Maria, you are wrong and you have hurt Daniil Matveevich." I would never have expected such illogical words from her—she was an intelligent and slightly fussy person.

I will not give you all the details, but we did go to see Father Arseny. The conversation was long and difficult, but he gave his blessing for us to register as "husband" and "wife," which we did a month and a half later. Lord, how all this turned out to be clever—how that apartment came to be useful later both for me and for my daughter.

Two months later, Daniil Matveevich became bed-ridden. His pain was agonizing, but he bore it like a man. Each afternoon a nurse would come to give him an injection, each evening Georgy Alexeevich would, and each night my mother would give him the needed injection—she cared for Daniil Matveevich very much.

He stayed and died in our apartment, in the room that had been Anya's. Several times Father Alexei came from Kaluga and heard his confession. Two days before Daniil Matveevich died, Father Arseny was brought, confessed him, and gave him Communion.

His death shocked me as much as my husband's and son's had. I knew that he was going to die. My mother and all our friends were amazed at the way he prepared for his death: he never complained, never blamed anyone, never got irritated at anyone around him. The way Daniil Matveevich behaved influenced my mother who used to complain constantly about her infirmity, her useless life. Now she bore it all without a word.

Lena, her husband Yuri, Georgy Alexeevich, and some of the women from our community[25] took care of Daniil Matveevich. I was surprised by my daughter—she used to spend all her free time by his bed, although she was only eleven and impatient by nature. So our contact with Daniil Matveevich brought love into our family, and an understanding of each other which we had never had before.

This tall, strong, enormous man had a strong faith, an unusually golden heart and tact. He had one quality, or perhaps was it a gift, which scared me at times. Sometimes we would all be sitting around the table with some guests. He would not be participating in the conversation, but might suddenly say to one of the guests, "You want to go visit your daughter tomorrow (and he would say where)—but it would be better if you went on Thursday." People would ask him how he knew, though he would never say, but what he predicted would happen. There were many examples of this, and we started to pay attention to him. Some of his actions never could be explained.

During one of my visits to Father Arseny I told him about this. He replied, "I had noticed this even when I was with him in the camp. It is a gift of God to a man of great faith. Of course you have heard, Maria

---

[25]The "community" formed by Father Arseny was a group of friends—men and women in different towns—committed to a Christian life under his guidance. They gave each other help and support.

Adrianovna, that there were saints in Russian lands who were called 'fools for Christ.' Their saintliness is great, their faith knows no limits, they can foretell the future and perform miracles. They usually behave strangely when they are with other people; these days we would say they are not quite normal—some more so, some less. You have seen a lot of him and I am sure you have noticed how strangely he can behave around other people. The kindness with which he treats people comes from his perfect understanding of their souls. He knows what a person needs most at any one time. For instance, for birthdays people usually bring flowers and candy which might be the last thing the person wants; Daniil Matveevich will bring precisely what that person needs most, and he will say the words that will warm his soul most deeply. Do you remember the first time you met him and he said, 'Masha is a good person, but she is not one of us . . .' He was seeing you for the first time, but said it as if he knew you well. In the labor camp, at work, in life he seemed to many to be naive or infantile—at the same time he is an eminent specialist in geology—all this is combined in one man.

"Don't be surprised when I will tell you that he is a modern day 'fool for Christ.' His soul is as devoted to God as were those of the 'fools' of the fifteenth and sixteenth centuries. His behavior among his contemporaries is that of a twentieth-century man. Behavior is determined by the period in history in which one lives. If somebody behaved today like the 'fool' Vassily Blazhenni, he would not be understood, and would most probably end up incarcerated in a mental hospital. Don't be surprised at my words: God has sent you the joy of knowing such a man. He was always a man of deep faith—what he says about losing his faith while traveling on geological expeditions is only so much talk. Wherever he went he protected the weak, the poor, and the sick; he always earned a good deal of money but he always gave it all away. He prays constantly: he prays the Jesus prayer,[26] but never talks about it. Once he met Hieromonk Seraphim here and Father Seraphim later told me, 'This is a man of God, a very spiritual man—I believe he must be a monk.' It must be true, because Father Seraphim is himself a prophet.

---

[26]"Lord Jesus Christ, son of God, have mercy on me a sinner," a prayer said with each breath, all day and even while sleeping. — Trans.

Don't be surprised that Daniil Matveevich kisses everybody, that is also part of his 'foolishness.' Don't forget that he can read people's thoughts, that he knows what their future brings. He sometimes says it, and later feel embarrassed that he said it, but he will have spoken the words of God.

"Maria Adrianovna! He entered your family—can't you see how everything has changed for you? Your mother and daughter have become different people; peace and calm have entered into your house. Wherever Daniil Matveevich goes there is joy and God's own grace. He may not have long to live and his suffering may be unbearable, but he tries not to show it. I, Hieromonk Arseny, find myself amazed at the mystery of his life and at the secrecy of his good deeds, and there are many of those. So much is contained within the one man!—a famous scientist, a man of prayer, a doer of good deeds who brings joy and light to others just by showing up, a man who knows the day of his own death and goes toward that death in prayer and repentance. He is now living in your apartment and you have probably seen him pray many times before the icon of the Mother of God of Smolensk, which is his most beloved icon. You immediately feel the urge to pray with him, so strong is his prayer."

"Yes," I said, "when Daniil Matveevich prays, my mother, my daughter and myself all feel the need to pray with him!"

"I am happy that God has let you meet him." Father Arseny gave me his blessing. I am deeply thankful to him for asking me to take care of Daniil Matveevich.

I want now to go back to my first visit with Lena to Father Arseny, a visit which completely changed my outlook on life. That evening (the evening of our first visit), Father Arseny spoke to us for half an hour about prayer and its importance in man's life. He told us what the Fathers of the Church said about prayer and its importance in man's life, and stressing the relationship between prayer and love for one's neighbor. I then left Rostov another person entirely. I was no longer angry, no longer irritated or angry at God—I was at peace. Of course the grief remained, but I was calm. When I returned to Moscow, I applied myself to raising my daughter, to caring for my mother and, under Father Arseny's direction, fulfilling the two great commandments of the Lord: love for God and for others. Whenever I could, I would visit Father Arseny in Rostov with Lena, Yuri and Daniil Matveevich. When at home in Moscow, I often went to church with Anya and sometimes with Georgy Alexeevich and Daniil Matveevich. At home I prayed with Anya and my mother. As Father Arseny had asked me, I took care of Daniil Matveevich—he lived five minutes away from me, and he came by almost every day, and then moved into our apartment.

Half a year after the death of Daniil Matveevich, Georgy Alexeevich asked me to be his wife. We went to Rostov, where Father Arseny gave us his blessing. Soon after that we were married in church. Mama and Anya had no objections. At that time I was thirty-two years of age.

I later discovered that the prayer "My beloved queen, my hope, O Mother of God . . ." was beloved by Father Arseny and he prayed it and taught it to many who came to him in sorrow.

Maria Tropareva (1964–1975)
Daniil Matveevich's memoir about his stay in camp
and the way his life was saved were written down
in 1965 by Dr. Irina Nikolaevna.
(Part of the archives kept by V.V. Bykov; received in 1999)

⊰ 6 ⊱

A Talk

July 28, 1965

THIS IS THE THIRD TALK of Father Arseny's that I wrote down as I heard it when I visited him. I know that there were more notes taken down by others who came at other times.

In his talks, Father Arseny always based his teachings on the teachings of the Church, its canons and established traditions. He did not like to talk about such "mystical teachings" as theosophy, anthroposophy, Yoga, Indian gurus, spirits or other pseudo-religions.

Once I went to visit the home in Moscow where he had come to see his spiritual daughter Anna Fedorovna, who was sick. Many of his spiritual children came by and he had to talk with each one of them in turn and give advice, so he stayed for six days. One evening was completely wasted.

Anna Fedorovna was visited that evening by her nephew, a middle-aged, handsome professor at the University of Moscow. He met Father Arseny and was happy to discover that he was a priest. He said that he had for a long while been wanting to talk to a priest in the privacy of someone's home. The six of us looked at him with some interest, but were not expecting the conversation to be what it was about . . .

"I am listening," said Father Arseny.

Then something happened and the questions just started pouring out of the nephew as from a cornucopia: "Masons, yoga, the teachings of Roerich,[27] anthroposophy, spirits, Theosophy, gurus" and on and on and on. We sat there listening as he kept up the talking, nonstop. He compared these "mystical teachings" to Christianity, to Orthodoxy; you could not stop him, you could not fit a word in edgewise. "You are a priest and so must know something about such issues," he ended.

But as soon as Father Arseny tried to answer, the nephew started

---

[27]Nikolai K. Roerich (d. 1947), a painter and philosopher. —Trans.

talking again. His aunt, sensing the awkwardness of the situation, said, "Kiryusha, let Father Arseny answer!"

"But I haven't said half of what I wanted to!" answered Kiryusha and kept right on talking. "Father Arseny! You have probably run across this kind of human mysticism which is so important and which is so popular nowadays throughout the world?"

"Yes, I have," said Father Arseny and started to reply. He did not just reply, but also posed questions that Kiryusha himself was unable to answer, showing that he did not really know all that much about those mystical teachings. He knew their names, but when he used them to criticize Orthodoxy he showed their inconsistencies and got himself so entangled that everyone started to laugh.

Angelina Nikolaevna, a doctor of physics and mathematics and one of Father Arseny's spiritual daughters, was a no-nonsense person. She grew irritated at the waste of the evening, an evening we all had been looking forward to, and said: "Kiril Mihailovich! It is now obvious that you don't know much about these subjects. May I ask you why you wanted to talk to Father Arseny about them? Every one of us who is sitting here knows more than you do! I can tell you in Father Arseny's stead what anthroposophy and theosophy are." And she talked on for the next fifteen minutes and ended thus: "All these teachings were invented by the dark powers to distract people from Christianity. You are a Russian and a professor in the University of Moscow, and your aunt is a believer—you should feel obligated to know the teachings of Orthodoxy. I know that your grandfather was a priest. I am ashamed of you!"

The nephew, hurt, said good-bye and left. Anna Fedorovna, his sick aunt, said, "Thank you, Angelina, for putting him in his place!"

Father Arseny smiled a little and said, "You came on a little too strong perhaps, Angelina Nikolaevna!" It was late and we all had to leave, so the evening was wasted.

I remembered this conversation in particular because on July 28, when we had gathered in the dining room and were awaiting an interesting talk from Father Arseny or the remembrances of one of us, a similar situation occurred.

A woman whom many of us did not know came from Kostroma with one of Father Arseny's spiritual daughters. She asked a question about dreams, prophecy, revelations, and even conversations with the departed. She was absolutely serious and was certain that her dreams were truly visions of the future, and that having shared them with a priest she would get his approval and clarification. Her name was Valeria Valentinovna. She started by telling us that her mother had died three years before. She had always been very close to her mother, they had been nearly inseparable, and she found it painful even to go to work. They had done everything together; now she still constantly saw her mother, talked to her, asked her for her advice, and could almost sense her physical presence.

Deep in thought, Father Arseny looked at Valeria Valentinovna, made the sign of the cross, and said, "I am not a medium, and I am very leery when I hear about dreams in general, and particularly about dreams that are supposed to foretell things. Dreams in which dead people appear, speak to the living, and give advice are dangerous, spiritually speaking. They are often the products of an unhealthy state of mind or of dark forces. I consider conversations with the dead, revelations, prophecies, or the constant appearance of the dead especially dangerous.

"Even in the time of the pharaohs, the interpretation of dreams was taught in special schools that were headed by heathen priests. The temples of ancient Greece and Rome always had both men and women who were interpreters of dreams. During the middle ages as well as in the eighteenth and nineteenth centuries, the interpretation of dreams was very popular. In Russia books about the interpretation of dreams were already being published as early as the seventeenth century.

"All such interpretations were nothing other than a mystification, a crude fraud based on the fact that it was impossible to verify whether the interpretation was correct or not. If the interpretations did not coincide with what really happened, the medium could say, 'You changed what you were going to do some time between the time we met and what was going to happen so that the gods became angry, and they changed their judgment.' In the eighteenth and nineteenth centuries representatives of different mystical schools tried to explain dreams scientifically. Silly books appeared that felt like a series of bad anecdotes. For instance, if you see a hen it means that you will travel; if you see a dog, something bad will happen to you; if you see your dead mother, you will die. Before 1917 I had such a book in my hands and felt nothing but disgust at its foolishness. I don't want to try to explain your dreams. I believe that you must pray seriously and deeply to God, the Mother of God, and the saint whose name your mother had. Tell me her name and I will pray for her."

Valeria Valentinovna said, "Galina, in memory of the martyr Galina who is commemorated on April 29."

"Go to church more often, arrange memorial services, remember her during liturgy. And pray for the repose of the servant of God Galina and those dreams will not come any more. Never think for a minute that God sends the soul of your mother from the other world to talk to you! It is not God who sends such things, but your own grief, the memory of your mother, your nerves, those are what cause your dreams. It may even be the powers of evil appearing to you in order to divert you from your path to God. Pray for her and I, Hieromonk Arseny, will also pray for the servant of God Galina."

I was watching Valeria Valetinovna's face and saw that she did not like Father Arseny's answer. She firmly believed that her mother was coming to her sent by God. "Father Arseny, the priest in my church in Kostroma had another explanation for these apparitions of my mother. He said that they were the grace of God, but you say that they might be from evil forces. How can I understand which is right? I love my mother and cannot accept that she could be sent to me by evil powers, nor will I allow anyone to even say such a thing. Everything that has to do with my mother is sacred to me, and I find myself very surprised at what you have said to me."

Nadezhda Petrovna then asked Valeria Valentinovna, "If your parish priest gave you a satisfactory answer, why did you come to talk to Father Arseny?"

Silence reigned in the room. Father Arseny sighed deeply and, as though Valeria Valentinovna had said nothing, started to talk about visitations in dreams that were mentioned in the Holy Scriptures, in lives of saints and in stories about the finding of holy icons. He pointed out that these visitations mostly happened to very holy people. Sometimes these visitations were sent to help someone get back on the straight path to faith. Whatever he said seemed useless, since Valeria Valentinovna continued to insist and argue.

Father Arseny got up and left, but we stayed on and kept hearing about her dreams. In the end, she said, "A strange man, your Father Arseny—he obviously does not understand!" All evening she talked about dreams and made reference to foreign authors. We were tired and the evening we had been looking forward to was lost.

Towards the end of the evening, Father Arseny came out again and said, "You are unhappy and hurt, but I am a priest and I cannot think differently than I do about your dreams. Pray to God, and pray to the Mother of God and to Saint Galina, and the appearances of your mother will stop. Pray!"

I cannot say whether these words convinced Valeria Valentinovna, but some two or three years later I saw her again, and she was no longer talking about dreams.

From the notes of Xenia Galitsky
From T.N. Kamenev's archives

☙ 7 ❧

The Crossword Puzzle

AFTER I HAD TRIED to convince her to take me there, Natalia Vladimir-ovna finally agreed to take me to see Father Arseny, whom she had found only in 1965 and whom she had been telling me about, telling me he was a true elder, a *starets*, and that he led people on a spiritual path. There were serious troubles in my family: my daughter and her husband were about to divorce, the problem of the apartment had come up, and of who would have the children (there were two of them) and all the other problems that always arise in a divorce. My life was spoiled. I hated my son-in-law, and made sure he knew it.

Apparently Natalia had received permission to take me to Father Arseny, so I made the journey joyously: I was on my way to see a saintly man who would solve all our problems, he would tell us what to do and show us the will of God.

We arrived late at night, slept on mattresses on the floor, got up at six, washed up, and went to liturgy in Father Arseny's room. After liturgy we were invited for breakfast with six other people. We had a simple meal of kasha, fish and tea with honey.

In front of Father Arseny stood a decanter of red wine. As we started to eat, Father Arseny poured himself a glass of wine and drank it while eating his kasha. When the glass was empty, he started to pour himself seconds, but one of the guests told him, "Father, you should not have any more. You've already had enough!"

"Well, some elder," I thought, "he drank down one glass, wanted a second, and his own spiritual children have to stop him. I am a fool to have believed that he was a real *starets*."

We finished the meal and Father Arseny went to have a rest. The women went off to wash the dishes and prepare the next meal, while the men remained in the dining room. Father Arseny was either resting or talking with someone, so the men pulled out a newspaper and started to work the crossword puzzle. They worked on it for fifteen or twenty minutes, but were unable to finish it. Father Arseny came out of his room, saw them, and said, "Let me help." He came up with a few words and then said, "Now they want the names of football players; that is something I know nothing about . . ."

And again I thought, "So what is this? He drinks wine, he works on crossword puzzles . . . why did I bother to come?"

When we sat for lunch, the same decanter was again next to Father Arseny. He suddenly pushed it in my direction and said, "You keep on looking at this decanter. Perhaps you are thirsty and want to drink?" I started to refuse, but my neighbor poured me a glass and, when I started to drink, I realized, to my shame, that it was blueberry juice . . . I felt so ashamed of my suspicions that I sat there humbly in silence.

After the meal, Father Arseny invited me into his room. Moved, I started telling him all my problems, I even cried when I described my son-in-law. I spoke for a long time, and pointed out how much I was doing for that family.

Father Arseny looked at me in silence for a long time. Then he got up, went over to his icons, prayed, blessed himself and said, "Anastasia Markovna, I look at you and I see that you are the guilty one in these problems. Try to listen to me seriously, even though this priest drinks wine and solves useless crossword puzzles.

"Well, listen carefully: your son-in-law, Leonid, is not a bad person—he is even a good person. He loves his wife, Svetlana, and his children. Yes, he does earn less money than your daughter, but he tries as hard as he can to help out at home, so what more do you want from him?

"You keep telling your daughter that he is a bad husband and your grandchildren that he is a bad father, and you remind everyone of your role in this household, and you want them to appreciate the 'enormous amount of work' that you are doing for them. Well, who could stand all that? If you want peace in that house, you are the one who has to change. When you get home tomorrow, enter it as a new person: as a new, good, true Christian woman. You are a believer, but you go to church and what do you ask from God? You ask for a divorce, or for a bigger salary for Leonid! Be warm-hearted and show your daughter and your son-in-law what it means to be a true Christian, and perhaps you will even bring them all into the church.

"You are not the only one who comes to me thinking that I will solve their problems, or make them disappear. Yes, of course, prayer will help, but *you* must be ready to see your own faults and be ready to correct them. When I see that the person who came to see me is in the wrong, it is my duty to say so!"

I fell on my knees and Father Arseny put his hand on my head and started to pray aloud. I did not understand some words of the prayers, but I did understand them later when I was in church and paid attention.

My visit to Father Arseny left an enormous impression on me. I asked myself, "How did he know my thoughts about the wine and the crossword puzzle?" At first I found it difficult to agree with everything Father Arseny had said, but after I looked carefully at the way I acted I agreed that he was right. I did change. I even became good friends with Leonid. I took my grandchildren to church and Leonid came with us. My daughter did not: her faith remained shallow.

I cannot say that it was easy to change in the way I had to. I wept many times and I visited Father Arseny several more times. But my family was at peace, and so was I.

⊰ 8 ⊱

Yuri and Kyra

August–September 1967

As I WAS READING over my memoirs, written in 1967, I can clearly see how unsatisfactory is my description of facts, especially concerning Father Arseny. I write so little about him and my description of him is so poor and so colorless! I got so involved in retelling my story with Kyra that I pushed away what was really important to write about.

The *starets* Arseny was a hieromonk, a man of strong will who was entirely directed toward God; he was a member of the Church who walked toward God under all of life's circumstances. He gave his entire life to his spiritual children and to any person who came to him. In ill health, at times almost at the point of death, exhausted, he would listen to them, talk to them, confess them—constantly praying. He lived for others, and took into his soul any grief or problem of others as if they were his own. When he prayed for others, he prayed for himself, because he took into his heart everything he heard. We, his spiritual children never took pity on him: we often came to him with unimportant problems which should not have needed his judgment, but were simply life's dust. We did not realize, or perhaps we did not want to realize, that we shouldn't be wearing him out with such trifles. We were cruel, egotistical, thinking only of ourselves.

I first met Kyra in Father Arseny's community. We were both his spiritual children; we met and became friends. I fell in love, I loved her so much that I myself was surprised. She was of medium height, slim, and elegant in her demeanor with a beautiful, charming face and appearance. Many members of our community loved Kyra and many had asked her to marry them. Twice she had almost agreed, but Father Arseny had not given his blessing.

One time, we left the church at the same time by pure coincidence and walked to the tram together. I was twenty-three years old (born in 1900), Kyra was twenty-one. We were both students. I asked Kyra once if she would mind if I accompanied her home after church. She accepted. Our relationship evolved and I realized that Kyra loved me. I was happy and surprised. I do not look interesting; I am not a handsome man. I am tall and thin, but strong. I started asking myself, can Kyra really love me? Perhaps she is just infatuated, perhaps she is mistaken? But I soon realized that her feelings were true. For a whole year we met at church, took walks together, met each other's parents. In the course of a year we talked about many things and told each other many things. Kyra wrote amazing poetry in which she expressed her soul. She described nature in such a gentle and fine way. Each poem revealed to me a little bit of her soul. I loved, and still love, each line she ever wrote. I advised her to send her poems to magazines, they were so much better than those you could read there, but she only laughed and read me new poems. Father Arseny knew about our relationship.

After a year, I asked her to be my wife. We went to Father Arseny. He heard us out and prayed for a long time. I got worried. But Father Arseny blessed us and said, "Carry each other's burdens and in that way fulfill the law of Christ." He repeated, "Carry each other's burdens." Kyra's parents and mine approved of our union. My mother and my sister Nadia became good friends with Kyra and loved her. We were married by Father Piotr.

Kyra was one of Father Arseny's active helpers in everything concerning his community. Therefore Father Arseny gave her more attention than he gave me, and often cited her as an example to the other women in the community. We moved to Molchanovka Street, to a six-story house, to a five-room communal apartment, into the room of a great uncle, Ivan Vassilyevich. He was very old and needed constant care; Kyra's parents decided to take him in so as to give us the chance to live on our own.[28]

There were so many problems and dangerous situations that I can't even remember them all. One of them was Father Arseny's arrest in

---

[28]In those days, newlyweds often had to live with their parents because of the scarcity of available rooms, even in communal apartments. —Trans.

December 1927, and his exile: we lost our spiritual father. Almost all priests were arrested at this time; many of the sisters and brothers of our community were also arrested and churches were closed down. Suppression of religion started in 1928 and was at its worst from 1937 to 1938. In those days you had always to be prepared to be arrested, exiled, shot—this was the way of life for the whole country, but for believers in particular.

Our community had to lay low, but it lived on in secrecy. We would pray and would all read the same chapter of the Gospel; priests who no longer had a church in which to serve, but who had not yet been arrested or exiled, used to celebrate joyous liturgies at home. Sometimes the liturgy was celebrated by brothers of our community who had been ordained by Bishop Afanassy. I knew that by 1924 Patriarch Tikhon had already asked trustworthy priests to select good people from their communities or parishes who could be ordained in secret, because he felt that the authorities intended to destroy all priests. It is well known that several bishops had made the same request of their parishes, but I know this personally only about Bishop Afanassy. I was not among those chosen for secret ordination.

During these cruel times my wife, Kyra, was extremely active. She visited Father Arseny several times in exile; she used to go on these trips with Alexandra Fedorovna Berg. With the help of other sisters she used to collect food parcels and money to help the needy, the priests and the friends of the community who had been exiled or sent to labor camps (this work was done mostly by our friend Irina Nikolaevna, whom we called Dunyasha). Younger brothers and sisters used to take these parcels to their destination. At times, this was very dangerous. I myself visited Father Arseny four times in exile and Father Piotr twice.

By the mercy of God not one member our own families suffered from the "punitive measures" instituted by the Government, and we lived until June 22, 1941 (the beginning of World War II), without any losses. From the day of our wedding until the day I had to leave for the army, our life—Kyra's and mine—in spite of the fear, or should I say terror, that reigned, our life was spiritually one and I can say without exaggeration that it was amazingly happy. My whole life was in my love for Kyra; you may think that I am exaggerating, but I can say that her

breath was my breath. We prayed together in the evenings, read the
services for matins, vespers, the hours, as well as the akathist to the
Mother of God, to Saint Seraphim of Sarov, to Saint Sergius of Radonezh, and to Saint Fyodosy and other saints. Some days we read the
poems of different poets with delight, and sometimes I listened with
delight to poems written by Kyra—she would write them on her way
to work, in the tram, or sometimes while she was cooking dinner. Our
only sadness was that we had no children. Relying on God's will we con-
sulted no doctors. We considered our marriage to be solid. We felt a
complete spiritual closeness and a complete unity of soul.

On July 6, 1941, on the day of my beloved icon of the Vladimir
Mother of God, I was called into the political section of the organization where I was working. They announced to me that I was excused
from military service, but was directed to the Ministry of Defense. I had
to be there the next day at ten in the morning, and I was given the
address.

I immediately went home and asked Kyra to come home from
work, and we went to bid farewell to our relatives. Late in the evening
we went to Father Georgy's home; he was a secret priest and our good
friend. During the night he served the liturgy, and confessed and communed us both. We prayed all night and in the morning, directly from
his home, Kyra and I went to the address provided. After the liturgy and
communion we both were calm. Our separation was difficult and sad,
even tragic. Tears were veiling our eyes.

I was received by high-ranking officials and I was told that, in view
of my specialty and my performance record, they wanted me to work
in the radio-detection of objects (now known as radar). They sat me in
a car and drove me to an unknown destination with three of my colleagues.

When we arrived, we were told that we were not to leave the
grounds, that they would feed us well, that we would be allowed to send
only one letter per trimester to our relatives. Reveille, breakfast, lunch
and dinner would be announced only by a whistle. We would be working fifteen hours a day. Any design that we came up with would immediately be executed in metal in their perfectly equipped laboratories. We
were told how we would be punished if we disobeyed any of these rules.

We would be working with prisoners who were important specialists in our field; we were instructed as to how we should to treat them. We realized that we had been sent to a kind of privileged camp which was later known as a *sharashka*.

We started work, but stayed in Moscow only one month. At the end of August we were flown to another city. I worked in this place for the duration of the war. I was sent to the front some twenty times to try out the result of our work on location. We were heavily supervised: no contact with anyone was allowed. The few letters we did receive from our relatives had heavy black markings blocking parts of the text.

The war came to a close at the end of 1945. At the beginning of 1946 we were transferred back to Moscow and worked under the same conditions. Many of us asked to be discharged and I was one of them. In April I was discharged with the high rank of Colonel (never having even been in the war!). I was then forty-six years old and Kyra was forty-four. They took me home in a car.

I arrived in an emotional state. A neighbor, a nice old lady called Maria Petrovna, who lived in the same communal apartment as we did opened the door. She saw a colonel and did not recognize me, but she gave me the keys to our room and seemed to be trying to say something, all the time looking at me in some panic. I put the light on, everything was as it used to be, but there was a child's crib in the corner and toys on the floor. I was trying to imagine what all this could mean, but then heard the door opening, a child's voice, and the words of Maria Petrovna, "He has come!" Kyra answered and came into the room, letting a little girl, age three, in before her . . .

I ran to her saying, "Kyra!" Before that I had been sitting at the table praying, thanking God that I was home and that I was about to see Kyra. She hugged the little girl as if protecting her; she looked at me with enormous eyes and she did not say, but moaned, "This is my daughter! She is mine!"

"Kyra!" I repeated, "Kyra!"

"She is my daughter, do you understand? Mine!"

The little girl was born while I was away: had she gotten remarried? I wondered. "Did you get remarried?"

"No, I did not, but she is my daughter."

I fell silent, not knowing what to do, what to say.

Holding back waves of growing irritation and anger, I went over to the little girl, picked her up and asked, "What is your name?"

"Katia!" she said confidently. A nice little face, she looked so much like Kyra!

Katia asked, "Are you my papa? Mama told me about you."

Should I just leave, I wondered, and never see Kyra again, never meet her again? But she is my wife, Father Arseny blessed us, and we have received the sacrament of marriage. Should I leave her alone with a child? Where is my faith? What did Father Arseny teach me? Yes, Kyra made a mistake, she has been unfaithful to me, she has broken all the laws of our faith. I am destroyed, I am crushed, but do I have the right to punish her, to make the life of the one I love even more difficult? And I answered myself, "No, I don't have the right to do it, and I love Kyra even now." I put Katia down, went over to my wife and said, "Let us pray to God and the Mother of God!"

She started to sob and said, "Forgive me: I am guilty before you, before God, and before Father Arseny. I know that I committed a mortal sin. I will tell you everything. Tell me what we three should do now. Tell me!"

I took her by the elbow, led her over to the icons and prayed with her. I was the one who said the prayers since she was sobbing. All that night I sat in an armchair, praying and thinking and thinking. Kyra put Katia to bed, lay down on the bed without undressing, and toward morning fell into an agitated sleep.

Who does not make mistakes? Who am I to judge my Kyra? In my thoughts I asked Father Arseny what to do and answered myself: I would stay with Kyra and Katia. I would care for them, I would never leave them. I had to reestablish our spiritual closeness, I would never condemn her, never ask her anything, as if nothing had happened and we would raise Katia together. But there would never be any physical intimacy, we would live together as brother and sister and take care of Katia. Only much later did I come to understand that in this way I was humiliating my wife; Father Arseny told me so many years later.

I said nothing to Kyra and we lived as before, as if nothing had happened. One thing surprised me: my parents and my sister, Nadezhda, never had a bad word to say about Kyra; they never condemned her, but kept on loving her and Katia. Kyra's mother did condemn her daughter; I said not a word.

Of course, we had to leave our room on the Molchanovka and move to another district. It was difficult to make the exchange; we had to pay, to pay too much money, but obtained two rooms in a three-room apartment. The third room was occupied by a young teacher named Alexandra Viktorovna Shilova who had a son, Seriozha,[29] who was a year older than Katia.

One night three men came, we thought they had come for us, but they searched Alexandra Viktorovna's room and took her away. The boy stayed there alone. Seriozha ended up living with us for three months, after which we decided to adopt him. We went to the authorities and asked if we could, but the answer was "No!" Three months later they wanted to send him off to a home for the children of the "enemies of the people." I went to them a third time: they gave me trouble and were difficult, but they did finally give me the adoption papers. We knew that this adoption was not a legal one, because his mother was still alive, but at the office one of the clerks said as a blunder that she had been put in prison for ten years without permission either to write or receive letters, and that is why they let us adopt the little boy. There were now four of us.

The three-room apartment was now all ours. We had no neighbors and so we could pray in peace. Priests would come and serve liturgies, five or six people would come to pray with us, sometimes seven—we were afraid to have more.

To outsiders, we looked like a couple: we loved each other, we took care of Katia and Seriozha, we told them stories, interesting stories, often based on the lives of saints. We each had a serial story going— Kyra told one about a kitten named Svetik, a swift, agile kitten who was always running into difficulties which he managed to surmount and who always helped others; my story was about a wolf and a fox, each of whom was always trying to be stronger than the other. Whenever Kyra or I would enter the house, we would hear, "Papa, Mama, a story!"

---

[29]A diminutive of Sergei. —Trans.

God help us if we did not tell them a story, the children would feel so hurt.

We borrowed books from friends, from Tatiana Nilovna who was working in the Lenin Library and took out books in secret to return them the next week. They were apocryphal stories about the childhood of Jesus Christ, the Mother of God, Nicholas the Wonderworker. The kids loved these stories. Starting at age eight, on their own they used to read books which had been lent to them by grandmothers and grandfathers, by my sister, Nadezhda and by Kyra. Kyra still was busy working for the members of the community, but could give them less time. She worked as a microbiologist, taught in Moscow University, and wrote "for the drawer."[30]

Katia and Seriozha were good students. They did their homework without our having to push them. They studied together, prayed independently, chose their friends well, and, what is most important, both believed in God. We loved both children equally, did not favor one over the other, and they knew it. Katia seemed to be more drawn to me and Seriozha to Kyra.

We were friendly and happy, we had the children to unite us, but there was an invisible line separating Kyra from me. One time, about two years after my return, I lost control. It was Christmastime. We had a Christmas tree and we were giving gifts to the children, and suddenly I grabbed Kyra by the shoulders, kissed her face, her lips, her eyes, her neck. Her warm arms hugged me, she pressed herself against me, and kept repeating, "Yura! Yura!" holding my head more and more tightly.

I pulled her arms from around my neck, nearly pushed her aside, walked away, and could only say, "I apologize! I forgot myself!" Having said this I realized the lack of honesty in my behavior. I loved Kyra, and had to remember that she was my wife, that we had been blessed by Father Arseny and in church, and I had placed my pride above love and forgiveness.

O Lord, how she sobbed, repeating, "Yura! Yura! Forgive me!"

Horror seized me. I took pity on her, I was so ashamed that I was

---

[30]Writers who did not want to write what was ordered by the authorities used to hide their manuscripts in a drawer—hence this expression. —Trans.

hurting Kyra, but my unexpressed anger, the feelings which I had never come to fully understand, did not let me tear through the invisible line that was separating us. I took Kyra by the elbow and started praying aloud while standing before the icon of the Vladimir Mother of God. Kyra kept on sobbing; she could not stop. Having finished praying, I sat her down next to me on the sofa, hugged her, and started to pat her hands and her head. I realized how wrong I had been, how cruel, how proud. I knelt before her and said, "Forgive me! I have been in the wrong, there will be no more of this artificial separateness. You know that I love you. My behavior has been the result of pride. This is certainly not what Father Arseny taught us!"

I lifted her up, stood her in front of me, and kissed her. It was all resolved. We had our faith, our children who united us and our love, a gift from God. I had been wrong, and I was guilty before Kyra since I had forgotten the blessing of our spiritual father and forgotten the fact that she was my wife. I had made her suffer and had suffered myself. All that was over.

I never did ask Kyra what had pushed her to do what she did and have a child. One day, many years later, she suddenly said, "Yuri! Everything that Father Arseny taught us—faith, God, husband—it all fell aside in one second of craziness. It only happened once. I was disgusting, weak, but when I understood that I was going to have a baby, I could not have an abortion—that would have been a mortal sin. Even if there had not been a baby, I would have told you all about it—I would have had to admit my unfaithfulness to you; that is also a mortal sin, but killing a child is worse—he has a guardian angel before he is born." We never spoke about it again.

In 1958, after eighteen years in a labor camp, Father Arseny returned. Our children had grown: Katia was fifteen, Sergei sixteen. I was fifty-eight, Kyra fifty-six, but she still was as beautiful and slim as before, you might have thought she was only forty. She always had the gift of looking at least fifteen years younger than she really was.

In June 1958, Kyra and I went to Rostov to see Father Arseny. We stayed for three days. I am not going to write about the joy we felt in seeing him—I think everyone can imagine what we felt. Father Arseny's health had been affected by his stay in the labor camp, his heart condition had worsened (he had had endocardiatis when young, at a time when they did not know how to treat it). His legs were edematous. He did look older, but spiritually he was even greater than before. You could especially tell that when he looked at you with his totally understanding eyes, and you knew that he could read your soul. He knew your soul. He was a good man, he forgave everything, he understood human weaknesses and the reason for those weaknesses. He approached each person who came to him in light of that person's inner structure and took into consideration his character, his upbringing and his life story. You seldom find a priest in a parish who can be so attentive to each person who comes to confession: they don't have the time.

He spoke with Kyra and confessed her for a very long time. She came out of his room lit up and joyous; her happy, wide-open eyes were filled with tears.

My conversation and confession were also very long. I admit that I was apprehensive about going to confession to Father Arseny. I started to tell him about what had happened to me, about the sins which I had committed before, but he stopped me with a gesture. "We will talk about this business later. Kyra told me in detail what happened to her in 1943, and also what happened between 1943 and 1946, when you came home again. I know all about it, so there is no need to repeat it. What she did gave you the right (even from a religious standpoint) to divorce her and to try to forget her. Nobody would have blamed you because the sin Kyra committed was a mortal one and only God in His great mercy can forgive it at the Last Judgment.

"Kyra is a person of strong will, she is very spiritual and a strong believer. Such people, when weighing their sins are liable to commit crazy actions under emotional stress. They think, 'There is no forgiveness for me, there is no return to the past.'

"She had three choices: The first was to throw herself on the all-forgiving mercy of God, to repent constantly, to pray, to be ashamed every moment, to be despised by her friends in the community and, most of all, not to know whether you would ever forgive her or take her back after she had had someone else's child, and she had to live that way for a very long time. Her second choice was the following: she could have gone with the other man—most women would have taken this path—

especially when he had loved Kyra for so many years (pray for him, his name is Dmitri). But everything that lay within her—her deep faith, her all-encompassing love for you, for her friends in the community, for the Church, for prayer, for the Lord God, for the Mother of God and for the saints—would not let her do that. She would have seen this as a second treason, a complete negation of her past, a plummet into life's chaos and into darkness of lack of faith. The third choice was a frightening one: under the influence of this new stress—I have seen such people in camp, in exile, as well as in the free world—decide to abandon life, so certain are they that there is no possible forgiveness on earth for them. They commit suicide.

"In the labor camp God sent me a great miracle: On January 27, 1943, I felt in my soul that Kyra was in immediate danger of perishing. I started to pray to the Mother of God to save her. I was especially worried and in prayer during the night (in Moscow it would have been daytime). I asked, I begged God to help, to send people who could give her support. These people did appear, and they were your mother, Elena Alexandrovna, your father and your sister Nadezhda. This was truly a miracle. Your family not only did not condemn Kyra, but did all they could to save her: they took her into their home, took care of her and loved her as their own daughter, as your wife.

"When you returned from the army, you accepted Kyra and Katia. To an outsider it looked as though you were living as husband and wife, people thought that Katia was your daughter, yet for two years you did not have relations with your wife. For her, that was a constant reminder of her sinfulness and it forced her to pray for God's forgiveness. Your decision was a good one, God inspired you, but then God, in His eternal mercy, united you again. You adopted Sergei, your family became stronger, stronger in faith and friendship."

My conversation with Father Arseny was a long one, memories kept on coming back to him and they seemed to revive him. He kept on remembering and told me many things that day.

For Kyra and me, Father Arseny was not only a spiritual father, but also a friend. We had helped to gather together our community, we had walked toward the same goal, walked according to the laws of the Fathers of the Church.

He confessed me many times, and each confession was another step up to a new cleansing of the soul and to a better spiritual understanding, but this one was a very special confession. We had not seen each other for eighteen years, eighteen years separated us from the last confession I had had with him in Arkhangelsk, but the inner feeling was the same, as though there had been no long separation and as though Father Arseny had been with us always. And in fact he was with us: he prayed for us, his spiritual children, in labor camp and in that way saved us and gave us support.

During one of our conversations Father Arseny told me, "Your accepting Kyra was the right thing to do. You knew her inner life, her character, her vulnerability and her spiritual outlook on life. You knew the depth of her faith, so you realized that her fall would for her be a constant prayer, a begging God for forgiveness, a constant repentance and sorrow for her deed. You also knew her love for you and yours for her. You will probably be surprised at what I am about to say, but I believe that this heavy sin, the constant repentance and consciousness of her guilt, has made Kyra an even better person. Yuri, this is surprising, but it does happen with people of strong character and deep faith. God's ways are inscrutable.

"God showed her that there are people who in difficult situations are ready to forget all conventions and are ready to help a person in pain. They thus uncover the beauty of their own souls and show the beauty of God's providence in a bright light. All this gave Kyra spiritual strength."

After Father Arseny was freed from camp in 1958, we met many times. Sometimes he would come to stay with us in Moscow for a week or two. In the summer we would rent a room in Rostov and stay there for our whole vacation. We would take Katia and Sergei with us. Those days were always days of joy: we heard many memoirs from Father Arseny and those of other guests, and we had interesting talks on spiritual topics.

In later years, Father Arseny felt weak. He would lie on a sofa or, in the summer, out in the garden on a folding chair, covered with a blanket. At times his heart would give him trouble, he would have difficulty breathing and his legs would swell; he suffered from an arrhythmia. We had many doctors in our community: Julia, Irina, Ludmila, Olga Sergeevna, Alexandra Andreevna and many others. By this time many of them had become professors or were chiefs of staff in some of the big hospitals. Thanks to them, and to the fact that they would sometimes forcibly take Father Arseny to the hospital (for observation and care), and of course thanks mainly to the mercy of God and the Mother of God, could Father Arseny, who had survived nine years of exile and eighteen years of camp, have lived another seventeen years in Rostov in the house of Nadezhda Petrovna, whose unrelenting care made it possible.

Father Arseny was weak and sick, but people kept on coming— almost every day at least five people came—he saw them all, talked to them, confessed them, served and prayed unceasingly.

The next part of these memoirs was written by Kyra.

Yuri Bakhmat
From the archives of V. V. Bykov (received in 1999)

In 1967 Father Arseny asked Yuri and myself to write our memoirs. I understood that he meant memoirs about everything related to the life of the community and also to my relationship with my husband. What Yuri wrote is absolutely true, there nothing which is not perfectly true, but there is a detail which is not exact, a detail that has to do with the subjective interpretation of some events.

I will start by telling that in the 1920s, when our community was living a deep spiritual life, I was the initiator of the "pure coincidence" through which we met. He could not have known this, and I think I fell in love with him before he did with me, but like most young girls, I tried not to show it. During confession I told this to Father Arseny and I remember vividly how he said, "God will put everything in its proper place."

✛

Our life has been described in detail by Yuri, so I will not say much about it.

From 1943 and to 1948 my whole life changed—it was full of constant worry, deep repentance, and a feeling that something terrible was about to happen. Each day was stressful for me, in spite of the fact that, starting in April 1946, my relationship with Yuri looked good from the outside. He loved my daughter, Katia, was attached to her, but I was constantly stressed.

In 1958 Father Arseny was freed, quite unexpectedly. Up to 1956 we thought that he had died in camp or that he had been shot, but God kept him alive for the sake of us, his spiritual children. In June 1958, Yuri and I went for the first time to the house of Nadezhda Petrovna in Rostov. We spent three days there, I will not attempt to describe the joy of our meeting—for Yuri and myself it was such a joy and Father Arseny was also happy.

On the second day of our stay I went to confession to Father Arseny. Fifteen years had elapsed since my fall. My husband's and my relationship had been reestablished, we were looking at life in the same way, and my sin had dissolved over time. But when I went to confession, my whole past lay in front of me in all its horror, and I was scared. How was I going to be able to look into his eyes, into the eyes of my spiritual father, of the elder Arseny? What could I say?

My soul was trembling with fear but I went into his room. At that time it was not yet full of icons, the famous portrait of the woman in the padded work-vest in front of barracks was not yet there (it was the work of the renowned M.V. Nesterov and was kept hidden somewhere); in place of the sofa, there was a bed covered with a dark bedspread.

I entered. Father Arseny was standing. I fell to my knees in front of him, my voice shook, and I could only say one sentence, "Father Arseny! I committed a grave sin, beg God to forgive me!" and bowed down, my head to the floor.

He helped me up, sat me on the bed next to him and said in a whisper, "Kyra! Let us pray."

We went over to the icons and started praying; I repeated every word of the prayers he said. I don't know how long we prayed, perhaps half an hour, perhaps an hour, perhaps even more. When he was finished, he sat me again on the bed, sat down next to me, and said, "Tell me!"

I spoke for a long time. I cried, hiding my face in my hands out of shame; I stopped; I started talking again and my past, this horrible past, this feeling of my dirty fall, lay again in front of my eyes.

This all came about because I was so sure of myself, I was sure that I was a good person, spiritually sound, morally straight. "Look, look! I will resist, whatever happens," all came from an awful womanly sinfulness. I played with fire right on the edge of the precipice, in front of a man who was in love with me—it burned me in one second and only then did I realize my sin, and true horror seized me. Barely dressed, I ran and ran, having scared to death that poor, puzzled man who probably thought that I was crazy. And this happened not when I was eighteen or twenty; no, I was forty-one years old; I was old.

In this state I burst into the apartment of Elena Alexandrovna, the mother of Yuri and his sister, Nadezhda. Why did I go to their apartment? I did not know then. While I was riding, running, walking, one thought kept coming back to me: they will drive me away, they will curse me, I am the wife of their son and brother. I have hurt him and shamed him by my deed. I fell into Elena Alexandrovna's arms and Nadia's and started telling them everything. I expected a slap on the face, I expected them to shout, "Get out of this house!" but what happened was the opposite. They put their arms around me and tried gently to calm me down, they tidied up my clothing, and they asked no questions. The only thing Elena Alexandrovna said was, "Kyra, you are sure to have a baby. You must keep it, so get ready to become a mother! From now on you will live with us. Nadia will go with you to your place to get your things."

I did not believe what I was hearing. I did not want to believe that I would have a baby, but ten days later I knew that Elena Alexandrovna had been right.

I lived with the family of my mother-in-law for three years and ten months. Can you even begin to imagine how I lived? I lived as a beloved daughter who was taken care of by the whole family: Elena Alexan-

drovna, Alexander Nikolaievich (Yuri's father) and Nadia. The birth of
their grandchild and niece Katia was a joy. They loved her, fed her,
played with her. When Yuri came home they continued to take care of
Katia, and later of Sergei. Katia loved Babushka Lena and Aunt Nadia
so much that I felt that Yuri and I were less important—that is probably the way it had to be.

That was more or less what my sinful and disorganized confession
to Father Arseny sounded like. When I fell silent, Father Arseny was
moving his leather prayer ropes and looking at his icons with concentration; the icons were lit by two oil lamps and a candle. Shadows were
running on the walls, and I was on my knees expecting stern and severe
words condemning me and perhaps refusing me forgiveness. It became
more and more frightening: my fate was being decided, my spiritual
fate. But Father Arseny put his arm around my shoulders and said to
me in a quiet voice, full of emotion, "In 1943, on January 27, the feast
day of Saint Nina, I was in the camp and praying for you intensely and
without ceasing. I was praying to God and the Mother of God and Saint
Nina to save you. Your downfall would have been not in the sin you had
committed but in what you would do next. I knew you, I understood
that you would be capable of committing suicide in order to save yourself from shame, guilt and horror of what you had done. You could also
have gone back to that other man. I prayed to God to save you from
both dangers and begged Him to send you people who would be able
to save you from sinking even lower. Answer me, did you have such
thoughts?"

"Yes, Father Arseny! The streets were dark and I was tempted to
throw myself under the tram. I was also tempted at times to go back to
the other man, who loved me without reservation. I had no hope that
Yuri would ever forgive me, but some irresistible power pushed me to
Elena Alexandrovna."

"I prayed to God, I begged Him and the Mother of God and Saint
Nina to help you, to save you and to keep you from making a horrible
mistake. They heard me and brought you to Yuri's family, that is why
you went to them. In normal human circumstances people don't go to
their husband's family and tell them everything!

"I remember that day very clearly. You were constantly appearing in my consciousness: I knew what you had done and could see you running through the streets of Moscow, having almost lost your mind. I knew your thoughts and I found myself at peace only when Elena Alexandrovna and Nadia took you in and kept you in their home. You told me that you did not know why you came to Yuri's family: now you know. Yuri and you are not only my spiritual children, but two of my closest friends. God heard my prayer and saved you, and His Holy Mother took you under Her protection. When you pray for your family, never forget to pray for Katia's father, Dmitri; he is a good man and he came to God."

I was shaken up, for no one else knew what had happened on January 27, 1943, no one else knew the name of the man, Katia's father, Dmitri—but Father Arseny knew.

"Fifteen years have passed and time has dulled these events in your memory. You have gone to confession to Father Piotr many times and asked for forgiveness; he forgave you, but your sin is a mortal one— God will ask you about it at the Last Judgment. Thy Will be Done, O Lord!

"I have no words of admonition, no advice to give; you lived through what happened, burning yourself with the fire of repentance. By the power vested in me by God, I forgive you, go and try from now on not to sin. And always remember that it is almost impossible to find people like Elena Alexandrovna, Nadia, and Alexander Nikolaevich. It is perhaps even harder to find a man like 'your Yuri,' as you call him. My friends and my spiritual children, I love you both. Call Yuri, tell him to come see me!"

I called Yuri. Father Arseny turned to the icons and we three prayed together. He asked us to kneel, blessed us with the icon of the Vladimir Mother of God, and we venerated it and the Cross.

As I read over these memoirs, I see how illogical they sound, how repetitious. I have read them again, but I am unable do a better job! Well, let this stay as it is. What happened in 1943 left an indelible mark on my soul; it will never disappear.

Our children, Katia and Sergei, were also under the spiritual direction of our Father Arseny, but in the last years of his life, he sent them more and more to Father Alexei (Alexei, the student) in the Kaluga region.

Almost every time Father Arseny came to Moscow or was "brought" there by his doctors for a stay in a clinic or in a hospital, he stayed with us (we had a three-room apartment, and Sergei and Katia had their own apartment not far from us). Sometimes he stayed with Natasha, Lyuda or Irina. All the Muscovites would go wherever he was for confession, advice and conversation. And then—something incredible would be happening! Our kitchen would be full of pounds and pounds of dried apricots, walnut meats, vitamin pills, tangerines, strawberries—anything and everything that people could find in that particular season. I remember one time Sergei Semenovich brought ten bottles of an excellent liqueur made with honey and aloe and insisted to one and all that it would certainly be very good for Father Arseny. Our dear Father Arseny laughed, and, to my joy, slowly but surely the guests drank it all. The days Father Arseny spent in Moscow were a celebration for everybody, but mainly for those in whose apartment he was staying.

There were days when Father Arseny would want to see some cemetery or simply to take a ride in the streets he knew and loved so well. Yuri or Vassily Ivanovich would usually take a taxi and ride around with him all over Moscow for entire afternoons.

I want to add that I did try several times to tell Yuri all that happened in 1943, but he always said, "Don't, it is over; I still love you as I did before and I don't want to stir up the past." Only Father Arseny, Elena Alexandrovna and Nadia knew everything that happened to me then.

Both Elena Alexandrovna and Nadia were amazing people. Their words, "You are our daughter," and their taking care of Katia and me in those hungry wartime years warmed my soul and helped me bear the weight of my sin, and gave me a certainty that Yuri would forgive me. I never heard a single word or hint of condemnation from them! All Yuri's family and I used to pray quietly together because we were living in a communal apartment[31]; Nadia was always the one who would say the prayers.

I want to tell something more about myself. Katia was born in a clinic where Olga was working. She kept me there for an extra month. My labor was a difficult one. I was forty-one years old and the doctors feared for my life, but God was merciful to me and I was able to return to Elena Alexandrovna's, where I lived a total of three years and ten months. My own mother and father were appalled by what I had done and by Katia's birth. They loved Yuri and knew well how I had hurt him by my behavior. Only after Yuri returned were we able to reestablish relations. My being pregnant and Katia's birth surprised my friends in the beginning, but everybody saw that I was living with my in-laws and a "legend" started that in 1942 Yuri had come home from the army for a few days and that Katia was his daughter. Yuri casually confirmed this theory, while I always stayed silent about it, which convinced people of their truth.

Sometimes I asked myself how I would react if Yuri had brought home a child from another woman? Human love can be very cruel and one can be tempted to retaliate. Only the love of a true Christian who has deep faith in his soul would have been able to forgive what a faithless or weak person never could.

As I am writing, Katia is twenty-four years old and Sergei twenty-five. I am a grandmother and I am helping them to raise Lena, who is three years old, and Nadia, who is two.

In 1964 something unbelievable happened. Katia and Seriozha had always been the best of friends, but then they fell in love with each other. When Katia became twenty-one and Sergei twenty-two they went to Father Arseny (on the day of Saint Sergius, July 18), who gave

---

[31]Group prayer was forbidden so the neighbors who shared the apartment could have reported them to the police if they had heard them praying! Those who reported would have been paid a reward.

his blessing for them to be married, but never told Yuri or me about it. They came back joyous and a bit shy on July 20 and told us, "Father Arseny has blessed us to be married and Father Alexei will crown[32] us in church in August." They also admitted to us that they had already spoken to Father Arseny the year before; at that time he had told them, "Wait so as to be absolutely sure and when Katia is twenty-one, do come see me again!" And that is what they did.

After we heard this we were more accepting. We blessed the children with an icon of the Mother of God of Kazan which Yuri had bought from workmen who had been hired to destroy a church. This icon was a miracle-working one from a church near Yaroslavl.

Sergei knew that he was not our son, but he loved both Yuri and me no less than did Katia. In 1957 we made some inquiries at the NKVD and got the following answer, "Alexandra Viktorovna Shilova died of pneumonia in 1950." When we inquired again in 1966, the answer was, "She was shot in 1948–1949, her place of burial unknown, she is restored as an honest citizen . . ."

That is how Yuri's and my life was. God was merciful to us, especially to me, a sinner. I do realize that almost all I have written about has to do with my family and myself, with very little about the community. The description of Father Arseny, our spiritual father and friend, is totally insufficient.

I can explain this by saying that I have also written memoirs called "A few short memoirs about Father Arseny and about his spiritual children"; there is also a notebook called "Memoirs of Father Arseny, January 9, 1975"; and I have also written together with Natalia Petrovna and Ludmilla "A description of the life of our community from 1921 to 1976," in which I have given the names of all our brothers and sisters, and our priests, even those whose ordination had been a secret. I wrote in them about the important events of this time, the dates of deaths, the appearance of new spiritual children, of Father Arseny's camp friends and others.

We gathered crumbs while talking to people and we wrote the biog-

---

[32]In Orthodox tradition newlyweds are crowned for a life together in this world and the next. —Trans.

raphies of many spiritual children who are still alive or have died. The biographies are extremely short, but we still have three notebooks of them. Of course the main person in all these writings is our beloved priest, the elder Arseny.

Father Arseny was benevolent and gentle, always even-tempered in his relations with all people. He loved them, but I witnessed his irreconcilability and sternness when he wanted to correct a mistake made by one of his spiritual children, when they were being unfair to others or committed other sins.

In the 1920s Anya K. was a very active member of our community; she helped many people and Father Arseny often commended her. At the end of one liturgy, Father Arseny came out with the cross, the people came up to venerate it, and he blessed some of them. Anya came up: he gave the cross to everyone but seemed not to notice her. "Father," she said, "bless me!" and Father Arseny said, loudly, "I am surprised that you came to church after what you have done. Do not come back until you have set right what you have done." Anya left in tears, but was there again the next Sunday, went to confession, and took communion. Everything seemed to have been settled.

Much later Anya told us that she had hurt her mother and father in such a way that her mother had to be taken to the hospital. Right after she left the church, she went to them and asked for their forgiveness. The fact that Father Arseny acted in this way was a life lesson for her!

In the summer of 1965 we rented a room and went to live in Rostov. I remember how guests gathered in the dining room of Nadezhda Petrovna. Father Arseny came into the room, said the prayers and we all came to be blessed by him. Lyubov Ivanovna, a lovely person whom we all loved, came up to him, but Father Arseny told her, "I am not going to bless you, leave here immediately, make right the wrong you did, and only then come back here." Lyubov Ivanovna started to cry and Father Arseny went back to his room returning only when she had left the house. A week later, Lyubov Ivanovna was here again; she went to confession and then returned often. I don't know why Father Arseny refused to bless her.

When he felt that his spiritual child was in need of correcting his behavior, or in need of help in overcoming sins, strengthening faith or learning to love others, Father Arseny was inflexible and strict. He always knew the inner world of the person he was dealing with, the depth of that person's faith. He never pushed him away with words of admonition that were overly stern. He did not want to hurt the person, but only to help him understand the evil he had to correct within himself.

To end my notes, I would recall Father Arseny's saying, "Faith in God and the love of others are truly alive in us only when we pray sincerely to our Creator, to the Mother of God and to the saints. We must also live within the Church, do good deeds and love our neighbor."

In the memoirs written by Father Arseny's spiritual children you will find differences, such as different dates; or the same events may be retold in a slightly different way. Each person wrote from his own memory, his own interpretation. Many events were described years after they had happened. But the most important thing is that even today Father Arseny remains our teacher and everything that is written about him is equally precious.

Written by Kyra Bakhmat
From the archives of V. V. Bykov (received in 1999)

❧ 9 ❧

The Archbishop

I CAME TO SEE FATHER ARSENY with a lot of questions and doubts I had about my family situation, my nephew, my brother and his family. I came early and rang his doorbell at six in the morning; I planned to leave for home on the nine o'clock train that night. I spoke with Father Arseny in the afternoon, and told him that I was leaving that same evening. To my surprise, he asked me to stay until the train that left at two the next afternoon. Of course I gladly agreed.

That evening was August 4, 1970, the day of Saint Mary Magdalene. We gathered as usual in the dining room after evening tea: there were seven of us. When we finished talking, Father Arseny said that he would tell us about something that had happened to him in the labor camp in 1942.

"One evening, for no known reason (but in camp there is never a known reason for anything) ten or twelve people were brought into our barracks. They had came from very far away; they were all in very poor shape and unable to work. I noticed an ancient man who staggered over to the lower bunks. The old man looked tired and sick, but in the morning he was walking freely and could even go out for roll call.

"I knew that at that time there were two priests in our barracks, Father Arhip and Father Panteleimon (a Ukrainian Uniate[33]). I do not know why, but neither of them wanted anything to do with me. I could understand why Father Panteleimon did not want to talk to me: it is well known that Uniate priests hate Orthodox priests. Any conversation always ended in insults to Orthodoxy. I noticed that Uniates easily befriended Baptists and other protestants, but that they hate Orthodox people. But I do not know why Father Arhip used to avoid me. I heard that he came from Voronezh; he seemed pleasant and warm-hearted; he was polite and talked to other people easily.

---

[33]The Uniates are Eastern-rite Catholics. —Trans.

"Fifteen or twenty days had gone by since the evening the new prisoners arrived. In the evening, probably around ten o'clock, a man walked over to me and said, 'Listen! That old priest is dying. He is still able to talk and is asking for you; you had better hurry, he might croak' (prisoners never said to die, but to croak). I went.

"A very old man lay on a lower bunk. Paralysis had hit him in the morning, so that he could no longer walk, but he was still able to talk. His speech was not clear, but I managed to understand him. I sat on his bunk. He started his confession by giving his name and saying, 'I am an archbishop.' Then I remembered everything I knew about this man. He had been consecrated a bishop by the Holy Synod before 1917 and was considered to be a honest son of the Church. He had participated in the election of Patriarch Tikhon. Then he had suddenly joined the *Obnovlentsi*, the 'Living Church,' and had led a fierce fight to dethrone Patriarch Tikhon and many bishops. He was later arrested, spent time in labor camps, came out, and made his repentance to Metropolitan Sergius.[34] He was welcomed back with the title of bishop; he was again arrested several times, and sent to different labor camps. I had never met him in person.

"How had this exhausted old man found himself in a labor camp? Such people were never sent to camps but were simply shot during the next 'cleansing.' Now this man lay in a regular barracks, he did not go out to work: the trustee in our barracks had been told to keep him in. I remembered that this bishop had suddenly disappeared in 1939. People made no mention of an arrest, but he was no longer talked about in church circles.

"It was late, and the neighbors of the dying man might have protested that we were not letting them sleep because we were talking. But in the camp people 'respected' death. If a priest were to be caught giving confession to a dying man, he might be punished and sent to a special cell for a few days, or they might add a year to his time. This extra year was an absurdity, anyway, because most prisoners died in camp. No

---

[34]From 1925 on Metropolitan Sergius (Staragorodski) headed the Russian Orthodox Church. He replaced Metropolitan Piotr (Polianski) who had been established according to the desire of Patriarch Tikhon, but was arrested in December 1925.

effort was spared to that end: hard labor and poor food. Nobody was ever freed from our camp, only members of the Communist Party had any chance of it, but such an order had to come directly from Stalin. In the seventeen years that I was in this camp I know of only twelve or fifteen people who were ever let out. In camps of less strict regime, people were freed far more often.

" 'Why did he say he was an archbishop and not a bishop?' I thought and, as if he had overheard my thoughts, he said, 'I was promoted to archbishop by the "Tikhonovians." ' These words put me on the alert.

" 'Before the 1917 revolution I realized,' he said, 'that it would be necessary to make changes in the Church, in its administration, its canons, its services and even the sacraments. We would have to switch to the new calendar, translate the services into Russian, and make many other changes. I voted to elect Metropolitan Tikhon (Belavin) as Patriarch. I knew him and even loved him in a way, but when the Living Church sprang up and most of the bishops were in support of him, I was happy: I saw that the Church could be saved, that it could be renewed and I actively supported that. I joined that movement especially because the government was in support of it; I considered that the time was right for it. I thought then and I think now that Orthodoxy must soon undergo big changes, and I spoke about this many times.

" 'A representative of the OGPU (the secret police), Evgeni Alexandrovich Tuchkov[35] called me in to his office. We had a long talk and met again several times after that, then we met with Karpov and others. Don't think that I was naive, but I did considered that any method was good in the fight against stagnation. I started to work against Patriarch Tikhon, against Metropolitan Peter (Polianski), against Metropolitan Agafangel (Preobrazhenski), against Archbishop Ilarion (Troitski), and against the many other metropolitans, archbishops, bishops, reactionary clergy and active lay believers who were against praying for the authorities which only created a split. The "Tikhovians" could not

---

[35]E.A. Tuchkov (1892–1957) was a member of the secret police, and from 1919 on he fought against the Russian Orthodox Church. He followed the line of Lenin, Trotsky, and Stalin. He interrogated Patriarch Tikhon and the Metropolitan Piotr and was awarded a medal of honor. In 1940 he became the head of the Union of Militant Atheists.

understand that "all authority comes from God."[36] I perfectly well understood that the self-appointed "metropolitan" Alexander Vvedenski and the archpriest Vladimir Krasnitski were crooks who only wanted to attain a high position in the Church. They had no thought of renewing Orthodoxy, but they were active in their fight and therefore were useful to the "renewal" movement.

" 'I was suddenly arrested. Solitary confinement in the Lyubianka prison, interrogations with beatings, and a meeting with Tuchkov—not the Tuchkov I had met before, but a cruel, authoritative man who told me, sardonically, "Your Grace, we need you in another position: you will do some work for us. I am going to send you to a labor camp. I will let you out in a year, and you will become a martyr. You will change your tune, you will come back to the Tikhovians and repent. They love people who repent, so they will forgive you and you will remain a bishop. You will then start to talk against the renewal movement, and then you will have a new stay in a camp. We will do this several times: camp, freedom, camp, freedom. And wherever you find yourself, you will be reporting to us every word you hear. You didn't even know it, but you have already been working for us. Keep one thing in mind: in the eyes of the Communist authorities it doesn't matter whether it is the Tikhon Church or the Living Church: both are harmful and we will eliminate them both. Before you are sent to the camp in Butirka, you will 'rest' for a month or two; during that time our people will 'work' on you so that you don't forget that double-crossing is not an option."

" 'They beat me up several times to teach me that lesson, and then they sent me to a labor camp where most of the prisoners were members of the clergy. In those days such camps did exist; I stayed there for a while. I was freed, left the renewal movement, and repented. They accepted me back at the rank of bishop, and I gained their confidence and wrote what I had to write to the Interrogator. I suffered horribly. I prayed to God and to His Holy Mother begging them to save me, to help me. I did realize that it was because of my own weakness that I had been caught in this trap. Each time before they sent me to a new camp,

---

[36]"Let every person be subject to the governing authorities; for there is no authority except from God" (Rom 13:1).

they would beat me to help me remember that you don't play games with the Secret Police.'

"After these words, I got up and said, 'I am not going to hear your confession. I am a simple hieromonk and I cannot take your confession upon myself. Yours is a sin against the Church, its foundation, its canons and against the lives of thousands of innocent people.' I turned around and went back to my bunk.

"After some twenty minutes, the same prisoner came back to me and said, 'That priest, the mullah is dying and calls for you. Why did you leave him? He die very soon, and he not letting us sleep. Go, he want to say something.' The prisoner was a Tartar and spoke a mixed-up Russian. I did not go. The man came a third time, swore filthily, and said, 'You are a mullah, he is a mullah, a priest. Why you no go? He going to die. Go!'

"I went, sat on the bunk next to the dying man and repeated that I could not accept his confession, and that I would not. 'What do you want to tell me?'

"Around us, we could hear swearing, laughing, talking. The barracks was not yet asleep. To my surprise, the archbishop's voice suddenly became clear, but there was almost no life in his eyes. 'I realize that you will not confess me, that in your understanding I am a great sinner.'

" 'That's right, I will not,' I answered.

" 'Then do me a favor: listen to me. In the Russian Church there used to be a tradition: if a man was dying and there was no priest nearby, the dying man could tell his sins to a friend, and that friend would retell those sins to a priest, and it was that priest who had to decide whether to accept this confession or not. This mostly happened during the war—these retold confessions were heard on the field of action. I am now in the last hours of my life. In the name of God, I beg you to listen to me, and when you are freed from this camp you will tell it all to a bishop. He will confer with other bishops and decide whether he will be able to accept my confession or not. I rely on the mercy of the Lord.'

"I answered that I would listen to his confession, but that I did not know whether I would ever get out of this camp or not. The archbishop said clearly, 'God will free you, He will free you for sure.'

"Slowly, sometimes through harsh breathing, he started to tell me his confession, and to my great surprise I realized that he truly believed in God, that he loved Him and had done a lot of what he had thinking that he was doing it for God. How enormous were his mistakes!

He started naming those he had denounced, who had been arrested, destroyed. He gave their names, and there appeared before me all the horror of betrayal, of reporting to the enemy. If the Archbishop had not been dying, I would not have believed everything he told me. He did not repent: he told me what he had done and he was only sorry that the Church had not accepted the renewal movement. The intelligent demonic work of the secret police and their desire to undermine the Russian Orthodox Church was clearly evident. You could see how they chose and used people who wanted to move ahead, who wanted power. At the same time, you could also see metropolitans, bishops and priests who preferred to be tortured, insulted and put to death than to go back on their faith in God; they protected the Church, its canons, its sacraments—there were many thousands of those! By enduring all these sufferings, by spilling their blood, by having given their lives they saved the Church. They not only saved it, they breathed new strength into it.

"At times, the archbishop stopped talking. He was obviously tired, and I kept thinking, 'There is no other criminal who has betrayed so many, or who has killed so many as this man, who claims to believe in God, this bishop of the Living Church. He worked with the OGPU and the NKVD to destroy the faith and corrupt the people.' He worked closely with the OGPU. He was not only their secret agent but also their consultant on church affairs—he himself mentioned this.

"I sat listening silently, but I could not resist asking him, 'Tell me. Before 1917 you were a bishop. If, at this time, a man had come to you and repented that he was a traitor, that he reported and destroyed thousands of people who were sent to forced labor and into prisons, all of it because that one man had cooperated with the police and the tsar's militia. Would you, then, have forgiven him his sins?'

" 'Oh, yes, you are right, but I am renouncing my past, I am asking for forgiveness. God is ever patient and ever merciful. I repent what I did and hope for salvation.' And suddenly he began to sob bitterly.

"I got up and said I would come back soon. I went to see Father Arhip. I woke him up and asked him to come back with me to the archbishop. Father Arhip answered me rather rudely, 'After the head count, the Tartar came to me asking me to help the man. I went and found out that he had been a member of the renewal movement. He started telling me his life story and I turned around and left. So that means he has now decided to try to ask you. My thinking is, "He is the one who messed up, he is the one who has to get out of it!" I hate members of the Living Church. It is because of them that I have spent twelve years in labor camp, and it is because of them that I am now in this most strict camp and I have no hope of ever being free again. I am not going to go!'

"I returned to the dying man. He lay there motionless and tears were running down his face. I made the sign of the cross over him three times and said that it was not up to me, a simple hieromonk, to forgive those sins. 'If God feels I am worthy of it, and if I am freed, I promise to retell your confession to a bishop and he, with the help of others, will decide. I believe that if the heretic Arius had come to a priest asking him to forgive him his sins, that priest would not have had the authority to forgive them. I feel the same way about myself.'

"I bowed low before the archbishop and prayed all night for him. I asked my Lord Jesus Christ and the Mother of God to enlighten me, a sinner. In the morning the Tatar came to me and said, 'You there. That one is already cold, I will go inform the man in charge!' No one ever reported me for having spent half the night at the archbishop's bunk; everything was all right.

"But this story left a heavy impression on my soul. A sincere faith in God seemed to have lived within this strange man, I became convinced of it while listening to his story-confession. But at the same time, there was the immeasurable baseness of reporting innocent people and a satanic desire to break down the Russian Orthodox Church, whatever the cost, by whatever method, disregarding everything else. He wanted it all to be the Living Church. His becoming an agent was not only due to the weakness of his character and will, but it was one of the sinful ways he chose to help him achieve his plans.

"I think that evil forces possessed the soul of the archbishop; in his delusions he sincerely thought that he believed in God, but the evil that held him destroyed his faith so that he became a toy in the hands of evil forces.

"During my first meeting with Bishop Afanassy, I told him the whole story-confession that I had heard from the archbishop as well as his request that Vladyko[37] would consider this confession together with several other bishops. While I was talking, Vladyko Afanassy did not interrupt me one time and asked me no questions. He said to me, 'I knew this archbishop, and had a dual impression of him. I will not share my impressions. I did think that he was a good man, but his confession has shown me a different side of him. You, a hieromonk, were not the one to grant him forgiveness. I know it may look like a cruel and unchristian act. When Patriarch Alexei sees me, I will speak to him about this. You, as a hieromonk, did the right thing.' "[38]

---

[37]This is a word, meaning "master," that is used for a bishop or archbishop. It is often used in an affectionate way. —Trans.

[38]Some readers may question the accuracy of this testimony about Father Arseny since it seems alien to the image and spirit of his person revealed in the other memoirs about him. It also seems to indicate an understanding of Church teaching and practice out of keeping with Father Arseny's knowledge and experience.

There is no reason why a hieromonk could not hear the confession of an archbishop and grant absolution. This was commonly done in the Russian Orthodox Church. Most Orthodox hierarchs, as a matter of fact, have priest-monks as their spiritual fathers and confessors. It is not necessary, nor is it the common practice, for bishops to confess to bishops, or for bishops to receive absolution only from other bishops. It is the case, however, that an apostate bishop would have to be reconciled to the Church by another bishop, and perhaps even a synod of bishops. If the hierarch in the present testimony, though having apostatsized and gravely sinned, had already been reconciled to the Church and received back into canonical communion, there would be no reason for Father Arseny not to offer him absolution. Also it would be completely impossible for any priest, and surely for Father Arseny, to deny absolution and comfort to a penitent church member at the point of death, whoever that person might be, and however grievous his or her sins.

It may also be noted that the attitude toward ecclesiastical reform and ecumenical activity of the schismatic Living Church, as well as that of certain members of the Moscow Patriarchate during the Communist period, was very different from that of the Russian Orthodox Church before the Bolshevik revolution, and the Russian Orthodox Church (and most other Orthodox Churches) today. The answers of the Russian hierarchs to preparatory questions for the All-Russian Church Council at the beginning of the last century, for example, as well as the acts of the 1917–1918 Council, testify to this. So do the lives and teachings of great Russian Orthodox Church leaders like Saint Philaret of Moscow, Saint Tikhon the Confessor, Patriarch of Moscow, and Saint Elizabeth the New-Martyr. The understandably conservative attitude of

One of the people who heard this story asked, "Father Arseny, you have not told us the name of this archbishop."

"I told his name only to Vladyko Afanassy."

Recorded by T.N. Kameneva
From the archives of T.N. Kameneva

the Russian Church under Communism, especially after the tragic episode of the Living Church, has sadly cast a negative shadow over innocent, acceptable, and even necessary changes in church life and activity (such as use of the new calendar, the use of contemporary language in the liturgy, and dialogue and cooperation with non-Orthodox Christians) supported by many faithful and intelligent Orthodox people, including bishops and saints. —Ed.

⊰ 10 ⊱

Loneliness

BEFORE I START TALKING about Father Arseny—how I saw him for the first time in 1971, then came to see him often and became his spiritual daughter—I feel I must tell something of my previous life.

I was forty-eight years old when my husband Mikhail, aged fifty, died after a short and difficult illness. At that time my daughter, Marina, was already married and living with her husband. My husband's mother, Ekaterina Fedorovna, a person of amazing character and deep faith, had always lived with us and helped raise her granddaughter, Marina. I will talk about Ekaterina Fedorovna again later; she died two years before her son, Mikhail. She was then seventy-eight years old.

I was left alone in my apartment. We used to be so happy together: we all loved each other, but now each object in it reminded me of our past. The sofa, the armchair, the cup my husband used to like to drink from, a dress of Ekaterina Fedorovna's, things Marina had left behind. I seldom saw Marina now.

Her husband's mother was looking after her little son, Vitia. It was only very seldom, when someone had fallen sick, that they brought me my little grandson to watch. That is how my life had turned out.

During the first months after my husband's death I was busy: I had to set up a monument on his and his mother's grave, take care of a lot of paper work, sell the *dacha*[39] which I no longer needed, and so on and so forth. On top of it all I was working.

My whole family had believed in God and Ekaterina Fedorovna had raised her son, Mikhail, in the faith. As for me, I had known nothing about the faith when I got married. I had been an active member of the *Komsomol*[40] when I was studying in school and in the Institute. I became a believer through the influence of my husband and his mother.

---

[39] A house in the country. —Trans.
[40] A communist club to which young people belonged. —Trans.

Ekaterina Fedorovna was an exceptional person; she was the pillar on which all our spiritual life rested. It is hard to believe that during the twenty-four years we lived together we had not one fight, even though I explode easily. Sometimes as I would be walking back from work upset, tired, despondent, I would feel so close to exploding that I would be afraid to go home—I realized that I might start shouting at my family to no purpose! I would open the door, take my coat off, and go to the kitchen. Ekaterina Fedorovna would just glance at me, understand my state of mind, hug me lovingly, and say, "You are tired, my Nastenka!" Angry, I would want to tear myself away from her, but she would hold me closer, kiss me on the cheek, make the sign of the cross over me three times, and my anger would simply disappear. She behaved the same way with my daughter, Marina. She was always gentle and loving, but she knew how to get her to obey. A sense of babushka's superiority, and of respect and love for her grew in Marina's soul as well as in mine.

Ekaterina Fedorovna's behavior was absolutely sincere, and she was not the least manipulative—this is just the way she was. She believed in God and went to church often, mostly on Sundays. She prayed for at least an hour every evening, even when she was tired; she read her rule of prayer, and on the feast days of icons of the Mother of God she would also read the akathist.

My husband Mikhail went to church with me on feast days and we went to confession and to communion only once a year, during Holy Week.[41] My husband worked as a scientist; I was a chemical engineer and worked as such in a factory.

Feelings of abandonment and loneliness, plus the empty apartment almost destroyed me. I felt better at work with people around me, but went home sad and depressed. I tried to combat my state of mind by going to visit friends more often; I also invited people over, watched television, read, went to church on Saturday evenings and Sunday mornings. I started to pray at home in the evening but the feelings of despondency and loneliness did not leave me.

I suddenly remembered that Ekaterina Fedorovna had had a friend

---

[41]The last week of Great Lent, the week leading up to Easter. —Trans.

named Varvara Semenovna who used to go with her to Rostov to see a priest, a Father Arseny who had returned from a labor camp in 1958. She would even occasionally spend a night there. I searched for and found my mother-in-law's old address book, called Varvara Semenovna, told her about myself, and asked her to help me meet this priest (she knew that my mother-in-law and my husband had died, and had been at their funerals). She listened to me and said she would call me soon. In a week, the telephone rang and Varvara Semenovna said that we would be able to go together that next Sunday.

We left Moscow by early train and were in Rostov by two o'clock. Rostov is an old town, but very decrepit. You could see the domes of many closed churches. We arrived, we were greeted in a very friendly fashion, and were immediately asked to sit down and eat lunch. I had a feeling that I had been in this house before and that I knew the people there. There were nine of us that day who sat down at the table; Father Arseny came out of his room, prayed, and blessed us all.

The month was September, the date the twentieth, so the next day would be the feast of the Nativity of the Mother of God. When we finished eating, Father Arseny spoke to us about the childhood of the Mother of God; he reminded us that his information came mostly from apocryphal writings and legends he had read in Greek a long time ago. The weather was warm. Father Arseny went out into the garden and called for me to come out about five minutes later. He blessed me and showed me to a chair that was standing nearby. I sat down and he said in a gentle voice, "Tell me about yourself."

I started to speak. At first I was fumbling for words, but then I made an effort and managed to tell him everything I could remember about myself before I was married, then about my life with my husband and our relationship, about Mikhail's faith in God, about my own faith and, of course, I spoke about Ekaterina Fedorovna—the person who had been closest to me and who had been better than any one of us. I reminded Father Arseny that she used to visit him with the Varvara Semenovna who had brought me today. I spoke for a long time. Father Arseny did not interrupt me, nor did he ask questions. I came to a close and fell silent. Father Arseny was also silent.

We were sitting under a large linden tree. The leaves were moving gently, spots of sunlight were running about the grass. It was warm, warmer than usual for September. Father Arseny's arms lay on the handles of his armchair; he was concentrating on his thoughts and his eyes looked beyond me to the sky. The silence lasted such a long time that I become nervous.

"Anastasia Vladimirovna," said Father Arseny, "I have listened carefully to you. You feel lonely, despondent, sad: this is in vain. This is an imaginary state that comes not from loneliness but from a way of life which is not spiritual enough. You used to live with your husband and could lean on him; you used to have your daughter with you, a daughter who required attention and care; you also used to have Ekaterina Fedorovna, who united you all through her love, her prayer and her goodness. You no longer have any of this and so you cannot find your place in this world. You are escaping into a state of depression and loneliness and hope that if you see me, a priest, that I will, by talking to you, give you instant help. Sometimes that does happen by the grace of God, but we must work together on getting you out of this despondent state; we will achieve this with the help of God, the Mother of God and your Saint Anastasia, the deliverer from bonds. Let us pray to Jesus Christ.

"I know that you loved Ekaterina Fedorovna and that you were amazed by her patience, her faith in God, her constant helpfulness to those around her. You were not able to understand how she could bear all this or where she found her strength. I will answer for her. God gave her strength because of her great love for others and her constant prayer to the Almighty God. Try to follow her path and all your miseries will fade away.

"I listened to you, but you spoke only about the surface of your life, your actions and your sins. You did not tell me the most important parts: you did not tell me about one thing that is hurting you, that is repulsive and that you do not want to remember. This thing you did not tell me, it remains in the depth of your conscience, perhaps because of a false sense of shame."

Father Arseny fell silent for a while, then made the sign of the cross and, looking at me, he repeated everything I had said. But when he said it, it came from the depths of my soul: all my life appeared with its disgusting deeds, sins and actions. With a sinking heart I saw myself in the words Father Arseny was saying. A wave of shame and disgust washed over me. I wanted to get up and run out of the house, out of the town— even a priest should not know me to be such a sinful person. He understood what I was feeling and gestured for me to sit back down on the chair from which I had leaped up. I had never even told my husband, much less anyone else what I was now hearing about myself. Fear gripped me.

I jumped up, fell on my knees, and said, "Father Arseny, I am ashamed. Forgive me!" And I started telling him everything that had been hidden in my conscience, even though he had already said it. Father Arseny put his hand on my head and said, "Anastasia Vladimirovna! I am not condemning you. God allowed me to go through the five steps to understanding life's way.

"The first step was the grasping of faith. That I received from my mother, Maria Alexandrovna, and the great elders of Optino, Father Nektary and Father Anatoly, who taught me how to pray and how to love people. I was helped onto the second step by a short talk of Patriarch Tikhon of Moscow and all Russia, as well as by Archbishop Ilarion (Troitski). The third step I owe to a simple priest named Ilarion (a namesake of Archbishop Ilarion). The fourth was the labor camp (which we called the 'death camp') where contact with so many different prisoners showed me both people with spiritually perfect souls and those who had the most frightening souls, possessed by immeasurably malicious anger and dark forces. The fifth step was my serving as a pastor and my contact with you, my spiritual children. This has taught me never to condemn anyone: as the prayer says: 'There is no man who lives and does not sin.'

"Remember, all our faith is based on our love of God and of the Mother of God and on our veneration of saints. We can express all this by loving all people and by never refusing them help. I always tell everybody the words of the Gospel, 'Love your God with all your heart and all your mind and love your neighbor as yourself.'

"Do you find yourself lonely? You have icons in your apartment— icons of Jesus Christ, of His Holy Mother, of our Saint Anastasia, of the Guardian Angel, of Archangel Michael, and probably you have others as well. If you feel seized by feelings of despondency, walk over to an icon and pray, and the dark forces will step away.

"Read a chapter of the Gospel every day. In the Four Gospels there are eighty-nine chapters, so in the course of a year you will be able read the whole Gospel four times. I started reading a chapter of the Gospel every day from an early age. I have been a hieromonk for fifty years and I celebrate the liturgy almost every day, but every time I read a chapter I find something new in it, something good and inspiring.

"Be with people and help them, whoever they are. They can be your colleagues, your friends, or your relatives. Help everyone and those around you will understand what a Christian is and will come to the Church, to God."

I will repeat a phrase that someone once said, "My soul forever lay in the palm of the hand of the elder Arseny." That next morning I went to confession and left with a peaceful spirit. Before I left, Father Arseny told me in front of all present, "Come to see me more often, you do not have to give me warning. When I am taken to Moscow, come over, you will be told of it."

Upon my return to Moscow I acted as Father Arseny had told me. I saw him at the apartments of his spiritual children six times, and went also to Rostov, but not more than once every two or three months.

Father Arseny was an inexhaustible fount of love. Those who thirsted could come, scoop up some of this love in their hand, drink, and rest from the pains of their life and from their sins; or they could fill a vessel brimful, take it home and drink from it there, slowly spending what they had received.

Having met him, you always left nourished with love, instruction, advice and help. My first meeting with him in 1971 was the basis for my rebirth.

Anastasia Vladimirovna Korsakov
From the archives of V. V. Bykov (received in 1999)

⚜ 11 ⚜

The Secret Service Agent

ON DECEMBER 10, 1972, the day of the icon of the Sign of the Mother of God, I went to see Father Arseny and while there met a comrade-in-arms called Innokenty Vladimirovich whom I had not seen for the past five years. We were both very happy to see each other. After a short while Konstantin Prozorov arrived. By the will of God, some time ago we had all found ourselves in the same labor camp, even in the same barracks; that is, the four of us, Father Arseny, Konstantin, Father Innokenty and myself, Seraphim Sazikov. The years had left their mark on each of us. The least affected by time was Father Arseny, but ever more frequently he had to lie down on the sofa while constantly praying or talking with those who had come to visit him. Every so often he would be taken to Moscow to be checked over in a clinic.

This time Father Arseny was feeling well and each of us were able to talk to him and receive his advice; we were all supposed to receive communion the next day. That evening eleven people gathered in the dining room. The space was tight, but it was cozy and everyone was well meaning. Father Arseny asked Father Innokenty to tell us how he had come to know God. In the course of years past he had asked the same thing of many people; he knew that this was important, even indispensable, for all the listeners. I was the only one who had never told my story. I had been a criminal, a professional thief, until I broke with my past and came to God, to His Church while still in camp but under the spiritual influence of Father Arseny.

Father Innokenty started his story:

"In the army, I was the leader of a reconnaissance group. They used to drop us deep to the rear of the German Army, where we were supposed to gather necessary information in crumbs and communicate it over a portable radio transmitter. Sometimes, if we were lucky, the Germans would not discover us and then we would be able stay for two or three months or even longer. We used to live in the forest, in foxholes, or in destroyed villages; we had to disperse throughout the neighborhood, talk to the locals and spend our days and nights lying under bushes near roads, or near railroad stations, airports and depots. We had to observe and then observe even more! The work was extremely dangerous. Soldiers would get killed—sometimes alone, sometimes in groups—especially when they were being parachuted behind enemy lines. The Germans were immaculately trained in fighting people like us. As a rule most of those who parachuted in died.

"This introduction is important to help you understand the work we were doing behind enemy lines. Our group was not made up of regular soldiers but of specially trained people, some of whom had to be able to speak German flawlessly. These people had either graduated from special language schools or institutes, or simply knew the language well. There were always women among us: it was easier for them to talk to local inhabitants and in that way gather information. All the participants carried top-of-the-line firearms and knives, civilian clothes and clean passports.

"We were sent far away from Moscow, beyond Minsk (Bielorussia), over near Lida. We found a deserted and destroyed village and settled in the basement of a burned-down wooden house on the outskirts of the town. We decided to make that our headquarters. There were eight of us, three women and five men; it was hard to gather up all the equipment that had been parachuted along with us, but we did and went to work.

"Our assignment was primarily reconnaissance, and sometimes we were supposed to sabotage something, but too much of that would lead to our being discovered. So that you could understand our work, you must realize that sometimes we had to capture German military men, interrogate them, find out where they were stationed, what they knew about the locations of their warehouses, and then we had to shoot them.

"Such executions were part of our orders and were always very painful for each of us: we were not killing in the heat of battle but were taking the life of a man, the enemy, who had been rendered defenseless. We would feel pity for them, but were not able to talk to each other about this feeling, since we were afraid. There was no choice, we had to execute the soldier or the officer—if we had let him go, he would have gone straightway to inform his own people about our group's location, which would have then been destroyed immediately. We had to do the same thing to local inhabitants if we felt that they had guessed who we were. Needless to say, the same fate awaited police officers.

"I believe you understand everything!

"In the month of October the mud was deep, the rain fell mixed with snow, a cold wind penetrated to the bones. We had been working without having lost a man; we had caught eleven German soldiers, gotten the information we needed and communicated it to our authorities. It was going to be hard to leave our burned-out village with its warm basement, but a German tank division had set up camp nearby. We went into the forest. It was difficult to get food and the German papers we had obtained before were no longer valid. That made it even more difficult to circulate in enemy territory; our rations were also coming to an end and our radio batteries were running low. We let our people know all this. One night an airplane, a U-2, parachuted containers that held everything we needed, but things got scattered, and it was difficult to find it all. The most important—the batteries—were intact.

"Now I am coming to essentials. We were living in foxholes in the forest, we were working separately and wearing civilian clothes, but we were armed. We could be absent for two or three days at a time. We always left a radio operator and a soldier in the foxhole.

"One night four of us went out: a lieutenant, a second lieutenant, a radio operator named Ira, and myself. We walked for some thirty kilometers[42] and came to a little church that had a house next to it. The rain was pouring down, it was freezing cold, our clothes were drenched, and we were frozen. There was no way for us to return to our base since it was much too far away, so we decided to go into the house claiming we were partisans. It was a risky thing to do, but we could not see another way. We knocked on the door and walked in. They let us in with no problem—they had no choice since we had weapons hanging all over us. Inside the house we found a middle-aged man, a young woman, a ten-year-old girl and a little boy about six years old. We took our coats off and hung them to dry near the stove, but kept our arms next to us. Our second lieutenant stayed next to the door to keep watch.

---

[42]About eighteen miles. —Trans.

The windows were curtained. The woman, a beautiful and welcoming person, asked no questions, but took out a pan full of hot potatoes, some bread and a bowl of cottage cheese. She said, 'Eat, please!' We ate a lot, adding some of our own canned goods; one of us then took the place of our second lieutenant to let him eat, too.

"We started to question the man: what? where? who? He answered calmly and, we felt, truthfully. We questioned them both for some two hours. We found out that the man was a priest called Father Piotr; his wife's name was Olga. We finished our interrogation and Father Piotr said, 'I know all the local partisans. They all stop by here in order to get one thing or another—how can I refuse them? The partisans and our parishioners have said that the Russian Army has parachuted a group of saboteurs. The Germans have been combing this place looking for them. You wouldn't be some of them, would you?'

"With this question Father Piotr signed the death warrant for himself and for his family. He had realized that we were not partisans.

"We stayed with them for two days, got ourselves warm, and ate to our heart's content. Olga allowed no one to come into the house; she told people that Father Piotr was not at home. She milked the cow and tended the animals; armed with a machine gun one of us always followed her. It came time for us to leave. Before we did that we were going to have to take the family into the woods and shoot them. The little boy, Seriozha, had gotten attached to me; little Genia loved Ira, who herself was such a young girl! Father Piotr, his wife Olga and the children often prayed aloud together. Father Piotr used to pray in front of his icons almost all the time.

"That evening it was time for us to leave. I told the family to get dressed and come into the woods. Father Piotr and Olga realized what was happening. They grew pale and Father Piotr asked permission to give communion to his family. I didn't know what 'communion' meant, I didn't know what the Holy Gifts were, but I gave my permission. They all walked over to the icons and prayed together; he communed Olga, Eugenia, Sergei and then took communion himself. He blessed everyone, including us. He walked over to a closet, took out some holy water and sprinkled some on each of us. He hugged each member of his family and, in a changed voice, he said, 'We are ready to die!' He realized that no amount of begging, no amount of tears would change anything. I looked around my group and saw that they were all against this killing.

"Ira whispered, 'Commander, maybe we shouldn't!'

"I kept silent. The lieutenant and the second lieutenant were disturbed: they did not know which of them I would ask to shoot the family. We had never shot children before and I also knew that neither Father Piotr nor his wife Olga were guilty of anything. All the members of our group were good people; they had been taken into the army because they knew the German language; they had been sent here, but they had no relations with the secret police, the NKVD . . .

"We went out into the woods and we walked for two or three kilometers to where there was a ditch. I ordered everybody to stop. The shooting of Father Piotr, Olga and their children was not going to be a military action because of some maneuver on their part; it would be the murder of innocent people. Even so, I did not have the right just to let them go—if I did, one of my group was supposed to shoot first me and then Father Piotr's family. I could see that both the lieutenants and Ira were against the shooting. I was sure that we would be able to agree to spare them. But I did not know whether one of my team might not be a member of the SMERCH (an organization called 'Death to the Spy'). If so, he or she could report me to the authorities and we would all be destroyed. We were all afraid of one another.

"I made up my mind. I ordered the lieutenants and the radio operator to go back to the old ditch, the place where we had agreed to meet, and to wait for me there. I saw pure joy on their faces; they were so happy that they would not be the ones doing the killing. They quickly turned and left, obviously afraid I might change my mind and tell them to do the killing. Father Piotr and his family stood close together praying. Olga's hands were on the children; she was not trying to protect them but to unite them. Father Piotr raised his hand to bless his family and even myself. I looked at them and started to shake. These people's faith in God was stronger than their fear of death; no one was crying, no one was begging me for clemency—me, who held their fate in my hands. They prayed, entrusting their lives to God, to His will.

"I walked over to Father Piotr. He did not notice me, but continued to pray. I caught a trace of fear and prayer on Olga's face. 'Father

Piotr, the cruel laws of war require me to shoot you and your family, but I can't do it and I will not—that would be murder. Go! But you must swear to me that you will tell no one that we were here. No one must know, no one!'

"'A priest is not permitted to swear, but I can promise you for myself, for Olga, Eugenia and Sergei that no one will find out that you were here. I promise!'

"He took out his pectoral cross, kissed it, and touched my lips with it, saying, 'I thank you, O Lord, for your great mercy on us sinners. O Holy Mother of God, I thank you! Hallowed be Thy name!' Then, looking at me, he made a prophecy: 'You will come to God! You will find the faith, the Church. You will have some difficult times, but God will save and protect you,' and he bowed to me. Olga walked over to me, blessed me with the sign of the cross, hugged me and, falling to her knees, kissed my hand. Genia kissed me. Seriozha hugged me. I warned them that I would shoot my machine gun into the ground for my companions to hear. I shot and, without looking back, I walked away. For the first time since the beginning of the war I felt joy, warmth and light.

"I know that you want to know who I am and where from. Who were my parents, what was my education? I was born in 1917 and raised in Moscow. I finished the University of Moscow in 1938 and went to work in a factory as a designer. Both my father and mother taught in the same university. My father taught the study of the strength of materials and my mother taught German and English. My parents had grown up in the milieu of progressive professors; their sympathies lay on the side of the revolution, and they considered it good taste to mock the Church and priests. That is how they raised me. For practice we spoke German or English at home, that is why I speak German perfectly. My army file states, 'He is fluent in English and in German.' That is what decided my fate when I was mobilized into the Army. They sent me to a special reconnaissance school and, in 1942, sent me to the other side of Smolensk. When the war started, I was twenty-four years old.

"The war ended. I returned to Moscow and got married to the radio operator Irina. I was offered work in espionage, but I refused and returned to the factory where I had been working before. Everything went on well until April 1952, when I was arrested as a foreign spy. It was alleged that I had been hired by the Germans in 1943 while I was in their territory.

"I spent time in the prisons of Butyrka and Tagansk. I was questioned for the first time two weeks after I was arrested by a handsome woman who said her last name was Voronets; I will remember her for the rest of my life. First she questioned me gently and seemed well-meaning in her attitude. The week after that, she called me in again and interrogated me in the Tagansk prison. But Voronets showed another side of herself: 'You have to confess, sign; I will make you talk.' I refused, so they took me to a cell, removed my pants and my underwear, threw me onto the cement floor with my back up, pulled my legs open, and started beating me with a rubber cane. The pain was such that I could not refrain from screaming. There were five men torturing me: one sat on my head, two others held my legs and two were doing the beating. The interrogator, Voronets, watched the torture and gave orders: 'Harder, more, more, hit him there.' I was unable to walk back to my cell, so they dragged me back by the legs with my head hitting the floor.

"Don't accuse me of being weak. A human being is not able to endure such torture. During the third questioning I 'admitted' that I was a spy, that the Germans had hired me, and that I was setting up a terrorist act. Voronets was present at all the torture and gave the orders to the torturers.

"Back in her office, as I was signing the protocol with my 'confession' I said to Voronets, 'You know good and well that I am not guilty.'

" 'You fool, we just need to gather up people to prove that there is a terrorist organization. You just got here by chance. People more important than you have also confessed. You are nothing, you are a louse, you are here just for the sake of the numbers. You just have to sign what the interrogator tells you to.' Suddenly she snarled evilly and poured filthy swear words over me. 'Lavrenty Pavlovich[43] is watching the development of the organization, and here I am, wasting my time

---

[43]Lavrenty Pavlovich Beria (1899–1953) was chief of the Secret Police. A most cruel man. —Trans.

with you, irritating my nerves for shit like you,' and she hit me in the face three times.

"They condemned me to be shot, but then sent me to the camp without ever taking away the death sentence. They sent me to the most strict camp, where the order was given that when there was going to be a 'cleansing' I would be the first to be shot. In 1952 I met Father Arseny, became a believer, found God, and saw the sinfulness of my previous life. I decided that I wanted to pray for my past and to become a priest. I will not tell you about life in camp; much has been written about that. For me personally, camp was the finding of God through Father Arseny. All the sufferings I had to endure there could perhaps serve to redeem the sins I had committed earlier—anyway that's the way I wanted to think.

"I was freed from the camp in 1955, before the big wave of freedom and rehabilitation. They gave me papers allowing me to return to Moscow. They had not touched Irina or the children—she was still in our apartment. Irina knew nothing about me. She thought I had died in the camp, or that I had been shot. When she inquired about me at the Police, they gave her no answer. I was unable to let her know that I was alive since no correspondence was allowed from the camps. God was merciful to me and I found Irina. The one-time radio operator in our group, she joyously accepted the faith and became a helper for the Church in many ways.

"I was let out of the camp almost exactly three years before Father Arseny was. He gave me then the addresses of several of his spiritual children. In December 1956, I met those people and told them that he was alive; they knew it already because they had received letters from him. Corresponding with him had by then been permitted; several of his spiritual children had even traveled to see him. I received most of the support I needed from Natalia Petrovna and Maria Alexandrovna. They helped me to get baptized in a distant church, go to confession and receive communion. They recommended that I attend the Church of Saint Nicholas—'Saint Nicholas of Kuznetz'—under the priest Father Vsevolod Schpiller.[44] They spoke to him about me and told him

---

[44]Archpriest Vsevolod Schpiller (1902–1984) returned to Russia from Bulgaria where he had emigrated and spent over 30 years. In 1951, he became the parish priest at St Nicholas. He

my life story. Natalia Petrovna came to church with me and presented me to Father Vsevolod. He said, 'Before I hear your confession, I want you to tell me about yourself. I will talk to you after the end of the liturgy. Wait for me.'

"The church was full of people, mostly women. The liturgy ended, but I had to wait a long time after it was over, so many were the parishioners who wanted to talk to Father Vsevolod. Every so often he would glance at me, letting me know that he had not forgotten me. Then, 'Let's go!' and we went. He asked me to sit down and then sat with me at a table. A middle-aged woman (I later found out she was his wife, his *matushka*) started feeding us lunch. The meal finished, but we continued to talk for a very long time. This talk was as much a conversation as a confession. I tried to open my soul to him entirely. Father Vsevolod seldom asked me questions, but when he did, he extricated the essential from the depths of my soul, things I had not even been aware of myself. I told him everything: my life before the army, my work in reconnaissance, getting ready for the shooting of Father Piotr and his family, the interrogations by the NKVD, the camp and my encounter with Father Arseny—the encounter that had brought me to the faith. Father Vsevolod asked me in detail about Father Arseny: where had he served? in what church? I did not know myself, but told him that Natalia Petrovna and Maria Alexandrovna—his spiritual daughters— would be able to answer his questions in detail. I was only able to talk about the spiritual help he had given me and about how many prisoners he had managed to bring to God in the camp of special regime. 'I came back to Russia only recently and have never heard of such a priest.' I became his spiritual son and my wife, Irina, his spiritual daughter. We followed all the advice Father Vsevolod gave us and often went to services in the church of St Nicholas of Kuznetz.

"During 1958, I began to feel the urge to become a priest. Father Vsevolod told me, 'Your path to priesthood will be a very long one. Think for a minute: you have no religious education; no seminary will

---

was a renowned theologian, an excellent sermonizer and a remarkable spiritual director. He created a community and raised a great number of students. Father Vsevolod had great spiritual authority and helped many people to find their way to God and His Church.

accept you because of your past, and then you are too old. No bishop is going to risk ordaining you, and I cannot give you my blessing. Your path to priesthood will be very long, you must be purified of your evil deeds' (he did say 'evil deeds'). 'This will be slow and difficult. You will become a priest, but only by the unique grace of God, and I don't know when. You must pray and repent; keep begging God for forgiveness, and the years will go by and God will decide everything.'

"Once, I tried to redeem myself by saying that I worked in reconnaissance and that we had saved the lives of tens of thousands of our soldiers. He said, 'That is true, but your hands are stained with the blood of those you either killed or that you ordered to be killed—this is a mortal sin and you committed it many times, even if you were obeying the orders of your superiors. Keep praying, keep asking for forgiveness, and keep repenting.'

"In 1958 I saw Father Arseny again. I told him that for the past two years I had been the spiritual son of Father Vsevolod Schpiller, the priest at the church of Saint Nicholas of Kuznetz. I asked Father Arseny to take me under his spiritual tutelage, in view of the fact that in the camp he was the one who had brought me to the faith. Father Arseny said nothing at first but, having questioned me extensively about Father Vsevolod, said that he was a priest with a great inner strength and spirituality so it would not be right for him—Father Arseny—to take upon himself my spiritual direction since Father Vsevolod had been my spiritual father for more than two years, and each person should have only one spiritual father. If you have two, you could get two different pieces of advice, and this could have bad consequences. You can have only one spiritual father, just as a child has only one birth father.

"I spoke several times with Father Arseny about my desire to become a priest. I did not get Father Vsevolod's blessing for more than nine years; Father Arseny was of same opinion. One day, after we had had a long conversation, I know that Father Arseny wrote a long letter to Father Vsevolod (Maria Alexandrovna transmitted it to him), and that Father Arseny received a reply from him. The question of my ordination was still not resolved, but in 1968 something extraordinary happened by the grace of God.

✠

"For some time Irina and I, remembering Father Piotr's family, had wanted to go back to Lida to see them and to ask for their forgiveness and for their prayers. More than twenty years had passed and much had changed. It took walking around for a while, but we did find the church; a service was going on, the priest was a new one. The house where Father Piotr had lived no longer existed; it had burned to the ground after the war. We started asking around, but we did not know Father Piotr's last name. The answer was that the priests were changed every year. As soon as one got used to being there he would be sent elsewhere. There had been several Father Piotrs. An old woman who was selling candles in the church figured out which Father Piotr we had in mind and gave us an approximate address.

"We traveled to northern Bielorussia, and in a small town found the only church that was still standing. It had suffered quite a bit, but a service was going on. We asked where Father Piotr lived and went to his house. Matushka Olga opened the door: time had covered her face with a net of wrinkles and she had become heavier but was still handsome. When she heard that we were looking for Father Piotr, she said, 'He is in church.' We asked permission to wait for him. Olga looked at us worriedly, fearing something, but allowed us to wait.

"It is important to mention that at that time and in the period that followed, the Orthodox Church was fiercely persecuted. The plan was to declare that republic to be atheist, without a God. We asked Olga about Genia and Sergei. Surprised, she replied that their daughter was married and living near Riazan; Sergei had finished school and was working in Minsk. Then she asked, 'And who are you? How do you know our children?'

"Then, of course, I did something silly. I walked over to her, took her by the shoulders, and said, 'Olga, don't you recognize me?'

"She was scared at first, pushed my hands away, and made the sign of the cross. Then she stepped back, flushed, and said, 'Is it you? Is it you?'

She hugged me and kissed me. Just at that moment Father Piotr entered and said, laughing, 'Eh! Matushka, who is it you are kissing?'

" 'Piotr, Piotr! Look who is here.' Irina walked up and we both fell to our knees and asked for their forgiveness for the past. Joy seized us and our faces were wet with tears.

"From that year on, Irina and I used to visit Father Piotr and Matushka Olga almost every year and would stay for four or five days. Of course I told them about my life in camp, about Father Arseny, who had made me a believer, about my spiritual father, the priest Vsevolod Schpiller (they had heard about him during their stays in Moscow), and of course about my desire to be a priest. Father Piotr and Olga visited us in Moscow several times. Once we received permission and all traveled together to see Father Arseny. After this first visit, they saw him several more times.

"In 1968 we went to visit Father Piotr and he told me that he had spoken about me to his bishop,[45] told him about my life, my work in reconnaissance, about my stay in camp, that I was a spiritual son of Father Vsevolod Schpiller (whom Vladyko had gotten to know in 1950 when he was a student in Moscow Seminary), and that I knew the services very well. Vladyko listened to Father Piotr and said that I must come to see him next time I was visiting Father Piotr. So I went. Vladyko received us, talked to me for a long time, and ordained me a priest on the feast day of the martyr Ignatius, February 11. I was ordained a deacon the day before that. Times are still unstable now so I will not tell the name of the bishop—it could harm him.

"I returned to Moscow a priest and went to Father Vsevolod immediately. He was very surprised that I had accepted ordination without his blessing. He was unhappy about it, but after he had prayed, he said, 'Thy will be done, O Lord!' He hugged me, blessed me, and kissed me. He knew that I was perhaps not worthy, but it had been done. I am now serving in Bielorussia, but my spiritual father is still Father Vsevolod. Father Arseny lives within me as a strong spiritual force in which I can dip to receive spirituality and strength. Father Arseny did not approve of my having a rushed ordination without Father Vsevolod's blessing, but said the same words Father Vsevolod had used, 'Thy will be done, O Lord!'

---

[45]In 1968 the bishop would have been Archbishop Antony (Melnikov).

"I came to understand that God existed in seeing the way that Father Piotr, Olga and their children were ready to accept death; only people of great faith could have gone to die that way.

"Well, I will not hide it from you: it has been difficult for me to tell you all my life story."

Deep in thought and not noticing the rest of us in the room, not noticing that Father Innokenty had ended his story, Father Arseny was sitting in his armchair. With a slow wave of his hand, he chased away something which was in his way and said, "In 1962 and 1963 I asked many of you to write your memoirs about your life in the Church, about how they had come to the faith or how that faith got stronger, and about the highly spiritual people you have encountered on the path of your life. During the course of these eleven years much has been written, some stories were retold right here, others were read aloud and everyone came to understand how different the ways that lead to God can be. Some came to God through suffering, some through a close encounter with death; for others it was the joy of meeting deeply spiritual people or seeing a miracle shown to them by God himself. For many this path has been difficult, full of doubt, disappointment, failure, hesitation: am I on the right path or am I mistaken? But there comes a moment when, with the help of God, the Holy Mother of God and the saints, that all obstacles disappear. Many came to God through human love, having become husband and wife.

"Look at Seraphim Alexandrovich" (Father Arseny was talking about me, Sazikov), "what an exceptionally difficult path he had to tread to get to God. He had to tear himself out of the terrifying world that surrounded him. We just heard the story of Father Innokenty—he had had no faith at all, no one to give him support, to advise him, but he still came to God, through a test of his conscience. The shooting of Father Piotr seemed unavoidable. Father Innokenty was faced with a dilemma: should he obey the orders of his superiors or should he let that family live? On one side of the scale he put the orders he had received, on the other the life of Father Piotr, his wife Olga and his children. He realized that no order could be compared to the value of human life. He resisted his military orders and let the family live, but he risked being shot himself.

"God placed Father Piotr's family on the brink of death. It was a heavy test, but since we know that this was given by God himself, this means that it was necessary both for Father Piotr and for Father Innokenty. This event brought Father Innokenty to God and to friendship with Father Piotr. Later, this same Father Piotr helped him get ordained to the priesthood. In this case we can clearly see the will of God. It has been said, 'A hair will not fall from your head without the will of God.'[46]

"During the war when your reconnaissance group caught a German soldier it was obligated to shoot him after he was questioned—there was no way you could have let him go. But killing an unarmed man made you into a murderer. From the army's point of view this is a necessary evil: he was the enemy, if you had let him go you would have been destroying the whole group that had been sent behind the German lines. Through your work you saved thousands of lives on the front. You can justify a lot, reason all you like, but you can never justify murder. You must pray and beg God for forgiveness. You were baptized after everything that happened to you and so you were forgiven all you had done; you have gone to confession and you have received communion, but you must pray, constantly pray, asking for God's mercy and forgiveness.

"Today I heard one of you say, 'Something happened . . .' Nothing ever happens by chance. Everything in men's lives happens through the will of God—everything, any meeting, any joy, any grief, any unusual event, everything that surrounds us is God's mercy, His will.

"To witness and see the inscrutability of the ways of God, I asked you to write memoirs showing how each one of you came to God. Listening to them or reading them, we delve into the souls of men who are tossing around, looking for God and we are always amazed at God's grace and his forgiveness for us sinners. A small spark of God, hidden under a load of sins, can become a flame, seize the whole soul of that person and sometimes influence the people around him or her.

---

[46]Mt 10:30; Lk 21:18: Acts 27:34.

"I know that I am very sick. When I go you must continue writing about your past and the paths that brought you to God. Let your children read them, let your relatives and other people you know read them. I am sure that much of what you hear here, if it is written down, will be kept and read and, by the grace of God, will be useful.

"Let the grace of God and the prayers of the Most Holy Mother of God and the saints be with all of you. Do write . . . !"

Addition by Father Innokenty

Rereading my memoirs as they were written down by Seraphim Sazikov in 1972, I find it important to add a few things. I realized that my spiritual fathers—Father Vsevolod, who is still alive now, and Father Arseny, who went to a better world in 1975—were right: my path as a priest turned out to be an arduous one. It was only thanks to the support of Father Vsevolod and to the warm support of my *matushka,* Irina, that I was saved from wrong steps. I think God was punishing me for my previous sins and for having become a priest in such a rush.

As I was telling about myself and about Father Vsevolod, who is an amazing person and spiritual father, who can read your soul, who is an amazing person and a good man, I thank God who, in His mercy, sent me the joy of contact with both Father Arseny and Father Vsevolod— with the help of God they practically made me into a man infused with faith in God.

When I used to visit the church of Saint Nicholas of Kuznetz I used to only speak with Father Vsevolod, never to other people; Irina, of course, being a woman, learned more, and sometimes talked of some of the difficulties faced by Father Vsevolod in his church.

Remembering and talking about my life, I unwillingly left out the image of Father Arseny. My plan was to write mostly about him because in the awful conditions of the camp it was he who breathed the faith into me. He was my spiritual forefather. I got so involved in remembering my life that I did not mention the colossal work he had taken upon himself in the labor camp where he was helping, giving support, and passing on the grace of faith to others who were ailing spiritually.

He saved so many people! Give rest, O Lord to the soul of the elder, Hieromonk Arseny.

Recorded on cassette and written up on
December 10, 1972, by Seraphim Sazikov.
Father Innokenty added his remarks in 1977.
(From the archives of T.N. Kamenev)

⊀ I2 ⊱

Father Seraphim

March 1972

IN 1972, IN MARCH, I cannot remember the exact date, but I went to see Father Arseny at an unexpected time and for an important reason. Nadezhda Petrovna welcomed me pleasantly and, when I had taken my coat off, said, mysteriously, "We have an amazing guest today!" and she smiled.

The dining room was empty, I knocked at Father Arseny's door and heard, "Come in!" Father Arseny was lying on the sofa, half-covered by a blanket. A man was sitting in the armchair; he rose when I came in. I saw a man of small stature, very pale with white hair, a big white beard, large lively eyes, and a good and welcoming face. I greeted him and went to get Father Arseny's blessing; he blessed me and said, loudly, "Now go to get Hieromonk Seraphim's blessing." I did.

Father Arseny looked at me and said, "Alexander Sergeevich, please write down the memoirs of Father Seraphim. Record his complicated life path, it should be included in the memoirs that we are collecting. Ask Nadezhda Petrovna and all the people who are here today to come and listen to his story. It will be good for them, especially since our paths crossed several times in the camps. Father Seraphim! I ask you please to talk without reservation; don't rush, tell us things in detail. I know that you are a shy person, but here we are all like family."

I asked permission to record the story on a cassette so as to be able to write it all down in detail. Father Seraphim looked around, made the sign of the cross several times, and, having said "So help me God!" began to talk.

"I am now eighty-nine years old. I was born in St. Petersburg in 1883 to an aristocratic family that descended from Rurik.[47] We are often mentioned in old history tales—we had some saints in our family, but

---

[47]Several aristocratic Russian families traced their origins to Rurik, a Viking chief who in A.D. 862 was asked to come and help the people of Novgorod govern themselves. —Trans.

127

we also had our share of evil-doers and we also had some traitors. Our last name is well known, but I will not mention it: you will just have to believe me. I was baptized with the name Alexei. I was raised as are all the children of rich families, with nannies, governesses, maids and butlers. I was the youngest of the family. I had three brothers, Vladimir, Vsevolod and Igor. I also had two sisters, Olga and Elena. My brothers were all handsome, tall and well built, and they served in the most select regiments; my sisters were extremely beautiful women. As for me, I stopped growing at age fifteen; my face was ugly, my hair untamable. My father and mother—God keep their souls—were proud of my brothers but never took me along to receptions, never showed me off to guests at home. I was embarrassed by myself, and I did not want to put my parents to shame.

"The whole family loved Russia. The names my brothers had received were those of Russian saints; my sisters, Olga and Elena, were named after holy princess Olga, who had received the name Elena when she was baptized. My brothers finished the best and most prestigious schools, as did my sisters. I could not apply to the Pages' School, nor even to the Cadets[48] because of my height and my looks; nor could I become an officer in the army. I studied in a regular school, graduated with a gold medal, attended the Polytechnic Institute, also graduating from it with a gold medal, but my parents did not think much of that.

"Starting at age eleven I used to go often to church and I used to pray fervently at home as well. At seventeen I went to Valaam[49] and later visited Solovki[50] and some Pskov monasteries. My parents, especially my mother, were passionately opposed to all this: here was this rich prince and he wanted to join the 'race of foals' (that is how some people used to refer to the clergy because of their long hair and beards). All my relatives were against me. There was talk that I should be sent to Ekaterinburg because the governor was a relative, or perhaps to England to the Embassy; all in order to separate me from the Church.

---

[48]Two highly prestigious military schools. —Trans.

[49]A well-known monastery in the north. —Trans.

[50]A fourteenth-century monastery on an island in the White Sea, far to the north of Russia. —Trans.

"After I finished the institute, I went to work in the Baltic Factory. The engineers had been influenced by the idea of revolution, as had been the intelligentsia in general. When they found out that I was a member of a well known prince's family, and that I had access to the tsar's court, they declared a boycott against me. They punished me by silence, spoke to me only about work, answering back only 'Yes' or 'No,' and, of course, mostly 'No.' I was miserable at home, but it was even worse at work. That I had finished the university with a gold medal only made my colleagues hate me the more. Many said, 'O little prince, did you get your medal because of your family or did you have to pay for it?'

"I kept thinking, 'What shall I do?' I went to the church where I always went. They had a good priest there, a Father Nikolai. I told him what was going on at home and at work and that I was feeling a strong desire to become a monk. The priest listened to me, kept silent for a while, then prayed with me and said, 'Alyosha! You are not fit for military service, you don't seem to do well at work, and now you want to go into a monastery: this is a good and God-pleasing plan. It is difficult for me to give you advice, although I do think that this would be a good thing. Go to Optino Monastery—but before that go to Kronstadt to see Father John—and do what they say,' and he blessed me. I went first to Father John of Kronstadt, there was such a crowd, I could not even enter the church, so I stood next to the door and asked for help from God and the Mother of God. The liturgy ended and the priest's horse-drawn carriage came. The priest came out of the church and people ran to get his blessing, some falling on their knees by his feet. I was standing in the crowd while the militia and the deacons were trying to clear a path for Father John. When he came to where I was—and I was deep in the crowd—he stopped, turned around and made himself a pathway, and came straight to me: 'You, little prince! You want to go to a monastery, do you? Well, first take yourself to Optino,' and then he blessed me and went on. The people around me began saying, 'So, you, servant of God, he is showing you your way!'

"A week later, I went to Optino. I went to the church, stood near the icon of the Holy Mother of God and prayed hard. I prayed, but I did not know whom to approach, whom to see. An old monk came to me and said, 'Why don't you go talk to the *starets* Anatoly?'

"I was surprised, but I followed him. I couldn't feel my legs under me, I was so scared. Who could have known that I was there and that I did not know how to find a *starets*? We got there and found a big crowd waiting to be seen by the *starets*. The sun was setting when a young monk came out and called me in to see the *starets*. I entered and received his blessing. The *starets* Anatoly looked me over and said, 'Alexei, leave your worldly life and go to the monastery of Nilo-Stolobensk, to the elder Agapit. Your life will be difficult, oh how difficult: you will pan for gold for many years. Go to your parents and tell them that you are going to the monastery.' The elder hugged me, blessed me and, joyous, I left for my home in St. Petersburg.

"When I got home, my father was not there. I told my mother that I had received the blessing of Optino to enter the monastery. There was an enormous falling out. My father returned from one of the tsar's receptions and Mama told him about me. My father started shouting, 'The doors to a monastery are closed to you: I will go to the Holy Synod and get them to give the order not to accept you anywhere.' My mother slapped me in the face many times and called me awful names. When my brothers and sisters came home, they started making fun of me and calling me a Fool for Christ. I patiently stood it all and then went to the factory to tell them I was quitting. They gladly let me go.

"I wrote letters to my relatives to tell them what I was doing and then left for the town of Ostachkov from where I boarded a small ship to get to the monastery of Nilo-Stolbensk. I spent one night in a hotel and the next day I went to the monastery church along with the rest of the pilgrims. I prayed, stayed for the liturgy and after that I went to a monk and asked him, 'Where can I find the starets Agapit?'

"The monk was surprised by my question and said, 'He lives in the skete.'[51]

"I asked again, 'But how can I get to see him?'

"He answered me, 'Not everyone is admitted to the skete, you must get permission from the monk responsible for the skete. He is now seeing the abbot. Go stand near the abbot's house and ask him when he comes out. If it is the will of God, he will allow you. He is very strict!'

---

[51]A small monastery, often comprised of smaller houses. —Trans.

"I asked where the abbot lived and went to stand by his house. Two monks came out, and which was the one responsible, I did not know. I walked up to them and said, 'Your Holiness, the elder Anatoly of Optino sent me to the elder Agapit at your monastery.'

"One of the monks said, 'Tell me what it is about.'

"They both listened without asking questions and the taller monk finally said, 'Your priest will need to get a paper from the Synod—but he will not get it.'

"So I guessed that the tall monk was the one responsible. He said, 'I am going over to the skete right now, and I will take you with me. Go to the pier, to the boats, and wait for me.'

"I found the pier and waited; after a while we boarded the boat and sailed off. It was about eleven o'clock. We arrived on the island, which was covered with woods, with tall pines reaching to the sky; and around the island lay the waters of Lake Seliger. Wide expanse, space, a blue sky—I could hardly catch my breath. The responsible monk called someone to take me to the elder Agapit.

"I entered his cell and received his blessing, but the elder did not even look at me. He said, 'So, Alexei, you have been traveling to us for a long time; we have been waiting for you. Tell me about it!' He did not offer to let me sit. I told him in detail about my family, my life in St. Petersburg and about my great desire to become a monk. I then fell silent, thinking that I had told him everything, but the elder said again, 'Tell me in more detail!'

"I started talking again, repeating myself, but I heard him say again, 'Keep on talking.' But all the while that I was talking he never looked at me. Then he started to ask me questions. I answered. A monk walked in—I thought perhaps he was his cell attendant. He brought the elder a piece of black bread and two bowls and I realized that that was the monastery lunch. The *starets* rose, prayed with the other monk for a long time, and then began to eat; I was still standing. He finished eating, prayed again, and then said, 'Keep on talking about yourself.'

"'Father,' I answered, 'I have told you everything.' I could barely stand on my feet any longer.

"For the first time he lifted his eyes, looked at me, and said, 'You have not told me everything. Are you running away to a monastery because you are envious of your handsome brothers? Perhaps if you also were handsome you would be attending social affairs and then you would not even think of a monastery.'

"I was silent; I did not know how to answer. Something stirred in my soul: 'Perhaps it is so.' Before that I had never thought of such a thing. I had been standing for some four hours when the *starets* got up and said, 'Wait, I will go to confer with someone.'

"I waited for about two more hours, then he walked back in and said, 'Against all the rules, you will stay on as my second cell attendant.' And suddenly he started to speak in English to me, then in French, and he said, 'You know languages well, they will be necessary in your life.' He then took out a book in old Slavonic and said, 'Read!' He listened, nodded his head, and said, 'You do know how to read, but you make mistakes in the stresses, the words jump over each other; you will have to study for a long time.' He started asking me about the Fathers of the Church, various Gospel and Old Testament texts and how I understood them. 'You know what, my dear, you only know the surface of things, your knowledge is immature, you have much to learn, but the main thing you have to learn is prayer. You will have to find joy, not effort, in prayer; in praying the rule every day, in addressing God, the Holy Virgin, the Mother of God and the saints you must find joy, spiritual happiness and a true understanding that you are uniting yourself to God. I look at you and I think, will you be able to exchange your princely upbringing and worldly knowledge for a monk's life? And I think, yes, you will be able to, let us praise God and His Holy Mother!

" 'You are tired of standing. Oh, that is all right, you will stand a lot in the monastery; you will get used to it. You will be my second attendant—Father Ieraks will show you what you have to do. You have a watch in your pocket: put it on this table, a monk does not need a watch, you will have to know the time by looking at the sun, you will get used to it.'

"That is how my monk's life started. I was then twenty-four years old; the year was 1907. I will admit that I am a sinful man. I was young and dumb. I did not know what real monk's obedience was, and at first I did not like the elder Agapit. I was so wrong, and I came to understand that only six months later. At first, everything was difficult, thoughts invaded me constantly, but under the direction of Father Agapit I overcame all difficulties and started loving him with all my soul. He was a true man of prayer. I was tonsured in 1911 with the name Seraphim. In 1913 I became a hierodeacon,[52] but my voice was not strong, so I was not often allowed to serve in the monastery. In 1914 I was ordained a hieromonk. Father Agapit taught me everything. He gave so much knowledge and strength to both myself and Father Ieraks. He taught us the church services, the teachings of the Holy Fathers, the Old and New Testaments. We would read a book, and he would then ask us in detail how we understood it. If necessary, he would explain everything to us, or would tell us what would be the next book to read in order to understand the first one.

"The most important thing he taught us was prayer. He taught us by praying himself and we followed, listening to every word he said; we plunged into a state of separateness from the surrounding world. At the same time Father Agapit was teaching us by saying, 'Man must grasp prayer, get into its Godly meaning not with his mind, but with his soul and his spirit; only then will his mind, his heart, and his soul separate from all material things, from daily concerns, sadness and even human joys. You will forget about your aching feet, which are tired from standing for so long, and you will reach delight in prayer—you, a sinner, will be closer to God, you who are so unworthy.'

"Father Agapit had been born into an aristocratic military family, served as a captain in the army, and then suddenly became a monk.[53] He had had no religious education but had spent years independently studying spiritual literature. His knowledge of the writings of the Fathers of the Church was amazing. He knew the Gospels and the Old Testament by heart, he loved the writings of Metropolitan Filaret (Drozdov) of Moscow, of Father John of Kronstadt; and he had corresponded with the elders of Optino, but had never visited them.

"Father Agapit was strict and inflexible if someone did not follow the rubrics or went against the teachings of the Church, or against his

---

[52]A hierodeacon is a monastic deacon; a hieromonk is a monastic priest. —Trans.

[53]The memoirs of Father Seraphim are retold the way he told them. Sometimes the events he describes are interrupted only to be returned to later.

rule of prayer, but he was fair and good-hearted. When he saw that a man had done something bad, he would blame him and punish him, and then he would suffer over it, even though his punishment would be well deserved and fair. He had a broad theological education, he knew the writings of the Fathers of the Church perfectly, he revered all the saints, but he had a special love for Russian saints: Saints Sergius of Radonezh, Savva of Storozhevsk, Fyodosy of Totemsk, Nil of Stolobensk, Seraphim of Sarov, Tikhon of Zadonsk, and many others. He considered that their lives were the highest spiritual achievement and thought that the Russian people and Russian monks had to learn from them especially.

"Father Agapit considered the Holy Mother of God to be the keeper of Russia, the protector of orphans, the despondent, those suffering from illness or torture. When he prayed to the Mother of God, Father Agapit was reborn. He would forget about his aching feet, get up and, if Father Ieraks or myself were reading the akathist to the Mother of God, he would start to sing the kontakia and ikoi[54] from memory. He knew by heart all the different akathists to the icons of the Vladimir Mother of God, of the icon of the Joy of All Who Sorrow, of Unexpected Joy and many others, and also to many Russian saints. When he prayed, he seemed afire, every word he pronounced kindled the faith in both myself and Father Ieraks and oriented us Godwards. He told us, 'We keep asking and asking from God, His Holy Mother and His saints, but what do we give Him in return? Let us praise His Holy Name, thank Him for His great Mercy, for being alive and for the chance of saving our sinful souls through prayer and love of others.'

"I spent almost thirty years in labor camps, three hundred and sixty months. Many people don't believe me: they don't think it possible to survive thirty years in a labor camp, and then no one ever had such a long term assigned to him. But I tell you that I did, yet I am here talking to you. Why is that? It is only because Father Agapit taught me and Father Ieraks how to pray; he also generously shared with us his spiritual fortune, which he had acquired during his long years of monastic life and constant prayer. When we prayed with him we were separate

---

[54]Kinds of church songs specific to each liturgical day. —Trans.

from all the emptiness of earthly life. Pardon me, I am repeating myself," said Father Seraphim.

He stopped and started to cry. Tears were rolling down his cheeks. We sat quietly, but Father Arseny got up, walked over to Father Seraphim, and hugged him. The silence lasted a few minutes. Then, "Forgive me, I was crying like a child, but remembering Father Agapit was so moving for me. I will not cry anymore. Forgive me!"

"One day, Father Agapit told us why he had joined the monastery. 'My father,' he said, 'was an aristocrat, a military man. He ended up a lieutenant general and could only imagine my brother and myself as officers in a regiment of the guards of His Majesty the Tsar, but for a lot of reasons we were never successful in being accepted in it.

" 'Our whole family believed in God: my grandmother, my father, my mother, my brother, and myself. We always used to go to church, we used to go to confession and to Communion three or four times a year.[55] My grandmother, Natalia, and my mother, Ekaterina, prayed a great deal and raised us—my brother and myself—in the faith.

" 'One time, I decided to spend my holiday in the Caucasus, on the shores of the Black Sea. My uncle's family had gone there to spend some time. It was hot but a light wind was blowing. My uncle suggested that we rent a boat and go sailing on the sea. I went to hire a large sailboat with oars and off we went.

" 'The wind was blowing in our direction, but the sail kept pulling us farther and farther from the shore. We could barely see the houses, and on the horizon only mountains were to be seen. The owner of the boat began to worry and, speaking in broken Russian, said, "We go back shore quick, look!" And he showed us a small cloud which was moving toward the shore. The wind suddenly changed and started blowing very strongly toward the shore. "Quick, it is storm, quick, Allah! Allah!" At first we could not understand what was so dangerous, but then the waves started to get larger and larger. The owner of the

---

[55]At that time this would have been more than average: most people would have gone only once a year. —Trans.

boat kept altering the direction of the sail and offered to lower it alto-
gether and use the oars to get us back as quickly as possible. Our boat
was being thrown to the right and left but had started to move faster.
The owner kept on saying, "Allah! Allah!"

" 'Several people were on the boat: my first cousin Anastasia, her
fiancé Andrei Sergeev, Sonia, a friend of Nastia's, her sixteen-year-old
brother Yura, myself and the owner of the boat, Ahmed. Suddenly the
wind grew strong, the sea grew turbulent, the boat was tossed and
started taking in water, and the sail was torn away. Where was the shore?
Was it near or was it far? The oars were wrenched out of our hands and
the boat was being enveloped by water and was rudderless. I started
praying aloud while removing my clothes and shoes; Andrei and Yura
were doing the same. The girls sat huddled together. I heard Anastasia
praying aloud, too, and the owner was calling on Allah. My Lord! I was
praying so hard, begging God to save us and, as I looked at the sky, I
saw the Mother of God with my mother kneeling in front of her and
praying. "Anastasia," I shouted, "do you see?" And I crossed myself
several times.

" 'Yes, I see it!' she responded. I realized that the Mother of God
would save us. An enormous wave struck us broadside and we found
ourselves in the water. I grabbed Anastasia and Sonia and struggled to
stay on top of the water. I looked to the sky and again saw a bright icon
of the Mother of God with my mother was praying in front of it. Suddenly a wave picked us up and threw us onto the shore. When I stood
up, I pulled the women away from the water and again saw the icon. It
was a real miracle, and both Anastasia and I saw the icon of the Mother
of God.

" 'Andrei was also saved, but Yura and the boat's owner drowned. The
vision of the icon of the Mother of God with my mother praying before
her shook Anastasia and me up. I immediately asked to be discharged
from the army and went off to the monastery of Valaam to become a
novice. Eight years later, by the will of God, I was transferred to the
monastery of Nilo-Stolobensk. Still later the abbot directed me to live in
the skete and this is where I live and pray. My cousin Anastasia was also
so shaken up by the vision we had that she refused to get married and
went to join a women's monastery; she is still alive and we correspond.

" 'That is how I became a monk, through the mercy of the Mother of God and the prayers of my own mother. I told my mother and father in detail what had happened to us and about the vision we had seen. "Pavel," said my mother, "on that day I was seriously worried about you, and at two o'clock I walked over to the icon of the Vladimir Mother of God, fell to my knees, and began to pray for you. I prayed and the tears were running down my cheeks. I did not know then why my heart was aching for you, but I kept on praying. You tell me now that you were in trouble at exactly two o'clock. Our Protector, the Mother of God, showed you a great miracle and saved you and Anastasia from drowning." My father and mother were not surprised that I had decided to enter a monastery and gave me their parental blessing. They also felt that the miracle was a good cause for prayer and monastic effort.'

"There were few books in Father Agapit's cell. He had all the service books, of course, the *menaia*, the lives of saints, such as Dimitri of Rostov, Theophan the Recluse and others. If he needed other books he had them sent over from the monastery's library. Father Agapit would rise early in the morning, pray all the required services, as well as the akathist. Every day Father Ieraks or I would read lives of saints and study them carefully with him. Father Agapit would stop at the most important parts and explain their teachings and their deeds to us. Every day we would read books about miracle-working icons of the Mother of God and, if there was an akathist for that icon, we would read it. Very few pilgrims were allowed in the skete. If somebody did show up, Father Ieraks and I would immediately leave the room.

"The skete was situated in a pine forest. Enormous pines reached for the sky. The silence was unusually deep although sometimes you could hear the sound of the handle of a pail or the sound of an ax striking a log. If the wind was strong, you could hear the sound of rustling pines and the gentle sound of the waves in Lake Seliger. The little houses in the skete were all identical and built of logs. The entrance to the skete was marked by two pillars with an arch between them, inscribed with a text which I have forgotten. The small house had a porch, a tiny entrance room in which Father Ieraks and I lived, a stove for cooking and heating the place, a jug of water on a washstand, a small samovar and a few cups. Everything was kept perfectly clean: we washed and dried everything every day. The meals were simple, almost ascetic. During Lent we ate almost nothing. We drank very light tea, but it had always to be very hot. We slept on beds made of boards that had been covered with a thin layer of felt. Our life was well-regulated and quiet. The sound of monastery bells announced the church services. Inside the cells, prayers were going on continually. It seemed our *starets* never grew tired.

"Winter was so beautiful. You would come out onto the porch and everything all around was white: the pines, the bushes and the paths between the cells, and you could see Lake Seliger, silent, calm, ice-veiled. Only rabbit tracks speckled the whiteness of the snow-shroud in numerous loops. Father Agapit would come outside and glorify God for the beauty He had created. Tears of gratitude often poured down his face. 'O Lord, My God!' he would say. 'I thank you for having created the sky and the earth. I thank you for this beauty which warms the souls of men.' He would stand there for a long time singing praises to God.

"We used to go to the monastery for services. In the summer we would travel by boat, in the winter we would go by sleigh over the ice; as for the deep mud of spring and fall, we would have to pray in our cells, since there would be no communication possible with the monastery.

"There was talk: 'Are monasteries useful? The monks are parasites, do-nothings, all they do is hit the ground with their foreheads. They would be better off doing something useful.' I hear this sort of thing and I am always amazed to hear this kind of talk coming from people who believe in God. Monasteries save the world; they save people. In monasteries there are constant prayers for men's salvation, for the forgiveness of their sins, for peace in the world, for the protection of our homeland. Morning, noon and night the monks pray for forgiveness for people's sins. Russia exists thanks to monasteries. And as long as there is at least one monastery, Orthodox Russia will live.

"In the beginning it was very difficult, so difficult that I had doubts: would I be able to bear it all? But I succeeded and walked in Father Agapit's footsteps. Then things got easier and I stopped even noticing the difficulties; prayer began to come naturally to me and was no longer a difficulty but a consolation. At first I was hurt when I received reprimands or obediences, but after a while I got used to them and began to accept it all as the way things ought to be.

"First I received a cassock to wear, then a *riassa* and finally a *mantia,* and there I was—a monk. All these were steps of joy; years passed and I became a hierodeacon and then a hieromonk. Each liturgy I celebrated was an indescribable spiritual delight—a miracle. The moment of the Eucharist is a great miracle performed by the priest. It regenerates you, lifts you up to unattainable heights, and you realize that God is with you.

"I have sometimes heard people ask, 'What is a miracle? I have never seen one.' It always surprises me and I say, 'But you have just come from the liturgy. Isn't the Eucharist, celebrated by the priest, a miracle? You did just see a miracle.'"

"Let me go back to my past. My family never tried to find me; they just crossed me out of their memory as an exile, unworthy of their attention. In 1957, ten months after I had left the labor camp, I found out during a trip to Leningrad that two of my brothers had joined the White Army and were now living in Paris. My oldest brother, Vladimir, had already been a lieutenant general in 1917 and had joined the General Headquarters of the Red Army. He was shot in 1938 or 1939, convicted as a spy and an enemy of the people. My sister Olga (the older one) left for the Ukraine in 1919 and disappeared there. Elena is still alive and working as a librarian; she did not suffer during the repressions of either 1933 or 1936.

"The Communists closed our monastery slowly and painfully. They arrested a few people at a time, shot them, dispersed others, took away all our treasures, broke and desecrated icons—well, they did to our monastery what they did with every monastery. In 1921, on August 1, the day of the finding of the relics of Saint Seraphim of Sarov, our *starets,* Father Agapit, fell asleep in the Lord quietly and peacefully. He had grown weak in the course of just one week; he could no longer get up and was losing strength day by day. We were not losing our mother or our father, we were losing the teacher who had given us, not our physical life, but our spiritual life, who had made me a man, who had taught me how to pray, and had breathed into me faith in Jesus Christ. I cannot tell you how greatly I grieved at his death, I cannot transmit it to you. If I try, my past will rise before me, before my eyes, and I will start to cry." Tears were rolling down Father Seraphim's face and he no longer seemed a small, plain man. He might have been sitting among us so sad, but he emitted light and his face was lit with an indescribably sad goodness.

"A few minutes before his peaceful death, Father Agapit suddenly had the strength to look at us. He called Father Ieraks and me over to him and said, 'Pray to God and His Holy Mother, beg her to forgive your sins, pray for all those who suffer and who are miserable. Love those around you and help them. Bear one another's burdens and so fulfill the law of Christ.' He blessed us three times, then his hand fell and he left us quietly."

Here, poor old Father Seraphim started crying. He was embarrassed and turned away from us. We wanted to leave, but Father Arseny stopped us. When he regained his composure, Father Seraphim began to talk again. "The monastery and even the skete were still hardly even existing, but I was chased out of the monastery and went to live in the village Nikolo-Rozhka, near the church. The church stood on top of a hill, all white and poised. When I went up the bell tower, there was a beautiful view of Lake Seliger with its numerous islands, and further away I could see the churches and bell towers of my beloved Nilo-Stolobensk monastery. They arrested me in 1923 and took me to the village of Ostachkov. I spent a long time in prison. They made mock of me in lots of ways and later sentenced me to five years of incarceration for being an 'anti-Soviet activist and a dangerous element.' Of course, there was never a real trial. I was in camp without interruption till 1956. When my five years ended, I was called in to be told that the decision had come down that I had to stay another five years. And so on.

"First I was in the camp in the Solovki islands. Prisoners had no rights in any camp, but at Solovki this was doubly true! They could take you around the corner of a church and without orders, or maybe just for fun, they could take you to the edge of a ditch and shoot you in the back of the head, or turn you with your face toward them, back up five or six paces so that you could not grab for their revolver, and shoot you in the face or in the heart and bury you half alive. I've seen this happen with my own eyes.

"At first they used to send me to do different jobs, but never to cut trees or work in the mines because I was so small in stature. They used me for menial but extremely difficult jobs: for carrying hundreds of pails of water, for starting bonfires in freezing weather to warm the guards and the working prisoners, and for other things I will not enumerate. Later the camp administration decided that monks, priests and bishops would be perfect for cleaning out the latrines and digging out human excrement. Twenty-eight of my thirty years in camp I spent working on that assignment! Whichever camp I was sent to, I was immediately assigned to this job—perhaps it was suggested in my file. It is heavy work, especially in wintertime: you have to chisel out the frozen mass and transport it away on sleds or carry it in pails. The smell penetrated your clothing, your hands, your face—people would avoid you, swear at you, and sometimes beat you up. The camp administration took special pleasure in sending clergy to do such work, saying, 'This is just the job for you, you are a priest, aren't you?' and they would add blasphemy about the Church and its rites. O, Lord! What lawlessness, what an outrage on the faith and what a desire to stamp out the Church and destroy the human soul.

"At times I was despondent—filthy and saturated with that awful smell. I could not get rid of the dirt. There was very little water, and what there was in the winter was frozen. I had to get my bread, *balanda*,[56] kasha, and hear people swearing at me. It was awful, but I used to suffer most of all because when I prayed I could not bless myself with the sign of the cross—my hands were too dirty and I was surrounded by filth. I decided that I should pray only when I could clean up, wash my hands, my face, my clothes, but I began to notice that when I was doing dirty work vain thoughts would possess me and take me away from my monk's rule.

"Archbishop Ilarion (Troitsky)[57] gave me some advice. We met in the Solovki prison where he was also forced to clean the latrines, 'Vladyko!' I asked him, 'What should I do? I am cleaning out excrement, but I am a hieromonk, so I have to pray day and night, but how can I

---

[56] A watery soup given out in camps and prisons. —Trans.
[57] He was incarcerated in the Solovki prison from 1924 to 1925 and again from 1926 to 1929.

do that when I am so dirty and disgusting? I cannot make the sign of
the cross. What should I do? Vain thoughts sometimes come to me.'

" 'It is essential to pray,' said Vladyko Ilarion, 'so that the surrounding world disappears and only your prayer remains. Do not cross
yourself with a dirty hand, but lift your eyes up, then down, then to the
right and to the left. You will have made the sign of the cross, but when
you are back in the barracks and are clean, do cross yourself with your
hand. When you pray during your work, when you are deep in prayer,
you will not see the dirt or smell the stink. That is what I do and it does
help me to bear the horror of it all. God will protect you from vain
thoughts: remember what Father Agapit taught you.' He blessed me
and, as if entering into something unknown, he said, 'Why should you
be asking me? You used to be with Father Agapit and you must know
yourself what you have to do: help everyone in any way you can—this
is the law of God.'

"I revered Vladyko Ilarion and religiously followed his advice. Very
soon after our conversation they moved him out of the Solovki, which
made me was very sad. In the beginning it was difficult to gather my
thoughts together, to concentrate, but in some two months, while I was
constantly praying, I stopped noticing the dirt and the smell and began
to live in another world. Next to me I could feel the presence of Father
Agapit, Father Ieraks, and my mother and I prayed as I had done in
Father Agapit's cell—I might have been doing dirty work, but I was able
to accept it as an obedience and forget about it. My soul was filled with
prayer and I blessed myself with my eyes as Archbishop Ilarion had
taught me. Of course, there were days when I was unable to concentrate, to depart from the surrounding world, but as the duration of my
stay in camp went on, these days became more and more rare.

"I stayed in the Solovki prison until 1928. After that I was sent from
camp to camp—dozens of different ones. I was in Visher, in Perm, in
Borkut, in several camps in the Ural mountains and in Siberia. Most of
these camps were created to build large factories or 'secret cities.'[58]

---

[58]Many such cities existed. People that the government required for inventions or secret
projects were locked up in these cities where they may have eaten and lived "well" but they were
allowed no communication with their families, nor were they allowed to come and go. These
were also known as *akademgorodoks*, "academic cities."

"When I was in the Solovki prison, they temporarily assigned me to tree felling. I stayed there for a long time and I remember with horror what went on there. In the fall there was an epidemic of typhoid fever, at least half the people died. The barracks were poorly built. Ours was very long and slept two hundred people—I had never seen such a large barracks. The camp administration declared a quarantine. I can tell you what happened in my barracks—it was one of the ones in which most people died. The doors were locked from the outside and they cut a hole at the bottom of the door so that you could push a cadaver out through it, or you could pass some logs into the barracks or some tar. There was a little window through which food was handed in to us. Five to twelve people died every day. They were dragged over to the door and we would shout, 'A dead one!' And they were pulled outside by a hook used by the grave diggers without. In the evening they would push in logs to heat the barracks. Twice a day the food window would open, and we would hear, 'Chow time!' The prisoners would walk up to the window, someone would pour the soup, kasha would be tossed into the soup, and we would get a piece of bread. Only those who could walk would receive food. Some were so sick that they could not even get up and were extremely weak. Other people took away the bowls of the sick ones, took away their food and fed it to those who were getting better; still others took away the food of the sick and ate it themselves—those were the majority.

"On the bottom bunk across from me there was a tall man called the Anchor. I did not know who he was. When he first fell sick, the criminals took care of him, but when they saw that he was dying they stopped. When he had been healthy, everybody was afraid of him, he was cruel to us all. I decided to take care of him and so I fed him for about two weeks. The Anchor got better, he started to walk again and instituted a strict discipline in the barracks. He forced people to care for the sick and to feed them. I was the one who had saved his life, but he never talked to me and simply did not notice me.

"The typhoid epidemic that had started so suddenly stopped just as suddenly. Out the two hundred who were in my barracks only about sixty survived.

"I forgot to explain about the pail of tar. Every man in the barracks had to anoint himself with tar, and the healthy ones had to anoint those who were sick. I had never heard before of healing with tar, but perhaps it was this that stopped the epidemic? Thanks be to God, I never caught the typhoid fever. I cared for the sick and continued to clean out the excrement as well as the whole barracks, because the prisoner who had taken care of that died.

"Then five days went by without any cadavers. They opened the doors and said, 'You won't be sick anymore. Those who were sick have acquired an immunity; those who never got sick were probably immune to start with.' They sent us to the sauna and gave us clean clothes (of course, the clothing had been used before by someone) and then the next day they sent us out to work cutting trees. God gave me strength. I took care of the sick, did my dirty work, cleaned the barracks, and still did not get sick myself in spite or the fact that there were thousands of insects that crawled all over me. But as soon as I started anointing myself with tar, they stopped.

"I remember how once, tired from work, I was lying on my bunk after roll call, and the Anchor came up to me and said, 'Well, it seems you saved my life. Thank you. Perhaps, when you are free again you might need help, you might be lonely or sick, so remember this address,' and he mentioned the town of Vladimir, gave the name of the street, the street number and apartment number. 'Repeat it all back,' he said. I did. 'You will go there and you will say that you come from Stepan Glushko. They will help you, don't worry.' He gave me his hand, shook mine, and left. Soon after that I was transferred. The criminals did not take anything from me because I had nothing for them to take; very seldom did they take my bread ration, but this was very seldom. God was merciful to me.

"I met Father Arseny in a camp in 1940. We lived in the same barracks till March 1941. We became friends. Our meeting was a true joy for us since we were of the same spirit. We used to pray together, but in such a way that they could not see us; they used to send people to the punishment cell for doing that. If you stood by yourself next to your bunk and prayed, but did not visibly cross yourself, they would not touch you, but if two got together someone was sure to denounce you. 'The priests are praying.' In 1941, they transferred Father Arseny to the camp of strict regime and I continued receiving my five-year terms one right after the other. My lack of health and my lack of strength should have killed me long before, but by God's grace I kept on living. You remember how the elder Anatoly of Optino said, 'You will pan for gold'? Well, my gold was my work in the camp. I saw Father Arseny once again in Rostov. By the grace of God, the Bishop of Yaroslavl gave me his address.

"God has been good to me. After many difficulties I was accepted as an assistant priest in a church in Tambov. I served several liturgies, and the senior priest allowed me to hear confessions when there were many people. At first nobody wanted to go to me, because I really did look like nothing, but later they all used to come to me. Father Gleb, the main priest, was a strict man, a good and prayerful man, but he did not like it that so many people came to confession to me. He forbade me to hear them by ordering me to help in the altar. I don't serve anymore, and now I receive a pension because I had been exiled unjustly. I went back to the Nil monastery, but they did not let me in. I could see it from the shore; there had been a lot of destruction and desecration. The locals told me that for a time the buildings had been used as an old age home, and then in 1938 it had been a camp for Polish prisoners, but now, I don't know. I have heard that they put an endocrinological institute in the skete, that they were making a vaccine for animals, and that later it became a secret factory or something, but no one could tell me anything in more detail.

"Then I went to visit Nikolo-Rozhk. It has been completely destroyed. On the shores of Lake Seliger you could see tourist camps, shouts, noise . . . I looked, I got sad and I left. My heart was bleeding. I prayed for my brothers, the monks who had been scattered, shot, tortured, who died during freezing treks, were killed by guards, died of starvation or illness, who lived through unbelievable suffering and torture. I could not even visit the grave of my beloved elder. The death of the *starets* Agapit was so painful for me. I am afraid to even tell you about the death of my friend Father Ieraks who had been a monk with me at Father Agapit's. I found out about it in 1943 by chance. I met a prisoner who had walked on the same trek as Father Ieraks, in Vorkut. He was sick with the last stages of scurvy. He could not keep walking, though he tried to; he fell several times, which slowed down the whole column, so the guards just shot him, threw his body in the bushes, and covered it with snow.

"Thank God I was sent to labor camp as a monk and not as the son of an aristocrat who had been close to the tsar and who had a famous last name. They did not know that two of my brothers were in Paris as White Army officers or that my oldest one was a lieutenant general shot as a spy. Probably the monastery's papers had been burned or they did not think of checking them. When I was interrogated I never said that I had lived in St. Petersburg, I said that I came from a peasant family. Otherwise in the twenties I would have been shot because of my brothers in Paris or in 1938 or 1939 for my brother the lieutenant general. In fact I myself found out about them only in 1958.

"Now, God has been generous to me. I live well. I have a room, a pension sufficient for me to live on, and mainly I can pray all the time. There is a church almost next door to my house, so I can be at all the services. The priest does not want me to serve, saying that I have not been assigned to that church.

"When I was freed from the camp in 1956 life was very hard for me. I had nowhere to live and my money had run out. I approached the church administration asking permission to serve in a church. Some thought I was lying about being a hieromonk; others said that most churches had been closed and that they did not need an extra priest— and they would give me a little money and I would have to leave. Finally I had to beg in the streets in Vladimir, and I was hungry and cold. They chased me out of the railroad station and did not let me get warm there. I prayed to the Holy Mother of God, the protector of orphans and the oppressed, and went to look for the address that Stepan Glushko (the Anchor) had given me so many years before. I had found out that he had been a professional thief. I found the street and the house, and rang the bell. An elderly woman opened the door. I said, 'Back in the twenties, Stepan Glushko gave me your address saying, if you fall on hard times, go there.'

"Anna Nikolaevna, who was Stepan's sister, was merciful and good-hearted. She let me in. I was very dirty and my clothing was in shreds. I washed up and she gave me some underwear. Later she bought me some clothing and forced me to accept a lot of money. She offered to let me stay with her. Apparently Stepan had written to her and told her how I had saved his life; she even knew that I was a priest. She told me his story. He had taken a wrong turn at age sixteen, went the wrong way, nothing had stopped him and he ended up a real criminal. He had finished his term and been freed. He came back to Vladimir, stayed with her for a week, then went to Rostov-on-Don. Since then she had not seen him. She received several letters, the last one from Canada where he had moved to in 1946. He asked her to join him in Canada.

"I lived at Anna Nikolaevna's for almost a month. She died two years ago, God have her soul. She was such a goodhearted person. She worked as a teacher almost up until she died. I wrote to her and visited her many times. From her place I went to Tambov and a miracle happened. The local bishop gave me an audience and we found we had friends in common. After hearing me out he directed me to serve in a large village where the church had not been destroyed. This is where I served as an assistant priest until it was time for me to retire—and now I have a pension. During all these years that I have been a free man, I have tried to find monks from my monastery, but I have not found one—they were all disposed of.

"Father Arseny, I have told it all as well as I could. I am tired. Give me the blessing to go and rest."

They walked over to each other, blessed each other, and Father Seraphim went to his tiny room, which used to be a pantry.

That same evening several people arrived from Moscow. There were ten people in the dining room after Father Seraphim had gone to rest. Father Arseny was in bed for almost the whole day, but after dinner he came out and told me, "Alexander Sergeevich! You recorded the memoirs of Father Seraphim on tape. Please let everybody hear what he said."

I brought out my machine, plugged it in, adjusted the sound, and Father Seraphim's voice entered the room. Everyone listened attentively. When the recording was finished they were all unusually silent.

✠

"I knew Father Seraphim in labor camp," said Father Arseny, "but I did not know about his life in such detail. I was in the same barracks with him for a few months and marveled to the depths of my soul at the way he was with the prisoners around him. He was physically very weak, and according to all camp norms, he should have been victim of mockery and beatings, and his food rations should have been taken from him. But that's not the way it was. He was not beaten, his food rations were not taken away, and he was even respected. An old man, tired from his filthy job, he was always taking care of someone. Whether a man was a professional thief, just a prisoner, or a double-crosser, they were all the same to him. They all realized that and accepted his help because of Father Seraphim's goodness, a goodness that has no limits.

"Notice that Father Seraphim never even mentioned the physical and spiritual help he was providing to other prisoners around him. He mostly talked about the importance of prayer for the soul of a man and for those around him. He spoke also about labor, but he never mentioned that he was helping others understand and make sense of their crooked ways. But I saw all this with my own eyes. I saw Father Seraphim—and perhaps you will think that I am overstating, but I think the image is right—as a restorer of souls who had been covered with dirt. Yes, he was a true restorer. Carefully, just like those who restore icons by removing layers of dried oil and dirt with a scalpel, taking care not to harm the original, Father Seraphim would carefully, gently approach a man and remove layers of sin from his soul, revealing first a small window of purity and then making this window bigger and bigger, and then finally clean up his whole soul. How careful you must be, how spiritually attentive to the injured soul not to harm it in trying to direct the man to the path of light. You must not hurt his pride, you must not show him how sinful he is—you could end up pushing him away so that he might think, 'I am such a sinner that I cannot be saved!'

"For a long time I used to observe Father Seraphim attentively. I wanted to borrow his spiritual experience from him and sometimes I could not understand how he could give light to the soul of a man who did not seem to deserve forgiveness. The elder Agapit had passed on to Father Seraphim all his spiritual experience which he had gathered from years of prayer, from attaining spiritual wisdom, from his efforts in directing others, from listening to them. I have already said that when a man comes to an elder, a priest, he receives a spiritual reserve which he carefully spends. The same is true for the priest, the elder who talks to people and receives something new from each one who comes, something spiritual, thus storing in his soul a spiritual wisdom—and this brings the elder what is sometimes called intuition or insight.

"There is intuition which is given as a gift by God, but there is also intuition which is achieved, through the mercy of God, by long, long spiritual experience, by prayer and close contact with many spiritually rich people or simply with people who suffer. Father Seraphim approached each one seeing his individuality, his way of life, his psychology, the degree of his sinfulness, and he could see and feel his whole soul using his own spiritual insight.

"You have just heard the story of a great *starets*, an unusually humble one. In his memoirs he never shows himself, he is always in the shadows, he never talks about himself but about those around him. When I pray with Father Seraphim, my soul is full of light, it is cleansed and I feel far from all earthly cares. The day after tomorrow I will be taken into a clinic where I will have to stay for more than a month. My spiritual children will be coming from far away, and I have asked Father Seraphim to replace me."

This was the end of the talk. When I got back to Moscow I listened to the tape, edited it as well as I could, and added words in places to make things clearer, but the whole structure of the memoirs is authentic, exactly as Father Seraphim told it.

Father Arseny soon left for Moscow. People were coming from far away and, when they did not find him, were upset. But Nadezhda Petrovna told them that Father Arseny was ill and asked them to talk to Father Seraphim instead. They realized that they could not change things, so they went to confession to Father Seraphim, an amazingly good priest, and they received spiritual help. Some reported that when they asked advice from Father Seraphim he would answer, "Why are you asking me, since you have already asked Father Arseny about this," and then he would repeat exactly what Father Arseny used to say, "Never ask the same question from more than one priest, since you

might hear different answers and it could trouble you." I met with
Father Seraphim three times, but by then Father Arseny was already
back. Father Seraphim stayed at Father Arseny's for four months.

Written by Alexander Briansky.
From the archives of V. V. Bykov (received in 1999)

❧ 13 ❦

Father Oleg

May 14, 1973

ON THAT DAY FATHER OLEG happened to be among those who were visiting Father Arseny. Father Arseny turned to him and asked him to tell us the story of his life. Silence reigned immediately, then Father Oleg (Oleg Viktorovich before his ordination) made the sign of the cross and started to talk.

"I was taken into the army in July 1941. Before 1944 I never was wounded or shell-shocked, though I participated in many battles and ended up as a sergeant.

"I knew that God existed and that He was always close to men, but my faith was not strong. We had lived in a communal apartment in Lefortovo. My parents never went to church but we often talked about God around the dinner table, but our talks were very casual. A young woman named Nadia (Nadezhda Vladimirovna) was living in another room in our heavily populated apartment. She was about twenty years old; I was eleven and considered her old. She was goodhearted, kind and hospitable; she would often invite my younger brother, Nikolai, and me to her room, give us tea with something sweet to eat, and tell us interesting stories from the lives of saints in both the Old and New Testaments. She would also tell us stories from apocryphal writings and from the books of the Finnish writer Selma Lagerlef. I found out all of these names only several years later, but the stories themselves I remembered and they formed the basis for my being certain that God existed and that He knew everything. She was a good storyteller. I heard about the words of Jesus Christ, the Mother of God, the apostles, information about the saints, and the concept of good and evil from her. Sometimes Aunt Nadia would also help us do difficult homework.

"Everybody in the apartment knew that Aunt Nadia was going to Church of Saints Peter and Paul on Soldat's Street. They all knew that she commemorated the feasts of the church and that she fasted when it was prescribed, but nobody reported her to the government. She was loved for her good heart, her readiness to help whenever she was asked or to care for someone ill. My mother and father were good friends with her. They knew that we visited her and listened to her stories, and they knew what the stories were about. Well, this is how my brother and I heard about God.

"I remember how Aunt Nadia asked permission from our parents to baptize us. My father agreed, but my mother objected, then unwillingly agreed, saying, 'If the children don't object, I don't care!'

"A priest from Saints Peter and Paul baptized us at home in Aunt Nadia's room; he was gentle and good. He talked to us saying that now we had two mothers, the one who had given us life and the other, Aunt Nadia, who would be our godmother. The priest was young (now he is very old and serving in another church; he spent some time in exile and in a labor camp).

"Aunt Nadia took care of us and sent us off to the army nine years later! I had been a member of the Pioneers and the Komsomol,[59] but for me they were just formalities. My brother never joined these groups and became a very pious man. My parents also came to the Church under the influence of Aunt Nadia.

"In 1944, after the war had already been going on for three years, I found myself near Leningrad. The Germans were in retreat after heavy battles and losses; the fighting was fierce. Our army was on the attack, while the Germans were digging trenches and building defensive embankments. There was strong preparation on their part, and then they came at us in tanks. We shot at them with heavy artillery; I was using an anti-tank gun. We hit two tanks, but the Germans came through and started to 'iron out' our trenches, which means that they were riding their tanks over our trenches and crushing our soldiers and arms with their powerful caterpillar treads, burying all and everything.

"The tank kept on coming at me. I was shooting, but it kept on moving. It finally reached my trench and climbed up onto the embankment. I could sense the approach of the caterpillar treads, dirt was flying all around, and I knew it was the end for me and that I would be crushed by the tank.

---

[59]Communist youth organizations. —Trans.

"Death itself did not scare me, but the idea that I would be crushed did. I cannot properly express that feeling of knowing you would be crushed. At that moment, Aunt Nadia's words came back to me. She had talked about God and the Mother of God and now her words caught fire within me and I said aloud from under the tank, 'Lord Jesus Christ, Son of God! Most Holy Mother of God, save me and help me!' My whole soul, all that remained of it outside that awful fear, went into that prayer. All those thoughts ran through me in one hundredth of a second and I saw my whole life in front of me. Yes, my whole life, but most clear was my prayer to God and my feeling of guilt before Him.

"Probably the tank was over me for only a few seconds, but an enormously strong feeling of the presence of God, His Holy Mother, of Aunt Nadia, her teachings and care, and also of my guilt in forgetting God coursed through me. It would take too long to tell you everything I felt in those few seconds, but I simply relived my whole life.

"The tank that was ironing out our trench kept on going, but it was damaged—I found out about that only later. We won the battle, my friends dug me out from under the ground, and gave me a shot of vodka. I was stunned, but could soon get up and move. The lieutenant came over to me. He was filthy, black with dirt, and he looked me and exclaimed, 'Look, comrades, Kiselev's hair has all gone white!' It was true that during the few seconds I was under the tank my hair had turned white. When I returned home after the war, my mother, father, Aunt Nadia and the other occupants of our apartment looked at me with surprise!

"On that same battlefield I made a promise to God that I would study the teachings of the Orthodox Church and become a priest.

"I returned to Moscow after the army. When I had finished Moscow University I started to study church history, the church services, patristics and much more, all related to Orthodoxy. I was preparing myself to become a priest. In those years that was very difficult, but my tutor and friend, Aunt Nadia, helped and supported me. She got religious books for me, she took me to meet deeply religious people who knew the services well. She passed on to me all her knowledge; she was my guide and my teacher. In 1950 she presented me to Bishop Guri of Tashkent, who was her friend and spiritual father. That same year he ordained me a deacon and three days later a priest. I retold my whole life to him in detail and how I had promised God that I would become a priest. Of course he had already known all of that from Aunt Nadia and from Father F.,[60] who was serving in Tashkent and who knew me well.

"The Priest M., who now serves in the Cathedral of the Epiphany in Moscow also recommended me for ordination. He knew my life and my miraculous escape from death, my promise to become a priest, and my preparation for it under the direction of Nadezhda Vladimirovna.

"In those days, being ordained a priest without a seminary education was a true miracle. But Vladyko Guri was not afraid of doing it. In 1953, Archbishop Guri was in charge of the region of Saratov and, in spite of protests, he allowed me to serve as second priest in one of the churches in a small town in his jurisdiction, where I serve to this day.

"I was brought to Father Arseny by the grace of God, by the Holy Mother of God, through the care of the nun Maria, and by the spiritual guidance of Archbishop Guri, who allowed me to become a priest. I serve in the church of Saint Nicholas and thank God day and night for the grace I have received and for those who helped me to find the Faith.

"I am now fifty-three years old. I have been married for a long time and I have two children, a daughter who is twenty-three and a son who is twenty-one. Aunt Nadia (the nun Maria) lives with us. She is now seventy-five years old. She helps in the church and sometimes goes to Moscow to stay with our daughter, Elizaveta.

"All through my life I have felt the protection of the Most Holy Mother of God for me, a sinner. I often pray to her and ask her to protect orphans, the poor, sinners, the persecuted, the unfortunate, and those suffering illness or calamity. Listen to the words of the prayer to the Mother of God and you will feel her enormous generosity to us sinners," and Father Oleg said this prayer:

"O my generous Queen, my hope, Mother of my God, friend of orphans and protector of travelers, joy of those who grieve, champion of those who suffer, see my sorrow, help me who am helpless, and feed me, a stranger. You know my pain, resolve it as you desire, as I have no

---

[60]Probably Father Fyodor Semenenko.

help but Thee, no other protector, no comforter. You will keep me and protect me for ever and ever. Amen."

While he was praying, we could hear someone crying quietly. Nadezhda Petrovna's face was wet with tears. Father Arseny got up, walked over to her, blessed her, and sat her on a chair. Father Oleg's reading of this prayer had somehow instilled grace in each of us and united us all.

There was silence in the room for over a minute. The silence was broken by Father Arseny. "God sent Father Oleg so many helpers, each one of whom helped him find the way to God. The nun Maria put in the first seeds of faith in the souls of some children who were totally foreign to her. She was not afraid to do this, even though in those days it was a truly dangerous thing to do. Pay attention to what clever ways this young woman used in order to bring the souls of these children to God. She did not use dry words of admonition, but read stories to them from the Old and New Testaments, the lives of saints, martyrs and ascetics. In that way she introduced them to the mystery of the Christian world, its spiritual warmth and depth. Once the souls of these children received the words they heard about faith, goodness, love for one's the neighbor, she began to teach them the words of prayers which remained with them their whole lives. In his memoir, Father Oleg forgot to mention that, but he has told me about it before in detail. Children who were born into a totally unbelieving family came to God and the oldest one, Father Oleg, became a priest. His parents also came to the faith and go regularly to the Church of Saints Peter and Paul in Lefortovo.

"I won't hide the fact that some of my spiritual children gathered here have children, or even fully grown sons or daughters, who do not go to church. Some are almost without faith, some simply do not believe at all. In the memoirs of Father Oleg you heard what brings children to God—warm Christian stories. Be an Aunt Nadia with her fascinating Christian stories for your own families.

"My own mother, Maria Alexandrovna," continued Father Arseny, "was a wise and exceptional person. She saw me not only as her own son but also as a creature of God whom she had to keep and raise in deep faith in the Creator. She felt responsible before Him because He had entrusted her with a human soul.

"During the whole of my childhood I was absorbing Christianity. Just as the nun Maria had, my mother educated me from early childhood in loving others and in believing in God. Stories about Jesus Christ, the Mother of God, stories from the Old and New Testaments, from apocryphal writings, from the lives of saints and much else entered into my soul and has been the foundation of my entire life. Every prayer I learned was explained to me many times. Like any other little boy, I liked to play, to misbehave, to have fun, sometimes even to fight, but my true self was filled with a faith in God. It is true, of course, that I had some difficulties, some doubts. I read a lot. Reading seized me and because of it I did not play outside enough and did not go on walks. Until 1917 there were many books published by 'progressive' professors with leftist tendencies. Under the pretext of conducting scientific research of natural phenomena and new discoveries, or simply through occult science, these books were, in fact, anti-religious propaganda, and sometimes they even preached demonic teachings. Work against Orthodox Christianity was active, everything was denigrated. Alas, this has been forgotten now; people are always saying, 'things were good before!' but that 'good' brought on the revolution!

"Of course I saw the anti-Christian literature, the speeches, the accusations against the Church, but what my mother had placed in my soul from childhood on helped me to see how dumb they were, how evil, how pseudo-scientific, and I could recognize the untruth of what I was reading thanks to my Christian thinking and my faith in God.

"I asked Father Oleg to tell what had brought him to God because I wanted to show that God sends helpers to those who go to Him— helpers and guides. I also wanted to show how important it is to raise children in Orthodoxy. It is indispensable to use stories from the Gospel and the Bible from early childhood on, to help children love one another, to help them to pray by explaining the words of prayer the way my mother and Aunt Nadia did.

"I have talked with many parents who tell me that their children know many fairy tales, but their content has no Christian value, no Orthodox value. There are stories about spirits, ghosts and so forth . . . what can they teach a child?

"Thank you, Father Oleg, for your good memoir! May God bless your whole family and that good-hearted, wonderful person, the nun Maria."

Written by Xenia Galitzkaya
From the archives of V. V. Bykov
(received in 1999)

※ 14 ※
Ilya Nikolaevich

I HAD NEVER SEEN this man before. He looked as though he might be sixty years old. He was of medium height, with white hair, a pointy beard, and amazingly warm and expressive eyes. He sat sideways from me and had a lively talk with Father Arseny about some shared friends. The meal was finished and the table had been cleared, but Father Arseny did not go back to his room, so we all stayed around.

"Let's listen to Ilya Nikolaevich. He and I were in the same camp for seven years—we were even in the same barracks. Later he was sent to the Ninth Labor Camp to dig out ore from underground mines. I was left in the Fifth Labor Camp. In the course of the years we had spent together, we had become close friends and, sometimes, after the lights were out, we were able to have theological discussions. Ilya Nikolaevich comes from a family of Germans in the Volga region;[61] he was baptized a protestant. He was a convinced atheist, finished the Political Academy and became an officer in the frontier guards. Ilya Nikolaevich took me by surprise because he started to talk about God before I did. He later admitted that he wanted to find out what an Orthodox priest was about: did he really believe in God? Was he sincere? I liked him and I was immeasurably sad that God did not live in is soul.

"Ilya Nikolaevich asked many questions and I answered all of them. First, I told him that without God man cannot have the fulness of life. I told him about Orthodoxy, about our services, the Gospels, the Acts of the Apostles. I quoted whole passages from memory and explained them, said prayers, and explained them. Ilya Nikolaevich never argued, he only listened, but I saw that what I was saying was not entering his soul. He was getting information. He was studying what the faith was, and what a priest was.

"My own memory can surprise me, but the memory of Ilya Niko-laevich was simply amazing, phenomenal. Everything I ever told him—

---

[61]There were quite a few such families, left over from Napoleon's times. They were russi-fied and forgot the German language. —Trans.

texts, prayers, events in church history, and much more—he remembered right away and could repeat it all word for word even a long time afterwards. I trusted that God would bring him to Himself. This is my short history of Ilya Nikolaevich; he will tell you the rest himself."

Ilya Nikolaevich began:

"I was sent to the strict regime camp without permission to correspond, just like everyone else. It was either that or being shot to death in camp. In the beginning it was difficult, especially since my last name is German, Schneider. Many hated me for it, but after about three months I found my 'place' in camp 'society.'

"Someone once told me, 'You see that man standing over there? He is a priest, and he is constantly helping everyone. We can't understand why he does that. His name is Father Arseny.' He was the first priest I had ever met in my life, and he had such a special way of living. I got interested, so I went over to him and said, 'Good evening, Father Arseny!'

" 'Good evening,' he answered, and that was the beginning of the friendship between a priest and an ex-political worker, an officer in the frontier guards. Everything that happens in life is according to God's Wisdom. Father Arseny told me many interesting things I had never heard about. I could remember it all in my intellect but it did not penetrate into my soul. We spent five years in the same barracks and suddenly I was sent to the Ninth Camp. It was big and we had to dig for ore deep in the mines. The first time I was lowered down into one it was rather scary. There was dim light in the main galleries, but no light at all in the shafts; the only light there came from the lamp on your own forehead. I worked there for five months and began to understand the planning of it all. I saw that everything had been done carelessly and in a hurry, that the supports of galleries were poorly made. Piles of wood designated as pit props were left on the ground. Safety rules were not obeyed. You could say nothing, you couldn't give advice, you were a zek.[62] If you talked, you were lucky if all they did was to hit you in the face with a fist; they could also send you to the punishment cell . . .

"We were following a sinuous rift in the stratum and a special

---

[62]A prisoner. —Trans.

brigade had been assigned to put the supports in place. One morning we went down into the mine and started work. The rock was giving off gravel, and suddenly we heard a loud cracking sound and a powerful blast of air knocked me to the ground. From there I could see an enormous boulder falling onto me. It was coming down slowly, and then stopped. I was lying as though in a pen case a foot and a half high, three feet wide; my left leg had been pinioned. From under the rubble you could hear moaning. Right next to me the *zek* Shiraev had been crushed by something big and was screaming desperately; then he grew quiet, and died. Moaning and crying went on for a while, and then there was complete silence. I called out, I screamed, but nobody answered. There I was, lying in this 'pen case,' I could even raise myself up onto my elbows, but I could not turn over because of my leg. I put the lamp out, and it became pitch dark. There was absolutely no hope of me being saved, and the most terrible thing was that death would be slow in coming and painful. What could I do? Well, there was nothing to do. I went through a period of despair, but then I remembered my talks in the barracks with Father Arseny. I knew about his deep faith in God and a thought came to me for the first time: if a man like Father Arseny believes in God, this means that He exists, and I started praying ardently, remembering everything Father Arseny had said.

"I lay there and I prayed and I repeated, 'O, Lord, help me! Help me O Lord!' hundreds of times. My left leg hurt, but while I was praying I fell asleep. I woke up and I felt terribly thirsty, but of course there was no water. I fell asleep again, praying. How much time went by, I do not know. I was helpless and my leg was hurting more and more but God gave me the strength to keep on praying, and I gathered all my spiritual willpower to enter into the words of my prayer. The pain grew less, I was no longer thirsty, nor was I hungry. I was dressed rather warmly, since it was always very cold in the mine, so I was wearing everything I owned to conserve the warmth of my body. I do not know how long I lay there; I was constantly passing from one state to the other: I was either praying or I was sleeping.

"All of a sudden I heard the sound of a pneumatic drill and the scraping of shovels, and very soon afterwards I was unearthed. I found out then that I had survived in this spot, without food or water, for seven days. My leg may have hurt, but there was no wound.[63] I was surprised that when they pulled me out and gave me two mugs of water to drink, they started interrogating me 'What happened? Why?' But then they very quickly stopped all that and sent me to a hospital. I had gone down that mine an atheist, but came out a true believer thanks to God's mercy and to the spiritual work Father Arseny had so thoughtfully performed for such a long time.

"Seventeen people died in that accident. I was the only one to survive from my brigade. A mine engineer—himself a *zek*—told me that in his experience and in all the literature he had read, he never heard of anyone ever surviving seven days without food or water at nearfreezing temperatures. God, through the prayers of Father Arseny and through His great mercy, performed a miracle and saved me.

"They sent me from the Ninth Camp back to the Fifth, and I spent another two years with Father Arseny. I was freed in 1956, Father Arseny in 1958. I found him through the help of his spiritual children and he watches over me to this day. It may surprise you, but in 1964 I became a deacon. That is another story. Father Arseny, who is sitting right here, is the one who blessed me to take this step."

Deacon Ilya got up, went over to Father Arseny, and said, "Bless me, Father!" Father Arseny blessed him, hugged him, and gave him a kiss. When we all were seated again, Father Ilya continued, "The accident in the mine was investigated. It just 'happened' that the supports were not done properly, which had been obvious to all even before the accident. They shot the engineer responsible for the work and five totally innocent prisoners who had done the work. The politicians probably felt that the law had triumphed and justice had been done!

"In the course of a year I was interrogated again several times. I was asked about the reason for the accident and how it was that I was the only one who survived."

Noted by Kyra Bakhmat
From the archives of V.V. Bykov (received in 1999)

---

[63]It is well known to specialists that people dug out from such mines, whose extremities were pinned for a long while, suffer permanent damage. The blood in the injured extremity starts to decompose, and after such people are dug out they almost always die.

❧ 15 ❧

The Poets of the Silver Age

MY WIFE AND I CAME to Rostov for a vacation and to see Father Arseny in August 1972. We were going to stay for about three weeks. We found a room with the help of some friends. We could not stay at Nadezhda Petrovna's; every day Father Arseny's spiritual children would be coming to spend one night, whereas we were going to be staying for a long time.

Not only had Father Arseny been my spiritual father since 1920, but we had also gone to school together: we were friends, our parents were friends, we visited each other often and loved one another.

I was born in 1893 and was a year older than Piotr (Father Arseny). We had been good friends since early childhood and this continued until 1915 when, at the age of twenty-two, I finished my studies a year ahead of him and immediately volunteered for the army. I was sent to infantry school to become an officer. I became a warrant officer and was sent straight to the front. I knew that Piotr would not be going into the army because of his heart ailment. He finished the university and, since he was his mother's only son, he would not be mobilized in any service.

I was active in the army from 1915 to 1920 and knew nothing of Piotr; I admit I almost forgot about him. I was wounded on the southern front and stayed in hospitals for a while, then they demobilized me as unfit for military service.

When I returned to Moscow, to my parents, I found out that Piotr had become a hieromonk. I was surprised. My parents told me that Piotr had spent a few years in Optino with the elders, had become a monk there and later a priest. He then returned to Moscow and was now serving in a small parish.

About three months after my return I finally found work in an office with good benefits. At the time, people in Moscow were seriously hungry and our living conditions were poor from all points of view. They took half of our apartment away from us, people openly called my parents "useless bourgeois" in spite of the fact that my father was a famous surgeon and my mother, who had received her education in France, was a psychiatrist who worked in a psychiatric hospital. In those days women psychiatrists were extremely rare. My father and mother were deeply believing people, which explains their friendship with Maria Alexandrovna, Father Arseny's mother.

I will talk again about the difficult lives we all led in the twenties. We could not get any firewood, so it was freezing cold in our rooms. We cooked and warmed ourselves with potbelly stoves. Its pipe was connected to an opening in the window, and the draught was so poor that the room was always full of smoke and our eyes were always red and full of tears. We used to burn books, chairs and slats which we had torn from fences. We would bring home the frozen potatoes that were our ration on children's sleds. Water would freeze in the faucets; we had brownouts and blackouts.

We would read lists of the hostages who had been shot: many people were arrested after being searched. Nobody knew who would be the next "useless bourgeois" to be arrested and shot.

During the six years from 1915 through 1920, I did not go to church. But one Sunday, in August 1920, I decided to go to the church where Father Arseny was serving. I was thinking, "My friend sure did estrange himself!" but I remembered that, even as early as 1913, he had been interested in Russian antiquities and in Orthodoxy.

I bought three candles and, after looking at the icons, lit one in front of the Vladimir Mother of God, one in front of Nicholas the Wonderworker and one in front of the Holy Trinity (I must say that the icon of the Vladimir Mother of God is the one I love and revere most). They were reading the writings of the Apostle Paul, the Royal Doors were open, and in the altar I could see a tall priest whom I recognized right away as Father Arseny. I stayed for the liturgy and was unspeakably amazed by the way he served. It is difficult for me to describe what I felt. The service was served exactly by the rules, so to the eye it was identical to what I had always seen in any church, but I had the impression that he was serving, not apart from the people who were standing in the church ("the service goes its way, and you parishioners just pray by yourselves" the way you feel in so many churches), but it was as if he were among them, uniting himself with each, and making each a participant in his serving. What I am trying to say is difficult to describe, to explain—you can only feel it in your soul. As I stood in that church I did not see my friend Piotr, but the Priest Arseny, who had a unique power which I could not completely comprehend. We had a meeting, lengthy and joyous, and I became his spiritual son and a participant in a small but united community.

It is now 1980 and I am 87 years old. Many of us have written our memoirs as Father Arseny has asked us to, and I have read them all. I am sorry to say that in ways unknown to me these memoirs found their way into the *samizdat*. As a result, there are mistakes, inexactitudes, wrong dates. Some texts were changed without the permission of their authors. While Father Arseny was alive I did not share my memoirs; only now have I decided to include my words with what has been written before. I am including the talk I heard in 1972 and wrote down then and there because that talk opens up several details of Father's life for us that were unknown till now, and retells some points of view he had not expressed before.

While I was living in Rostov in August 1972, I saw Father Arseny almost daily and was present at many of his talks. One of them, that lasted for two evenings, I especially remember.

That day there were nine or ten people as usual around the table. (I often wondered how it happened that the local authorities, who knew perfectly well about these visits to Nadezhda Petrovna's house, did nothing to stop them. I answered myself: the Most Holy Mother of God was protecting Father Arseny from misery and persecution.)

One of the guests that night was a man I did not know. He was of medium height, with a thin face, skin stretched over his bones and big, kindly, deep-set eyes and a pleasant voice. Among his noticeable traits were hands with long, restless fingers, an upper lip that twitched slightly, and a deep, wide scar on his left cheek. He was very nervous and seemed to hold himself in all the time—it was obvious that he was constantly very tense. He had probably lived a difficult life and suffered much. He addressed Father Arseny with utter respect.

In the beginning, the conversation was general, as it usually is after evening tea. Then somebody mentioned the poet Alexander Blok, then Sergei Yesenin and it was mentioned that they both believed in God and were Orthodox. Father Arseny looked at the guests and said, "This is a very interesting topic," and, turning to the man I did not know, the one with the large scar, he said, "Ilya Sergeevich was well acquainted with poets at the beginning of the twentieth century. And he was particularly acquainted with both Blok and Yesenin. I ask you, Ilya Sergeevich, to tell us about the poets of the 'silver age' and about their relationship with God, the Church, and Orthodoxy. I think Ilya Sergeevich must know this problem better than anyone else."

Ilya Sergeevich began recounting in an even voice:

"In 1906 I was twenty years old. I was born in St. Petersburg in 1886 and I am now eighty-six years old. I studied in the university and raved about such poets as Blok, Hodasevich, Brussov, Balmont, Bely and Sologub. I used to dream of meeting them, 'smelling the perfume of poetry,' and being close to those poets who brought light and joy to people. But all this was just a dream. It was impossible to get close to those 'masters.'

"Once when by pure chance I was talking with another student, I learned that he knew several poets and he offered to introduce me to Alexander Blok. And, in fact, after a few days this student—Yura Svetlov—invited me to a literary soiree and presented me to Blok. I probably looked at him with enamored eyes; he noticed this and, giving me his hand, said, 'I am glad to meet you!' and turned away to talk to someone else. That same evening Yura presented me to other poets and I was on top of the world with happiness. I became a regular at these literary soirees and people came to know me as a constant admirer of talent.

"My family was of the old gentry, old fashioned and truly, deeply believing. My father, mother, grandmother and two sisters went to church regularly and knew Father John of Kronstadt.

"For three years I absorbed the perspectives of these poets, imitated them one after the other in the poems I composed (though my poems were of poor quality); they would kindly say that they were good but never wanted to print them in their journals. Only Gumilev said, 'Young man! Here you are studying in the university and yet you write surprisingly dumb and flat poems. If you have no talent, you should take lessons in writing verse; perhaps some of ours could help you!' I was very hurt and started to avoid Gumilev.

"My family noticed my crush on the contemporary poets. I used to be out many evenings and my studies suffered (though I will still mention that I did graduate from the university). My parents tried to convince me to break away from those friends, but I still admired Blok, Sollogub, Bely, Brussov and others.

"I did nothing for a year after finishing the university, and then obtained a very small and poorly paid position as 'secretary' for a small literary review. I felt that I had broken into the big world of the silver age poets (a name that sprang up in the second half of the twentieth century). All these poets were surrounded by hundreds of admirers, both men and women; they were infected by a spirit of decadence, symbolism and other 'isms.' They swarmed around one poet, then another, and then their groups disseminated.

"In all the arguments, gossip and talk there was a dirty war, full of treachery going on. My father was extremely intelligent and good-hearted, and he never considered himself a member of the 'intelligentsia' (he liked neither the word nor the concept) but was a true intellectual raised in Russian culture, in Orthodoxy and in faith and he loved the Church. Seeing me floundering in literary circles caused him to have lengthy and serious talks with me trying to convince me to get out of all this. I exploded and shouted that it was my life, I was not a child, but my father said, 'I am not trying to convince you. Do remember that a few years back you liked psychology? So I am asking you please to conduct a psychological study of the people around you and write it down in a "journal" every day. Remember that you are Orthodox, that you are a believer and that you will make your deductions based on your faith in God. Could you promise me to do that?'

"I agreed. My father continued, 'I have read many of the poems and other writings of Briusov, Blok, Bely, Hodasevich and of the angry and sad Sologub and others. I realize that in most of their poems you can see the form and behind this form you can find the content, but a spirituality that warms the human soul, a faith in God do not exist in them. There is a warped personality and a pretense of genius. The only one who is a true genius is Alexander Blok, but in his beautiful creations you sense a certain deterioration in his psychological state.'

"I pursued my observations for a whole year. I wrote them down every day and finally noticed what I should have seen while I was an active member of that society.

"I surprised my relatives—and even myself—by getting married, having met a charming young woman, that daughter of a priest called Father Michael, who used to serve in the Church of Nicholas the Wonderworker. Xenia was a believer; she was good-hearted, responsive to other people's problems, and extremely intelligent. We met in August and got married in church in October. The wedding was small, and my parents and Father Michael were happy.

"I invited my wife to come with me to three or four literary soirees and presented her to important poets. She did not like these evenings and especially she did not like the poets.

"'You know,' she said, 'everything is so artificial, so forced, so strained, and I did not like your "masters" at all. They are so good in words but they look at women as rudely as if they were race horses,' and she gave me a perfect and exhaustive description of each evening she had attended.

"My conversations with my father, Xenia's skeptical, astute remarks, and my own observations brought me to the conclusion that I had been wrong about the people I had been spending so much time with those past several years. I had been so blind in spite of believing in God!

"Rereading what I had read or listening to them reading their poems, I saw that each of these poets often wrote about God, but immediately afterwards they would mention the evil powers and the devil himself—sometimes they would even celebrate them. If you looked deeper you could see that everything that they wrote led to negating God, making fun of Him, comparing the Holy Mother of God and the saints to fauns, Aphrodite, Apollo, dryads, nymphs and so on.

"Most of the 'masters' were Theosophists or anthroposophists (e.g. Andrei Bely); some became enthused with the teachings of Helena Blavatsky or of Buddhism, of Tibet. With earnest faces they spoke of the land of Shambala. They held spiritualist séances and served 'black masses,' believed in reincarnation and so on. They often mentioned the name of God among this mish-mash. But who was that God? It was impossible to figure it out. They did not declare their beliefs clearly, but you could read between the lines.

"Each poet hated one of the other poets. They often had arguments and their works were published in small reviews which were avidly read by their adorers, mainly young people who were influenced by their skeptical ideas about God, about Orthodoxy, about the Faith, and all this served to propagate revolutionary ideas, godlessness and atheism.

"Their teachings were packaged in beautiful words that were often difficult to understand, 'mysterious,' they carried the reader away to a world he thought superior. I later read many books analyzing their works, but nowhere did I find a study of their role in the destruction of Russia by preparing the intelligentsia for the idea of revolution. Of course, all these writings appeared in Soviet Russia, so they could not talk about their religious aspect. Perhaps something of the kind did appear abroad, but I had no access to such literature.

"I was totally insignificant among these poets, like a chair you get used to and forget the existence of. In 1930, we moved to Moscow and I went to work in the Soviet Writer publishing house. In 1936, I was arrested and given ten years in a labor camp. In December 1941 they switched my punishment to ten years in the camp of strictest regime, without correspondence. That is where I met Father Arseny in 1951 and became his spiritual son.

"I will now come back to talking about the 'spirituality' of the silver age poets and their influence on Russian society before the 1917 Revolution.

"I will start by saying that most of these poets were amazingly talented, some of them were even geniuses, and what I am going to say does not diminish their writing ability nor does it aim to lessen their work. I will simply look at their work from the perspective of an Orthodox man. Much written by them will forever be seen as a part of the treasury of Russian literature.

"It goes without saying that Alexander Blok was a genius. What he wrote was excellent but he 'sank' in his 'Unknown One,'[64] in his verse

---

[64]A very well known poem by Alexander Blok. —Trans.

about 'The Perfect Lady.' In all his work you could feel a crack, a pain deeply anchored in his soul, and he was never able to heal from it. In his poetry he mentions 'the Most Holy Mother of God,' but for him she is almost the same thing as his 'perfect lady.' I deliberately use the word 'mentions' because these words helped create images and created a shadow of mystery. Of course, Blok did believe that God existed, but it was his own god, and only his, not the Lord of the Russian Orthodox Church. If you read his work carefully, you can see this easily, although the word 'God' does appear often. Anyone who reads his work carefully has not seen the true God in it and that brought a great deal of harm to his readers. Perhaps the upbringing Blok received from his mother did not let him discover the true God; perhaps his relations later with his wife, Lyubov Dmitrievna N. Mendeleev, may have influenced him.

"I do not intend to talk about all the poets of this time. I have said the most important thing: naming Holy Names and using church words and quotes created sacrilegious attributes, rhymes and associations; all these expressions were very familiar to the Russian mind as they were used in church services and in conversation. The poets who had 'their own god' could use these expressions to mock and abase Orthodoxy. All this had a negative influence on their readers and often led to a loss of spirituality and faith, to nihilism.

"There was another group of poets which included Nicholas Gumilev, Anna Akhmatova and Tchulkovs. People thought that Gumilev did not believe in God, but I can affirm that he did. Anna Akhmatova and her friend Nadezhda Pavlovich were believers and never said anything against God in their work."

Ilya Sergeevich finished his story and was silent.

Father Arseny said, "You did not mention the name of Maximilian Voloshin, one of the most original and interesting poets of the period."

Ilya Sergeevich was about to speak, but Father Arseny said, "I will tell you about him myself.

"In 1924, one time after liturgy a thick-set man came in. He was not very tall, but he had a large beard, a lot of hair, a broad face, and radiant, kind, inquisitive eyes. Of course, I saw all this when he walked up to me. He said, 'Father Arseny! I have come to talk to you; where and when can we do that?'

" 'Let us go now!' I led him over to a bench which was next to the church wall; it had been placed there for the use of elderly parishioners. We sat down, I looked at this face. It struck me as familiar but I knew that I had never seen him before. I saw that he did not know how to start the conversation and that he felt at a loss. I decided to help him and surprised myself by saying, 'Maximilian Alexandrovich! I am listening to you.'

"He shivered and, moved, he asked, 'How do you know my name?'

"I did not know how to answer because the name had suddenly appeared in my head, probably with God's help. Seeing that I remained silent, he started to talk:

" 'My name is indeed Maximilian Alexandrovich, my last name is Voloshin, my "profession" is that of poet, watercolorist, unsuccessful philosopher-thinker, permanent seeker of truth, intercessor in other people's problems, inventor and a man with a not very successful (agitated) personal life. By nature I am a poet, a dreamer, an artist. I love beauty (including women's beauty), and I am aware of my sins before God. I live in Koktebel in the Crimea and have come to Moscow on business and to be able to come to your church and have a talk with you. Sergei Nikolaevich Dirylin, a believer and a good friend of mine, suggested that I do this. Father Arseny, I am constantly in search of God. I feel His nearness and even His mercy, undeserved by me, as well as his leniency—I am a great sinner.'

"He sounded calm, but I could sense his inner tension. I had read his poems before and had liked their inner meaning. I knew of his extraordinarily good heart and I knew that he had saved many people from being shot or imprisoned. I had heard that he sometimes tried to impress people by talking about himself, but now I found in front of me a man who was tired, moved and saddened.

"Sergei Nikolaevich Dirylin was an art historian; we were friends, we respected one another. I knew that he was a believer and I had seen him twice in Optino while I was spending time there with the elders. In 1920 he had become a priest and served in the church of Saint Nicholas in Kelnik in the community of Father Alexei Mechev, and later in that of his son, Father Sergei. He was arrested and exiled to Siberia; when he returned from Siberia (or was it during his stay there?)

he married one of the community's sisters, Irina, who had gone out to take care of him. After that, he no longer served in church but worked in the fields of literature and the history of art; perhaps he was no longer even a priest. But I believe he was still a priest, because the marriage was a fictitious one, so he could avoid being arrested a second time. Sergei Nikolaevich was too good a man to turn his back on God and the Faith, but anyway his behavior had a negative influence and was condemned by the clergy in Moscow; I heard about all of this back then.

"Anyway, he was the one who had suggested that Voloshin should see me. We went to my apartment where Anna Andreevna, a nosy old lady in whose house I was living, started giving us something to eat between lunch and dinner. Maximilian Alexandrovich and I talked almost until vespers. It was a confession, the story of his life and the people around him. Of course I will not tell you the content of his confession, but there was much I could not then understand; it was only my eighteen-year-long stay in the 'death camp' that taught me, by the grace of God, to understand the human soul.

"Much of what he said was similar to what exists in any person, but what was striking was the purity of his soul, as pure as the soul of a child. Every so often, while he was listening to what I was saying, he would exclaim, 'Of course that's the way it is, that is exactly what I thought.' After I had heard his confession I asked him, 'Maximilian Alexandrovich, you have come to confession and the weight of sin has been removed from your soul: tell me, will you try not to make the same mistakes you mentioned in confession?'

"And he—honestly, childlike—answered, 'Father Arseny, of course I will struggle with myself, but I am afraid that my nature is too earthy and that somewhere and some time in some difficult situation I might not be able to control myself.'

"Looking at Maximilian Alexandrovich I understood the purity of his soul and the honesty of his answer, so I gave him absolution and gave him communion.

"From 1924 until my first arrest in 1927, Maximilian Voloshin came to see me when he was in Moscow, and we became friends. He loved his mother, Elena Ottobaldovna, and called her 'Pra' (from the word 'pramother'—or superior mother), but I think that he did not tell her about his confessions because that would have been beyond the bonds of his inner self.

"During our talks he would sometimes read his poems to me and those poems went deep into my soul. I remember one of them called 'The Northwest':

> The demons dance freely
> All over Russia, right and left
> The cold Northwest
> Tears and turns the snowy curtains.
> The wind of flat plateaus
> The wind of tundras, forests and seas
> The black wind of frozen flatlands
> The wind of discord, beatings and pogroms.
> . . .
> Hundreds of years of dull and fierce torture
> The scroll is not entirely unrolled
> And the list of executioners is not complete
> The delirium of Searches and the horror of Special cells
> Neither Moscow, nor Astrakhan or Yaik
> Have ever seen worse times.

"The poem is long, I will not quote it in full. Voloshin was not published because his poems contained the truth about the Communist terror and the persecution of human souls. I don't know if some of them were secretly published.[65]

"In 1931, when I was exiled to the north, Kyra and Yuri came to visit me and brought several poems by Maximilian Voloshin. He had sent them to me specially, they were handwritten. One of the poems was called 'The Vladimir Mother of God' and I will quote it from memory. With this poem Voloshin sent me a note in which he said that he sent this poem to his best friends: myself and the art restorer Alexander Ivanovich Anisimov, who had been one of the restorers of this most sacred icon. I knew him well. I was deeply touched by Voloshin's letter

---

[65]The poems quoted here were published in Voloshin's *Selected Poems* in 1988.

and by his truly remarkable poem, which was remarkable both spiritually and historically. Of course, under Communist authority it was
never published and none of you, except Kyra and Yura, have ever heard
it. At the same time he sent some extracts from a poem about Saint
Seraphim of Sarov, saying that it was unfinished. I have forgotten much
of it, but I do remember a few lines:

> At age seven he was on top of a bell tower
> He stepped back. But somebody's wings
> flew right up to him, somebody's hands
> supported him in the air and, unharmed
> he was placed on the earth.
> . . .
> The Mother of God herself chose the place
> In Russia, between Satis and Sarov
> For Seraphim to lead his ascetical life
> . . .
> The landowner Motovilov was sick
> He was brought to Sarov by hand
> The elder asked him sternly:
> "Do you believe in Jesus Christ,
> That He is God and Man, and that the Mother of God
> Is truly ever virgin"—"I do believe"

"I never read the whole poem and probably never will, since all of
Voloshin's work was removed from circulation and placed in archives.

"Before I tell you from memory the poem about the Vladimir
Mother of God, I want to say that such a piece of work could only have
been written by somebody who felt God and the Mother of God very
deeply even if, in his poetical interpretation, he expressed something not
quite correctly, not like everyone else. For this poem alone much will be
forgiven Maximilian Voloshin. He instills a great love for the Holy
Mother of God in the soul of an Orthodox person. It is joyous and we
can see the history of Russia and God's role in that history, when Rus-
sians would often cry out, 'O Mother of God, save the Russian land!'

"I loved the poem called 'The House of the Poet,' which showed his hospitality, his love for man and for nature. It was published; find it and read it. It began this way:

> The door is open, cross the threshold
> My house is open to meet all roads
> In the cool cells, whitewashed
> The wind is breathing and the roll of the wave
> Lives . . .
> Enter my guest, shake off at my threshold
> The dust of everyday life and the mold of thoughts . . .
> From the depths of time you will be met sternly
> By the large face of the Queen Taiah
> My abode is poor, and times are hard . . .

"Voloshin brought goodness to people. He welcomed many into his house, though he was constantly under the menace of arrest, of death. Of course, his poetry is contradictory, but he cannot be blamed for that. He was a great poet, a son of his times and his society, but he was a believing Orthodox man."

While Ilya Sergeevich was speaking about the silver age poets, and Father Arseny about Maximilian Voloshin, some ten people had gathered in the dining room. Two of the women I had never seen before. They were both probably between fifty-five and sixty years of age; one was silent, the other impetuous and energetic, she was constantly trying to speak. The silent one, I found out later, was Elizaveta Alexandrovna, the other Lyudmilla Alexandrovna. During a brief interruption Elizaveta Alexandrovna said to Father Arseny, "Father! I have often heard about Maximilian Voloshin from my friends and members of our community. He is my husband's most beloved poet.

"One of our friends, Zoia Dimitrievna Prianishkova (the daughter of the academician) had tuberculosis of the bone in her right hip from her childhood; in 1918 her parents sent her with one of their friends to the Crimea for treatment. But the civil war started. It lasted nearly three years and they had to stay in the Crimea. They had no contact with Moscow, had no funds to live on, no protection, and no help, and they were starving to death.

"I cannot now remember how they met Maximilian Voloshin, but he, along with his mother, took them into their house, where they stayed for over a year, and then they helped them to get back to Moscow to the girl's parents.

"Another friend of ours, Elena Sergeevna Volnuhina (a daughter of the sculptor who made the monument of Ivan Fedorov, the first printer) came to the Crimea to be treated for weak lungs right after the end of the civil war. She was advised to take a room in Koktebel. In the morning she hired a Tatar with an oxcart, loaded her suitcase, the bags that held her clothes, and the purse with her passport and money and walked next to the owner of the cart.

"They were barely out of the city when the Tatar whipped the horse and ran off at great speed. Elena Sergevna was left behind in a light summer dress and nothing else, no money or papers. She walked along the road in distress. She walked and prayed to the Mother of God asking her for help, placing all her hope in her. Soon she saw a house that was unique in its architectural style. She went up to it and knocked on the door. She was let in and, crying, told her story to an elderly lady and a man.

"Years afterwards Elena Sergeevna (Lyolia) was always teary-eyed when she told how she was received: they fed her and gave her clothes. She stayed with them for three months, until she received money from her relatives to go home. Maximilian Voloshin got her a train ticket and took her to the station. Elena Sergeevna kept on saying that they were both amazingly nice and charitable people. Lyolia brought back many handwritten poems, which we copied. I wanted to tell these two stories because they reveal the souls of the poet and his mother."

The other woman, Lyudmilla Alexandrovna happened to know Andrei Bely well; she was also a friend of Nadezhda Pavlovich, had met Anna Akhmatova and knew Brussov and Nadezhda well.

The conversation about the poets, their literary value and their relationship with God, faith and Orthodoxy continued for two evenings. At the end of the second evening, Father Arseny said that he himself had for a while been carried away by the silver age poets.

"You know," he said, "being carried away by these poets was like an epidemic: it was fashionable, almost everyone who knew how to read knew these poems, especially Blok's—his poetry was recited everywhere. Wherever you would go, you would hear the familiar words of his poems: 'Under the embankment, in the grassy ditch . . .' or 'Why did you cast down you eyes, so shyly . . .'

"We loved Rigor and Nikolai Gumilev but I soon realized that they were empty and that they did not agree with the way I understood the world. But I still love some of Gumilev's poems. In one poem he foretells his own death:

> The bullet which they cast will whistle
> Above the gray and foamy river Dvina
> The bullet which they cast will find
> My chest—it came for me
> I will fall, and in pangs of death
> I will see my past so true.
>
> . . .
>
> And God will give me in full measure
> What I deserve for my short and bitter life.

"Gumilev was Orthodox and a believer; many people who knew him have told me so. Of course, his faith was not fully the faith of the Church. He believed the way most of the intelligentsia believed back then."

And, turning to Ilya Sergeevich, Father Arseny said, "I interrupted you and started reminiscing about Voloshin. Perhaps you wanted to say something more?"

Ilya Sergeevich said, "I was daring enough to critically analyze the works of many poets and perhaps some people will not agree with me, but this is how I see them now, with the soul of an Orthodox man."

It was getting late. We prayed, Father Arseny blessed each of us and went back to his room. We each went to our places: some of us were spending the night at Nadezhda Petrovna's. I went out with Elizaveta and Lyudmilla Alexandrovna. They were planning to spend the night at some friends who lived in Rostov. Because the evening was warm and calm I offered to accompany them. As we were walking I found out that they were first cousins and were members of a large Moscow community, that their priest had been shot,[66] and that God had now brought them to Father Arseny. They considered this to be a great spiritual joy, but regretted that they could not see him often. I saw them several times afterwards in friends' apartments, when Father Arseny was brought to Moscow.

I wrote down the content of those talks in 1972 immediately, while I was still in Rostov on vacation. It was not worked on until several years later, when I edited it. I copied the poem, "The Vladimir Mother of God," from the original, which I borrowed from Father Arseny.

THE VLADIMIR MOTHER OF GOD[67]

Not on a throne, but on her arm
Hugging her neck with His left hand
He looks at her, His cheek pressed against hers
And seems to constantly demand . . .
I am speechless—
I don't have the strength or the words . . .
And she, alarmed and sad
Looks through the moving ripple
Into the world's glowing horizon,
Where sunset resembles fire.
And such a sad emotion lay
On her pure virginal features, that her Holy Face
In the fire of prayer, every second
As if alive, changes expression.

Who opened the lakes of these eyes?
Not the iconwriter Saint Luke,
As it was told by ancient chroniclers,
Not an icon-dauber from the caves of Pechera:

---

[66]Father Sergei Mechev.
[67]John Hainsworth worked to make this translation a true poem. —Trans.

But in the burning furnaces of Byzantium,
In the evil days of iconoclasm
Her Face, out of the flaming elements
Was made incarnate in worldly colors.
But out of all the holy revelations
Made by art—this is the only one
That survived the bonfire of self-destruction
Among fragments and ruins.

From mosaics, gold, and monuments
From everything this era plumed itself about
You went, on waters of blue rivers
To Kiev, where princes fought.
And from then on, during people's calamities
Your Image, was lifted over Russia
In the dark ages, it did show us the way,
And in prisons—it showed a secret escape path.
You were there for the last hours
Of soldiers in the light of Liturgy . . .

The terrifying history of Russia
Passed before your Holy Face.
Is it not when you knew about the attack of Batiy,
About the steppes on fire, and the destruction of villages
that You left the hopeless Kiev
And took down the power of princes?
And you went with Andrew to Bogolyubovo
In the moldiness and depth of Vladimir's forests
Into the tight world of dry pine fellings
Under the net of beautiful cupolas.

And when the lame Ironman gave away
The shores of the Oka to be destroyed
Who but You did not let him get into Moscow
And blocked from him the roads into Russia?
From the forests, the deserts and the shores

All came to you to pray for Russia:
The guards of powerful killers,
The avid collectors of lands . . .
Here in the Dormition cathedral,
in the heart of the walls of the Kremlin,
Touched by your gentle appearance
So many cruel and cold eyes
Were wet with a light tear!

Old men and nuns would prostrate themselves
the incensed altars were alight,
The humble tsarinas kissed the ground
Angry tsars bowed before you . . .
By death and bloody battles
The virgin cloth was lit
The cloth before which all of Russia
Prayed for eight centuries.

But the blind people, in a year of anger
Gave up itself the keys of its strongholds
And the Most Holy Virgin left
From its desecrated holy place.
And when red dais
Raised their voices next to desecrated churches—
From under rizas and pious riches
You showed your true and Holy Face.
The bright Face of Wisdom-Sophia
Crumpled and dried in miserly Moscow,
And in the future—the Holy Face of Russia itself—
Against all slanders and gossips.

The Holy Kremlin does not tremble any more
From the drone of bronze; and flowers do not bloom:
The world has lost the blinding miracle:
The revelation of eternal Beauty!

O Faithful guardian and zealous keeper
Of Our Mother of Vladimir—to you—
Two keys I give: a gold one to Her abode,
And a rusty one—to our saddest fate.

Maximilian Voloshin (1925–1929), Koktebel, Crimea

Here are a few words added by Father Arseny (1961): "I presume that the last four lines refer to A.I. Anisimov, who restored the Vladimir Mother of God icon and protected her from those who wanted to try to remove more layers of paint. Alexander Ivanovich Anisimov was shot in 1937."

⌇

N.T. Lebedev
From the archives of V.V. Bykov (received in 1999)[68]

---

[68]This chapter was slightly shortened, omitting comments on less famous poets who are largely unknown abroad. —Trans.

❧ 16 ❧

Memoirs of Father Arseny
and His Spiritual Children

Talks of Father Arseny
Recorded by Kyra Bakhmat

I WROTE THESE MEMOIRS over the course of about twenty years, starting in 1958. They are fragments, separate from and sometimes unrelated to one another. I wrote them down as they came to my memory.

MEMOIRS OF A.F. BERG (1980)

SINCE THE VERY FOUNDING of our community, I met and became lifelong friends with Alexandra Fedorovna Berg. She was an amazing person, goodhearted, believing, and prayerful. My relationship with her was always one of respect. We were only some four years apart in age, and we had joined the community at the same time but, I cannot explain why, I always called her by her patronymic, Alexandra Fedorovna, while she simply called me Kyra. Alexandra Fedorovna wanted me to simply call her Alexandra, but something would not let me do it, nor could I use the familiar "you" with her. We loved each other. We were good friends who helped each other and prayed together—Yuri, Sasha[69] (as I called her when I was not with her), and myself. When, late in her life, Alexandra Fedorovna could not see well, she dictated some of her recollections about Father Arseny and about her own life to me:

"My family was an old noble German one that always served the Faith and the Fatherland. At the end of the sixteenth century, Peter the Great invited my great-grandfather to serve in Russia, he never went back to Germany. German nobility was transferred to Russian nobility, that is, the Emperor gave us rank and title. My great-grandfather

---

[69]Sasha is a very common diminutive for both Alexander and Alexandra. —Trans.

married a Russian woman and forgot his German roots, so only our last name reminds us of our long-forgotten past.

"My father, Fedor Ignatievich, knew our genealogy well and inscribed all its important events into a large leather-bound notebook: who was born when, who got married, who died, medals received, lands sold and bought. The first thing that appears in this notebook dates to 1743. The heavy, yellowed pages of this book commanded respect. Now several decades have passed since this notebook was seized by the authorities during my first arrest. Perhaps is it now in the archives of the KGB or of the NKVD, perhaps it has been destroyed. When I was later 'pardoned,' I asked for the notebook to be returned to me. The answer was vague: the notebook was considered to be of historical interest and was being kept in the government archives. I asked where it was exactly, but received no answer.

"I can remember the stories my father used to tell me. When I was a little girl, he would sit me on his lap. I would be joined by my sisters, Nadia and Vera, and he would say, 'I will go to the country of the forgotten and of fairy tales. I will pull something interesting out of there and I will retell it.' He would be silent for a while, probably gathering his thoughts, and then he would start talking and we, his children, would go with him into the magic world of Russian wonder tales, which were modified by my father to have Christian deeds and meanings. When I got older, Papa would read to me from apocryphal writings, or he would pick up his leather-bound notebook and tell us about our ancestors and their heroic deeds, or he would explain the genealogy of the Berg family, or he would read us short stories by different writers. I specifically remember a story called 'The Signal' by Garschin.

"When I was a little girl and I used to ask Papa to take me to the 'country of the forgotten,' he would smile and say, 'You will have your own "country of the forgotten" some day.' When I grew older, I understood what that country was. I am now eighty-two years old, and my 'country of the forgotten' is my past. It is enormous and I will try to talk only about the good parts, about the part of my past that was illumined by faith and the directives of Father Arseny, the gift of God throughout my life. I will retell my memoirs as well as my old memory is able. You, Kyra, know that at my age the past appears in chunks, perhaps tied to the way I am feeling both physically and mentally, and perhaps also influenced by the weather, good or bad. I am now almost blind. I sit in my armchair or I lie in bed looking at my past and what I did earlier, and I judge and evaluate it all differently. I see my mistakes, the wrong things I did, the injuries I inflicted on people, my sins, my insufficient striving to God. I cannot correct anything now. It is all in the past, the only thing I can do is pray to God and constantly repent in confession, asking forgiveness for what I did some time ago. It is so painful to remember the sins I committed and the bad things I did."

"I was born in 1898. At age fourteen, people around me said that I was a real beauty; at sixteen, I became aware of my 'privilege' and turned the head of many a young man. I tempted many men, and several husbands offered to leave their families if I would promise to marry them! When I remember these days, I am ashamed of myself. I turned the heads of many, and yet remained untouchable. You should know, Kyra, that a woman's beauty, and especially a 'blinding beauty' is a very unhappy thing, it is a heavy cross to bear. My father became angry at me. He talked to me several times, but my mother was proud in a way to have a beautiful daughter, especially since my sisters were not beauties, to put it mildly.

"Mama and Papa were deeply believing people, but their outlook on life was a mere reflection of the society that surrounded them. They were intelligent and educated, members of the intelligentsia. Our family went to church and, of course, we went to confession and took Communion twice a year. In spite of my lack of seriousness, I knew and understood church services. Once, when I went to confession, I was not met by my usual priest, Father Ioan, but by an old priest called Father Theodosy. I said a few sentences about my sins and expected the prayer of absolution, but the priest started talking to me as if he knew my life. He spoke calmly, gently reminding me of the laws of God, explaining them to me, teaching me how I should live, how I should pray, how I should prepare for confession. Father Theodosy spoke to me for a long time, even after the service started. At the end of our talk, he told me that I was not ready for confession and he advised me to look at my life and come again in a month's time.

"My father was angry at his refusal of confession and communion, so he went to see Father Theodosy. He talked to him with passion and, some twenty minutes later, came out with a serious face, sad and ashamed. He walked over to me and said, 'Father Theodosy is right, you are not worthy of confession. Your mother and I have not raised you right. You will come to confession again in a month.'

"I was very hurt by what I heard from Father Theodosy and from my father, but I started to think. In a month's time, I went to confession again and, before going, I carefully prepared what I was going to say. I spoke for a long time. Father Theodosy listened to me carefully, without interrupting. When I finished he said, 'I have listened to you, and I had the feeling that you were reciting a lesson you had learned by heart. Remember learning something by heart in school but not having any real understanding of what you are saying? Your preparation is formal—I don't feel any soul, any Christian understanding of sin, there is no desire not to sin any more. To prepare yourself, you probably used Dobrovolsky's brochure, *Questions and Answers about Confession.*

" 'Yes,' I said, 'I used that brochure to prepare myself.'

"Father Theodosy stood next to the Cross and Gospel, silent. His lips were moving slightly; he was probably praying. 'Here I stand and I wonder, may I give you absolution and let you take Communion? It is strange, but I have to tell you that your beauty is destroying you. Forget about it: it was given to you by God and you have no merit in it. Years will go by and your face will get covered with wrinkles. You will no longer be beautiful and then you will see the emptiness of the life you have lived. If faith in God, the Mother of God, and the Church stay alive within you, then you will retain your spiritual beauty, a beauty that cannot fade and get old. You will then remember me, the unworthy Father Theodosy, and gratefully pray for me. Not because I am hard of heart, but for your own good I have to tell you again: go home and come back next Sunday for confession. I trust that you will not hold a grudge and you will certainly come. As for Dobrovolsky's brochure, please burn it.'

"My family was good friends with Father Arseny's mother and we used to play together as children. Maria Alexandrovna often visited museums and theaters with her son and she used to take me along. I knew that Maria Alexandrovna was a very pious person, so I went to see her and told her that the priest had refused my confession three times. She listen to me attentively and said, 'Sasha, Father Theodosy is right. Confession is the outpouring of one's soul to God, absolutely openly, with nothing hidden and with a sincere desire not to do bad deeds again. Don't feel hurt, Sasha, you live surrounded by love. Nonetheless, you are charmed by your own beauty, which was not given to you for confusing other people. Look with your soul at your confession, look at your actions as though from the outside—only then will Father Theodosy accept your confession.'

"That evening Maria Alexandrovna told me many very important things. A week later, on Sunday, I went back to confession with Father Theodosy and, after Communion, I was overwhelmed for the first time in my life by a feeling of true joy, not an earthly joy, but a spiritual one.

"I have already said that our family was close to Maria Alexandrovna's family: Father Arseny, who was then called Petya, was my friend and we used to play together. Sometimes Maria Alexandrovna took us children to exhibits, museums, the theater. My parents were always happy to let me go on these outings. For three years in a row we spent our summers in neighboring *dachas*. I was very friendly with Petya, although he was three and a half years older than I was. As far as I can remember he was always interested in Russian history; he collected books on religious art and Russian monasteries, on icons, and on Moscow's old churches; he was interested in architecture and took notes on books he was reading. He read, and read, and read.

"When we lived in the countryside, Maria Alexandrovna would gather us children together and take us for long hikes in the local forests. She would want Piotr to come, but he would always say that he had something to finish writing; but he would still come and then would be delighted by the beauty of the sights. He loved nature, understood it, and often said, 'O Lord, everything is so wisely and amazingly created.'

"He was always a brilliant student. He finished high school early and with high honors (a gold medal). He went to university and also finished it early. For a few months he was ill with endocarditis and a high fever. In serious scientific journals he published long articles in which he absolutely rejected the 'western' outlook on Russian architecture and iconography and affirmed the originality of its provenance, its purely Russian roots.

"The end of 1916 was a spiritual turning point for him. He became less involved in art and started to study Orthodoxy in depth. He was always visiting churches in Moscow, searching for a spiritual father who could understand his inner world. One of the well-known Moscow priests advised him to go to Optino 'to see the elders,' as people said then. He went and spent two years there under the tutelage of Father Anatoly and Father Nektary. In 1919 he returned to Moscow, with the blessing of the elders, already a hieromonk.[70] Maria Alexandrovna, his mother, was conflicted about this. She was a firm believer, and therefore she was happy that her son was a hieromonk, but in the depth of her soul she had had a desire to see him married, to know his wife and her grandchildren. I think she would have been more happy had he decided to be a married priest, Father Piotr, with the same faith that he had acquired at Optino. This bitterness stayed with her for a long time, but I don't know whether she ever talked about it with her son. By the end of 1919 Maria Alexandrovna had realized that Father Arseny had chosen the only path that was right for him.

"During all these years I was friends with Maria Alexandrovna and loved her at least as much as I did my own mother. To be honest, she had more spiritual influence on me than my mother did and I learned a great deal from her—she was thirty years older than I.

"The whole of Father Arseny's life unrolled before my eyes. Only the two years he had spent at Optino, the nine years he was exiled, and the eighteen years he was in labor camp separated us. I visited him more than once when he was in exile.

"Never in my whole life will I forget the trip I made to visit him during the winter. The train took me to Vologda; once there I had to

---

[70]A hieromonk is a monk who is also a priest. —Trans.

find a driver with a horse-drawn cart, which I did. We rode along for a long time; night was falling and the driver suddenly stopped the horse, tossed out my luggage, and said, 'There are eight more miles to your village. You can see over there a pier: you can wait there overnight and you can do the walk in the morning.'

"I said to him, 'But it is nighttime and my luggage is heavy, I will never be able to make it!'

"But he whipped up his horse and left. It was −20° and there was a piercing wind. I suddenly saw a barge standing on the shore, so I started walking towards it, pulling my bags with me one at a time; I wanted to get some protection from the wind. I climbed onto the barge and saw the word 'Cashier.' I entered and smelled the strong odor of cheap tobacco. I heard someone say, 'Hey, guys, look, a woman has come here to hide from the wind!'

"I froze. I realized from the voices that there were three men in the cold booth. I was scared: who were they? Only God could save me, so I started praying, asking for help from the Mother of God, from the saints, but my prayer kept getting interrupted since the men asked me one question after the other and I had to answer. 'Where are you going? What for? Where from? What are you carrying? How old are you? Are you married or still a maiden?' Question after question; I decided to tell only the truth. If I survived till the morning, they would be able to see anyway where I was going and whom I wanted to see. I answered all their questions, and prayed to the Mother of God in between.

"They finished their questioning, and fell silent. It was cold, but at least there was no wind, although I could hear its howling outside. One of the peasants said, 'You know what, girl, don't let yourself fall asleep; it is so cold you could die in your sleep.'

"We left the barge at sunrise. Two of the men were going to the same village I was, so they took my luggage onto their shoulders and carried it for me. The wind stopped and we talked as we were walking along. My companions were about fifty years old. 'You probably got scared when you entered the barge yesterday?'

" 'Yes, I did,' I answered honestly.

" 'I will tell you, girl, around here you should not be walking by yourself. People could steal from you, or they could rape you. There are many camps around here and there are many criminals on the roads; in the forests, they attack and rob. You were lucky you met us!'

"They carried my things up to the house where Father Arseny was living and I thanked them. The owner of the house came out and right behind her I saw Father Arseny. We threw ourselves into each other's arms. 'I prayed for you all night. Did you sleep on the barge?' Turning to the hostess, he showed her my bags and said, 'Ekaterina Nikolaevna! Just take all this and distribute it!' I never went alone to see Father Arseny again. I was too afraid."

We like to remember how we accompanied Father Arseny to Bishop Afanassy (Sakharov) in Petushki.[71] This was in the year 1960 or perhaps the beginning of 1961. These meetings were touching. We were present as Vladyko Afanassy and Father Arseny served together. They had the same opinion of Metropolitan Sergei.[72] As soon as Alexei became patriarch, this problem no longer existed, and now Vladyko Afanassy would sometimes serve in church, even in Vladimir.

It was obvious that Bishop Afanassy and Father Arseny were friends and knew each other well. I wanted to ask about this, but never found an appropriate moment. The strange thing about this was that their severe terms in labor camps had torn them out of normal life for a long time. So the question was: when and where could they have met? Alexandra Fedorovna did not know.

During her last years, Alexandra Fedorovna lived with us. Her chil-

---

[71]Bishop Afanassy (Sakharov) (1887–1962) was one of the remarkable bishops of the times of persecution. He said himself, "Out of my thirty-three years of being bishop I spent thirty-three months serving my diocese, thirty-two months free but out of commission, seventy-six months in prison, and two hundred fifty-four months in exile and forced labor." After he was freed from labor camp in 1954, Bishop Afanassy lived with his spiritual children, first in Tutaev (near Yaroslavl) and then in Petushki near Vladimir.

[72]After Metropolitan Sergei (Starogorodski)'s Declaration of July 29, 1927, many bishops, priests, monks and laypeople refused to obey him and would not pray for him during liturgies that named him as being "In the seat of the patriarchal throne." They only prayed for Metropolitan Piotr (Polianski), who had been exiled at the time. Metropolitan Sergei's declaration was interpreted by many as compromising the leadership of the Church and therefore unacceptable.

dren worked and her grandchildren had grown up and were studying. It was impossible for Alexandra Fedorovna, who had become blind, to stay by herself. Yuri was working, but I had already retired and was at home, so her presence was a joy for us. Her children and grandchildren never forgot her, visited and cared for her.

Alexandra Fedorovna was a gifted person with encyclopedic knowledge. She was familiar with the writings of the Fathers of the Church and church services, and was at ease with spiritual questions. She gladly shared her knowledge with people who wanted to be ordained. Sometimes she helped students at religious academies or seminaries who had been sent to her by priests who knew her.

Once Alexandra Fedorovna recalled how Father Arseny's mother had raised him, but he retells this himself in his memoirs about Father Oleg. I told her about this, but she wanted me to write what she herself remembered:

"Maria Alexandrovna considered that the foundation of faith had to be established in a child by his mother during the first days of life. Before his birth, it is important that the mother pray constantly, because prayer penetrates the child while he is in the womb. Then praying aloud before the baby's cradle will have a lasting influence on his soul.

"When a child is born, you assume responsibility not only for his bodily health, but also for his soul. It is possible to raise a physically healthy child with a disfigured soul. When such a person becomes an adult, he will be lost; he will become a liar or a criminal. Had the mother shown him the presence of God, even if he were not in perfect health, he would be spiritually rich and would find his path in life. She said, 'I saw Piotr both as my biological son and as a creation of God, and I felt responsible before God because He had entrusted to me the raising of this person. I was always against children learning prayers by rote. It is important to explain everything to them. You must show the child pictures related to the prayer and appropriate to his abilities, which the child is able to understand, so that the prayer will be also understandable to him. Folktales are also important in raising a child. Most people tell stories about witches, mermaids and the like, or else they read them the folktales of the brothers Grimm. But that is not what is needed for building the foundations of faith within a child's soul. You should often read them stories about Jesus Christ's childhood, of the Mother of God and of the saints; you can read legends by Selma Lagerlef about Jesus Christ; you can retell your child lives of such saints as Sergius of Radonezh, Seraphim of Sarov, Nicholas the Wonderworker; you can also read apocryphal writings by Leskov, even though a certain fog of Tolstoy's ideas sometimes appears in these stories.

" 'Of course, you should also tell your children Russian folktales—skipping the passages you judge inappropriate. When the child learns to read by himself, he will read what you skipped, but he will already have in his soul the foundation of faith that will permit him to throw out the bad.' This is what Maria Alexandrovna used to say about raising a child in the faith.

"When Maria Alexandrovna took Piotr and me to the theater, she used to choose plays that would influence us in a positive way. I will never forget how I saw *The Blue Bird* at the Moscow Artistic Theater. My imagination was deeply impressed and I continued for a few days to be mesmerized by what I had seen. Dog, Cat, Sugar, Water, the Trough full of dough, Till, Metill, Death holding an enormous scythe in her hands were in front of my eyes day and night, but I was mostly impressed by the way it took me into the world of shadows. Enormous white columns rose to the ceiling (when I grew up I realized that these had been made from tulle hanging from above which was lit by projectors, but the effect was unforgettable), a light fog rose and Till and Metill were almost lost in the Great Chaos and walked through the passageway—even the sadness that the Blue Bird had not been found did not sadden them. Everything was so mysterious and perfect.

"I remember that when an enormous room from the world of shadows appeared on stage, I said aloud, 'Aunt Masha, is this paradise?'

"We came home excited, talking about the play the whole way home. We asked, 'Why? What was this?'

"Maria Alexandrovna answered, 'I will explain it all when we get home.' At the dinner table Aunt Masha told us, 'Children, you saw that Till and Metill were looking for happiness: they looked for a long while, persistently, but they did not find it. They did not find it because true happiness can only be found through faith in God and loving Him. We must tell God our thoughts and we must pray to Him: happiness is understanding the will of God. Till and Metill looked for happiness on earth and forgot God. Happiness is loving one another and helping others.' "

"I will tell about a few things that happened to me. (Father Arseny always said that nothing happens by chance, it is only by the will of God) and which I consider miraculous.

"On Vorkut, I don't know why, they moved me from one labor camp to another. I was dying of scurvy and utter exhaustion. After a trek, we entered the barracks, and I was so weak that I fell down. I regained consciousness on a bunk while someone was taking my clothes off me. 'They will probably steal my backpack,' I thought, but I did not care. I was dying. Through the fog of semi-consciousness I heard two women talking, 'You rub her chest and abdomen, I will do her legs and then we will turn her over.' I felt the hands of strangers were rubbing my body. My strength and conscience slowly returned, and I came to. It was almost dark in the barracks so I could not see the women's faces. They gave me a piece of bread and some hot water, put some clothes on me, covered me with a blanket, and I fell asleep.

"In the morning I heard the command, 'Get up!' and heard the usual swearing all around the barracks. A woman bent over me and said, 'You should stay in bed at least one day, otherwise you will die. I will go talk to the *starosta* (as they called the woman in charge), and perhaps she will help.'

"She came and said, 'I will help, but she needs not just one day, but three days, in bed' and then she went away. I do not know what this *starosta* did, but I remained in the bunk for three days. In all that time those two women cared for me and cured me somehow and brought me food. So you see I survived and here I am talking to you.

"Those women were Anna Alexandrovna, from a collective farm in Tula. She was a woman of faith and a golden heart; intelligent and strong, she knew how to stand up for herself. Her face was round and had a slightly upturned nose and enormous, beautiful, gray eyes. The other woman was called Larissa. She had been a thief. She had a beautiful face and a surprisingly attractive appearance. Very intelligent, she had very caring and loving eyes. She had dozens of names and last names, but her real name was Ekaterina. She was a thief, a real criminal, and among thieves, she had a special alias. She could be very caring and goodhearted, but she could also be very cruel. In the barracks she held sway among the criminals and many were afraid of her. The fact that two prisoners who were total strangers to me saved me and cared for me was one of God's real miracles.

"Many years went by. The year was 1939 and I was working in Moscow. I had finished the University of Moscow and was working in the Institute of Sciences making experiments on white mice and rats and testing different drugs, viruses, and microbes on them. I married Viacheslav. One day while I was shopping in a store I heard, 'Good morning, Alexandra Fedorovna.'

"I turned around and saw before me a woman with a charming and pleasant face who was well dressed. I looked again and realized that she was the criminal, Katia.[73] We hugged and kissed, and I wanted to ask her how she was, but she only said, 'Give me your address.'

"I did, and she disappeared into the crowd without saying good-bye. I was surprised and stayed in the store for a while longer. Ten o'clock that evening my apartment bell rang, and I opened the door. Katia walked in, took off her coat silently, and said, 'I am sorry I did not say good-bye, but I couldn't,' and before she even entered the room she asked, 'Would you let me stay with you for two months?'

"I don't know what my face was saying, but I answered, 'Of course, Katia, do stay.' But I thought, 'She will rob us.'

"You remember, of course, that at this time I had to take the children to my husband's parents and pick them up again in the evening. Katia stayed with us for over two months. My children and my husband loved her, and she was never a burden to anyone. In the evenings when we used to pray together, we did so in front of her. Father Piotr came down from Yaroslavl and served the liturgy, and we were not afraid of Katia. When we prayed she always stood but only seldom made the sign of the cross. After Father Piotr served, she walked over to him and asked him to give her a little time for a talk, but it took a long time. Later,

---

[73]Short for Ekaterina. —Trans.

about a year later, Father Piotr told us, 'An amazing woman, your Katia. She has a surprising soul, it is truly Christian, but her life is so complex and difficult.'

"Katia would come home at different times of the day or evening, sometimes even around eleven at night, so I just gave her a key to our apartment. One morning Katia came to Viacheslav and me and asked us to give her a blessing. She hugged the children, venerated the icon of the Mother of God of Kazan and, as always, just left. Do you remember her? You met her once at our place. You were both at a liturgy celebrated by Father Piotr and you even said about her, 'What a good, intelligent, and beautiful face this woman has.' " (I could remember my own words as well as the nice and attractive face of that woman.)

"What Katia was doing and where she went I never asked," continued Alexandra Fedorovna. "On the day that Katia had asked us to bless her, I went as usual to take the children to their grandmother, after which Viacheslav and I went off to our respective places of work. When I came home that evening, I saw a clean cup in the middle of the table and under it a note:

> My dear ones, thank you for your trust, and for everything.
> I love you, remember Ekaterina.
> Katia.
> P.S. The bundle is for you, it is clean.

The word 'clean' was underlined. Next to the note I saw a large bundle wrapped in newspaper. I opened it and could not even speak: I had never in my life seen such a large amount of money. We prayed for a long time and asked Father Herman's advice. He said, 'Give a third to the poor and keep the rest.' Everything in life has a purpose and Katia's 'clean' gift helped us. Is this all not one of God's miracles? A thief, a criminal, who had done time in prison more than once, suddenly behaves like that. I did not see Katia again, but in 1961 did I receive an amazing letter full of love and gratitude.

"I told all this to a friend of ours and I heard, 'You committed a sin in taking money from a thief.' I thought that this was a person who did not know much about people, and did not know what a labor camp was. Of course in 1958 I also told all this to Father Arseny and he said, 'You were right to accept the money. Katia told you the truth that the money was "clean." She simply wanted to let you know, "There is no blood or pain for others connected with this money." ' "

"I will tell you about another miracle. I was walking at eleven thirty at night on Malaya Nikitskaya Street. It was windy and cold and there was no one else in the street. The houses were old ones, with deep gateways. I prayed and thought, 'I have to get to the tram stop as soon as I can,' but I was going to have to walk for five or six minutes more to get there. I was scared. I passed a tall house and suddenly two men came out and pushed me into the gateway. I was trying to say something when a third man grabbed me by the throat, pulled out a knife said, 'Shut up or I will cut you up! Let's take her to the basement quickly!'

"They pulled me into the basement, took the shopping bag with my purchases and my purse with my money (I had just received my week's pay). They started searching me to see if I had any other valuables on me. I had a large gold cross on a chain hanging around my neck. They took off my jumper and I was left in a dress with a torn collar. The cross on its chain was still on me. It was light in the basement. It was useless to scream, to ask, to beg—they were merciless. I felt like a compressed knot and put all my spiritual ego into a prayer to God, to His Holy Mother, and to my spiritual father, Father Arseny. I was not afraid of death, but of dirty violence done to my body. Two of the men were standing next to me while the third, obviously the chief, was pulling money, documents, and pieces of paper out of my purse. Under the light of a hanging lamp he was carefully reading everything, but put the money in his pocket. I could only pray to God in a disorganized way, asking for the assistance of His Holy Mother and of Father Arseny. The third one was attentively reading a little piece of paper he had pulled out of my purse. He suddenly asked, 'What labor camp were you in?'

"I was so shocked that I did not understand his question. 'How long did you stay in a labor camp? And which one were you in?'

"I answered. He looked at me attentively and said, 'Hey, guys! Give her back her clothes.'

"He pulled the money out of his pocket and put it back in my purse saying, 'Go home, and know that you'd better not say anything about us!'

"I realized that the Lord and the Birthgiver of God, as well as the prayers of Father Arseny, had saved me. I walked over to the third one (the chief), bowed low to him, made the sign of the cross, gave him my hand, and said, 'I thank you.'

" 'Go, go quickly. I thank you for your thanks and for yourself. I realized that you were in camp from reading your papers. I know camps well, go!'

"It was such a miraculous liberation, an indescribable miracle! I walked and glorified God and His Holy Mother, as well as that protector of humans, Saint Nicholas the Wonderworker. I walked along calmly enough, but when I entered the house I started sobbing and I couldn't stop. I went over to the icons, prayed, and peace came back to me and I was able to tell Viacheslav everything in full detail. I could only think, what a mercy God has shown to me, a sinner. I was on the brink of death. This was a miracle."

That is how Alexandra Fedorovna remembered her life.

MORE ABOUT OUR COMMUNITY

PEOPLE HAVE WRITTEN memoirs of our community, its life, and about Father Arseny from as early as the 1920s. They were sincere and fresh, full of the spiritual atmosphere in which we lived in those days. But the massive arrests of believers then started and that forced us to destroy what had been written or else we had to hand the notebooks for safe-keeping to people who were not members of the community. Very often they also destroyed them for fear of being arrested.

Two sisters and their brother, members of our community were arrested and some memoirs were found in their apartment, which brought bad consequences for many of us.

The worst years, the hardest years for the life of the community were from 1928 to 1937. There were arrests, exile, labor camps, the closing of churches, the arrests of priests and also of their parishioners in great numbers. No one knew what to expect the next day. At the end of December 1927, on Christmas Eve, Father Arseny was arrested and exiled to Arkhangelsk. He was frequently transferred from one village to the other; they never allowed him to stay in one place for more than four or five months at a time.

Until 1929 our church was not shut down and our priests, Father Stepan and Father Vassily were still serving. Then they were arrested and a priest from the Living Church was assigned to the parish. We went to other churches, those that were still open, and our community lived on in secret.

It was extremely difficult to go visit Father Arseny. We knew that those who were in exile were hungry, so we tried to bring him as much food as we could. We also brought him letters from his spiritual children and, of course, we talked with him, but two serious problems arose.

After the second visit of one of his spiritual daughters, the police came and started interrogating her in detail. Why were people coming? Who were they? He forbade all visits. Besides, the women in whose houses Father Arseny was living, seeing that we brought him so much food, felt that our visits were a treasure that allowed them to feed their entire family, especially since Father Arseny always gave her the food and since she cooked for him. When one of us came we would hear, "You did not bring very much!" Almost all the hostesses behaved this way in all the places. I once said to one of them that I felt that I was feeding six people and she said, "So what? Here I am feeding your pops as well as my whole family. You have a lot of money there in Moscow— I have children. Do you want me to talk to the police? I will go and tell how many of you come and visit!"

He had to move to another house, but soon a man from the militia came and made threats; he had obviously been drinking. I gave him a hundred rubles and in those days that was a lot of money. He took them and said, "All right, I will close this dossier; as for Varvara, she is a bad woman!"

After his term of exile was finished, he still spent time being forced to live at least a hundred kilometers away from Moscow. Father Arseny went to live in a small town, close to Moscow, where a small church was miraculously still active. The priest was Father Alexander, who was an old and sick man. He allowed Father Arseny to serve, and he must have had the permission of the authorities. Father Arseny did not serve often, so his spiritual children were able to come, but we all knew that this was only a temporary situation. The persecutions had gotten stronger and were intended to annihilate the Church, destroy all the priests, and defile and destroy all the churches.

In 1931 Father Arseny was arrested again and exiled to the Vologda region. In 1939 he was arrested yet again. He was sent to Siberia for a while, to the Ural Mountains, and then for a year near Arkhangelsk. Father Arseny speaks about these times when he writes about Father Ilarion. At the end of 1940, Father Arseny was imprisoned in a labor camp and until 1956 we, his spiritual children, heard nothing. We did not know whether he was dead or alive, or whether he had he been shot. We lived in anguish. We were interrogated more and more often, some of us in the Lyubianka prison. Some of us were arrested, others were sent to labor camps, or exiled out of Moscow. Even Boris Timofeivich was arrested; he had been secretly ordained a priest on Father Arseny's recommendation. Only a few of us knew about this ordination (Natasha, Yuri, Vera), but he used to serve the liturgy at K.S.'s place because he was so generous. K.S. invited several people to join us for this liturgy, without asking Father Boris' permission. From the questions that were asked during the interrogation, we realized that one of us was a double-crosser and scrupulously analyzed each step of every person who had been present at that liturgy.

We discovered who the traitor was. It was disgusting, but we had to know. We created closed groups of seven or eight people, people who knew each other well, and decided that we would not inform the others about the services that were going to be served, or about the readings of vespers, matins, or akathists. All community affairs were decided by the leaders of the groups and money was collected by these leaders for each group individually. The arrests stopped, but we had lost the confidence in each other that we had had before.

Many of us noticed that they were being followed (this was called "being tailed"). If we noticed it, we never went to visit members of our community, but some neutral acquaintance or relative. We all became very careful. Sometimes one of the people suspected would arrive, without prior warning, and say, "I have come for the service." Then our answer would be, "We regret it, but Mama is sick, and we don't serve at home."

Up until 1941, the old spirit of our community united us and we tried hard to maintain our previous ties, friends, meetings and home liturgies. After 1941, we could no longer celebrate these liturgies, so we gathered in groups, talked, read the works of the Fathers of the Church, or one of us would present a short lecture on some spiritual topic; that this was our "light in the window."

We confessed and took Communion in "working" churches, but our confessions were not always understood by the priests. If one of us asked advice about spiritual or everyday problems, or opened up completely, speaking about sinful thoughts, the priests would very often be surprised, take this for a kind of hyperpiety and, without any lengthy conversation, cover our head with their stole and forgive our sins.

We still had heard nothing about Father Arseny. We thought that he must have been shot or died in labor camps. I remember how, on April 7, 1956, the day of Annunciation,[74] Julia and Lyuda ran in or, more precisely, tore in, shouting, "Yura, Kyra! There is a letter from Father Arseny!" We telephoned Vera (Danilovna) and Natasha (Natalia Petrovna). We gathered and our joy had no bounds. We immediately wrote him several letters, but he had not given us the address of his camp.

First Olga went to see him, then Yuri and Natasha, Julia and Lyuda. Father Arseny wrote that he was now allowed to see people. We collected food, money and clothing. Upon her return Olga told us that, to her joy, in the eighteen years in which we had not seen him, he had not changed much. She only reported that his eyes struck her with their special spiritual light, that he had become stricter, but at the same time more gentle. He gave everything away that we had sent.

He was freed at the beginning of 1958 and rehabilitated. Without warning anyone, he moved to Rostov. He was not able to settle there for a time, but then he moved into Nadezhda Petrovna's house, where he lived for the next seventeen years, protected by God, His Most Holy Mother and the saints.

---

[74]April 7 old style is March 25, the date of Annunciation. —Trans.

The number of people who visited him in those seventeen years was staggering. More than half of them were people he had met in labor camps or new people who had been introduced by one of his old friends from his community or from a camp. The people you might meet at Nadezhda Petrovna's house were also so different from one another: a white-haired academician, a retired general, a journalist, a peasant from a collective farm, doctors of medicine or other disciplines, factory workers, a renowned psychiatrist, an ex-member of the Communist Party, professional thieves who had gone straight under Father Arseny's influence, even Communist Party workers or secret service agents who had worked in labor camps and were later pardoned and reestablished in their previous jobs, but who had become believers. Young, old, working people, retirees and housewives visited him. How many tears, sorrows, emotions entered Father Arseny's room, and how many people came out renewed, full of hope, enriched by true faith and love. Sometimes he received a one-day visit from a governing bishop, dressed in civilian clothes; retired bishops sometimes stayed for weeks. Priests whom he had met in labor camp came; they had become his true friends. Of course, he also received visits from brothers of his community who had become secret priests between 1935 and 1940 and could now serve in churches of different dioceses. Some people remained secret priests; at the same time they might be members of the Academy of Sciences or might hold a doctorate of science, or might be designers of airplanes or motors. No more services were served in homes; they could visit open churches. When they came to see Father Arseny they concelebrated with him. God's will and the passage of time had put everything in its proper place. We had also suffered losses: seven sisters of the community had left during the years of persecution and only three or four of them had come back after Father Arseny returned.

As before, we collected money for the poor, cared for the sick, the homebound or the institutionalized. Spiritual children came not only from Moscow, but from all over the Soviet Union: from Magadan, Norilsk, Leningrad, Alma-Ata, Yaroslavl, Gorki, Harkov—well, it is impossible to name them all.

We had a chance to meet remarkable people so full of such spirituality that I felt unworthy of being with them. I can remember the hieromonk Seraphim, Father Evgeny Bogorodsky, Father Kiril, the Nuns Ioana and Evdokia, Alexandra Fedorovna Berg, Elizaveta Alexandrovna, the Nun Irina, the Hieromonk Filip, Father Alexei. Each and every meeting with these people was a true joy and filled my soul with spiritual warmth.

The year 1958 was a turning point in the lives of many of us: Father Arseny returned, but of course it did not prove possible for our community to be reborn. We had no church; the times were different. Father Arseny became our *starets*, who was almost living in a skete and whom we had to visit to receive advice and direction and to unload the heavy burden of our sins, be purified, and then return to the world to spend gradually the grace we had received. Then we would return to see him when the time was right. The rule was that we were not supposed to come more often than once every three months. Only Lyuda, Yuri, Natasha, Irina, myself, Father Herman, Father Alexei and several others were allowed to come any time; but of course even we, the "selected ones," did not go too often. Many of us would go to Rostov for our holidays, rent a room, and go see Father Arseny. We would take walks with him (when his health permitted) visiting the town and the countryside around Rostov.

Yuri and I used to go to Rostov every year. We spent a lot of time with Father Arseny and we even brought our grandchildren with us. Father Arseny recommended that we see Father Alexander Tolgodsky,[75] Father Vsevolod Schpiller, Father Serge Orlov,[76] who used to serve near Moscow, and another priest I cannot name because he is still alive and serving in the Church of Saints Peter and Paul in Moscow. In this church he was not liked very much, since he was quiet and did not behave like other priests. The main priest did not like him, but he was a very spiritual and kind man. He now heads a parish with a big church and is very influential.[77]

---

[75]Father Alexander Tolgodsky (1880–1962). For the twenty-six years after 1936, he was the main priest in the parish of Saint Elias Obidenni.

[76]Father Serge Orlov (1890–1975), who had been secretly consecrated a monk with the name Hieromonk Seraphim, was priest in the Church of the Veil close to Moscow. He was an erudite man and at the same time was a humble monk. He was confessor and friend of many bishops and priests.

[77]This might perhaps be Father Seraphim Golubtsov (1908–1981).

How Father Arseny knew these priests was unknown to me, but he always spoke about them with utter respect. When he directed his spiritual children to them, he asked them not to tell that it was he, Father Arseny, who had sent them. Father Arseny also sent many Muscovites to get instruction from the Nun Athanasia (Irina Nikolaevna).

Our community was unique in a way. From 1920 to 1930 it consisted mostly of cultured people, people with higher education, or young people who were studying at the university or were members of Christian groups. This of course was felt by all the members since it created an atmosphere of intellectuality in our relations, in the ways we understood and interpreted the church services and Father Arseny's teachings.

Sometimes this was a positive influence, but it also happened that being too intellectual got in the way of knowing God, of believing in him, of loving others; it got in the way of a spiritual understanding of the world or of the human soul. You could see this during the talks led by Father Arseny, you could see it in the questions that were asked and even in the heated debates. Some people lived their faith not with their soul and heart, but by rationally weighing it against the bulk of knowledge that they had acquired. Questions and arguments continued after the talks had come to a close while people were leaving to go home.

But the longer the community continued, the fewer the arguments we had. They were replaced by mutual understanding and love for each other. It would be wrong to think that the high intelligence of some of our members made them spiritually richer than simple workmen or peasants. Very often a person with little or no education at all was a few heads higher and better than his very intellectual counterpart, who might be a doctor, a teacher, or an engineer. Right from the very beginning there were many people in our community who were called the "former ones"—they were aristocrats, rich businessmen, merchants, even princes (whose surnames were world renowned) and their children, but nobody ever showed superiority because of his or her origins. We were all equal and became superior only through our level of spiritual upbringing, obedience, depth of prayer, goodness and love.

I have said before that Father Arseny never allowed anyone to have two spiritual fathers. He felt that this could be harmful and if Father Sergei, Father Vsevolod, or Father Alexander or any other priest from the church of Saints Peter and Paul had given a piece of advice, he never contradicted it but always said, "Do as he told you." He had great respect for Father Vsevolod Schpiller, with whom he sometimes corresponded through his spiritual children, and he loved Father Sergei Orlov, whom he knew well through Bishop Afanassy (Sakharov).

People who came to see Father Arseny after 1958 came when they had reached a difficult time in their life; sometimes they might have reached a crossroads, not knowing which way to turn; he would show them which way they should take. In grief, or in a spiritual fire, in the cases of the death of a close one—in cases of any loss—he knew how to console and direct the person. Praying together with him helped people to face life again. If someone had committed a heavy sin, Father Arseny would pray for the sinner begging God to forgive but it was the words that he himself pronounced as father-confessor that the person would remember for the rest of his life; he would try never to commit that sin again.

As has been said before, there were always four or five people in Nadezhda Petrovna's house. They might have come for one or two days, but during holidays up to twelve people would arrive! Father Arseny had to talk to each person, hear their confession, and give them Communion; all that required time and strength. He tired easily and his heart would give him problems, and then he would have to stay lying on the sofa and receive visits in that way. On some days it happened that the situation in Nadezhda Petrovna's house would be complicated. Those who were already there would have to leave to make room for newly arriving spiritual children. Tired and sick, Father Arseny still had to receive them and sometimes talk with them into the night. Father Arseny treated with equal attention small and large problems, sins, and thoughts brought to him by his spiritual children; he listened to each one with the same attention, gave advice and confessions.

I once tried to add up how many people had come to Rostov in the course of one year. I counted between 350 and 380 people. I saw twenty or twenty-five priests from various cities: they were either priests he had met in camps or members of the community who had been ordained and were now serving in churches. There were dozens of men who had been in labor camps with him and as many women, sisters of the community. Several of his friends did not live to see him freed: they had died either of natural causes or in camps; three of them had been shot—Father Igor, Deacon Evgeni and Valentina Petrovna.

Many people were absolutely new. They were between twenty and forty years of age, either friends of members of the community or of "camp friends," or they were simply people we knew nothing about who had heard about Father Arseny in ways unknown to us. Priests who knew him sent to him their own spiritual children. Father Arseny would get exhausted but would rest only when he was forced to go into a clinic. Then he suffered for his friends worrying how they were doing in his absence.

From 1966 on, every time Father Arseny had to leave for Moscow, he was replaced by a very old priest, Father Philip. He was a retired priest who lived in Yaroslavl and would be brought to Rostov by one of us. Father Philip was extremely well educated in spiritual matters; he was wise and would approach each person according to that person's own inner character, education, and way of looking at things. He was a hieromonk who had spent ten years on Mount Athos and then returned to Russia in 1912; he lived in the Pskovo-Pechersky Monastery. By God's will he was bypassed by arrests and camps. In 1922 he moved to Yaroslavl and lived a quiet life with some pious relatives; no one knew that he was a hieromonk. His own spiritual children visited him and he directed them, but he always said, "I have only a small family, about thirty people and perhaps that is why we were never arrested or sent to labor camps." In 1966 he was ninety-one years old, but was still active, quick and limber, and was always saying the Jesus prayer. He served seriously, strictly according to the rule, but he was inspiring. We all loved him and when Father Arseny was sick went to him with joy since they were of the same spirit. It was a rare occurrence, but it did happen that when several people truly close to Father Arseny, people he had known for decades, found themselves together around him then he might tell us about his life, his coming to God, the creation of the community, the people he had met, or his doubts and mistakes. We had known him since 1920, and had been with him practically all the time and had followed him, and we thought that we knew everything about him. But when he started, we realized that even though we had been so close to him, we had been blind, perceiving what we had seen through our own egos and missing the essential.

Father Arseny's memory was astounding. It happened that a person might have gone to confession with him some fifteen years earlier and, of course, have forgotten everything he had said then; but suddenly Father Arseny would remind him of big pieces of his confession. It was almost frightening. In memoirs written by his spiritual children about themselves or about him, you can often encounter the phrases "brought to the faith," "saved spiritually," "put faith into him," or other such expressions. Father Arseny did not like to hear such words. He felt himself to be unworthy, so he would get upset and ask us not to make him out to be a "righteous man" and insisted that he was simply a priest-monk. Knowing that, we asked the people who retold their stories not to use such words, but when we wrote things down, we added them because it was the absolute truth. That is the reason why there is sometimes a discrepancy between the words you hear on a tape and those you read; this occurs only concerning Father Arseny's words and actions. It is important to know this in order to understand the reason for the differences you encounter. I will note that some memoirs, written by different people who did not even know each other, are very similar in content: probably their circumstances were similar.

More than once I saw men and women who had met at Father Arseny's later get married; most of the time these families lived in the faith. That is why some of the memoirs have such a "family character."

Besides the long talks he would have with spiritual children who had come to visit him, Father Arseny also maintained an extensive correspondence with those who were unable to come. Letters from these spiritual children would be sent to Moscow to different addresses and would be brought to Father Arseny. He would read them and dictate answers to me, Anya and Nina (the one who wrote the beautiful story called "O Mother of God, Help Me!").[78] Father Arseny wrote seven to twelve letters a day. He would read attentively the letters we had writ-

---

[78]This memoir is found in *Father Arseny 1893–1973*.

ten under his dictation, sometimes making corrections, then we would put them in envelopes and write the addresses; those who were leaving would drop these letters in different mail boxes. Father himself wrote special letters, unknown to us, but there were not many of those. He would get so tired that he dictated even letters addressed to bishops and priests.

He would often tell us, "In Moscow, be sure to stop in on this or that person—and he would give us a name—they are having a difficult time." Sometimes early in the morning he would get up and urgently dictate a letter for a spiritual daughter or son living in Riazan, Torzhka, Leningrad, or Novgorod, saying, "They have big problems now." We would sit down, write what he said, and immediately drop these letters into mailboxes. Two or three times I sent off a telegram with just one word, "Come!" I suppose other of his children sent similar telegrams under his instruction.

In 1977 we had the idea of gathering from their addressees Father Arseny's answers to their letters in order to publish a collection of them, but we encountered quite a bit of resistance. Many people did not want to send the letters and even refused to make photocopies. We did have the addresses of those who had received the letters, so we asked them again, but we received only thirty copies and one original in his handwriting, even though he had written hundreds of them! Our plans did not materialize. It is a pity!

In all his talks and lectures on religious or philosophical subjects, Father Arseny never touched on the topic of "dark powers." If somebody tried to bring it up, Father Arseny would change the subject or would simply say, "God, the Holy Mother of God and the saints are with us and this is an inexhaustible source of light, love, useful advice and talk. It is not good to talk about the 'dark powers.' Such talk creates confusion in souls from useless and harmful knowledge." One evening, however, one of the newly arrived guests tried all evening to talk about these powers. Father Arseny did not say anything, but after a while this conversation became unpleasant to him and he asked, "Tell me, why do you keep returning to this subject?"

"I want to learn to fight against them."

"If you want to fight, pray. Look in your prayer book: there are prayers specially for this. Go to church more often, go to confession, take Communion, do good deeds, and often read Psalm 90 (91), 'He who dwells in the shelter of the Most High . . .' as well as the prayer to the Mother of God, 'O victorious Leader of triumphant hosts . . .' All that is evil will leave you. If these powers overcome you, it means that you are not praying well, are not going to church enough and are going to confession too seldom. I cannot give other advice and I do not want to keep on talking about this: it is harmful."

Father Arseny never liked or used familiarity in addressing his spiritual children, whoever they might be. Few were those whom he called by their first name or used the familiar form of address. He did that only with a few friends from camps and some long-standing members of his community; others he called by their name and patronymic and used the polite form of speech. He never used pet names like Katyusha, Yulka, Petya, or Lesha; there were never were any friendly taps on the shoulder or pettings of the hand. He hugged and kissed only when meeting special camp friends or brothers of the community. He did not like to use diminutives and never used affectionate phrases: he thought that they too often were used to cover insincerity.

The newly arrived would realize from his simple words that he had already understood why they had come, that he had entered into their spiritual world, that he knew their worry, their grief and the spiritual disarray that had followed it. The person would immediately feel close to Father Arseny and would open his whole soul without fear. Father Arseny's words came along with prayer to God and love for the person.

He said that many people try to help their acquaintances, their friends, or their colleagues, but not their blood relatives—mother, father, grandfather, sister, brother. He explained, "In helping your acquaintances, you show a yourself to be so good and responsive: 'See what a good Christian I am!' Helping your father or mother is dull, uninteresting, not noticeable to those around you. A rude word addressed to friends or acquaintances is something you simply know is considered unacceptable, but carelessness, rudeness, or irritation toward your relatives, especially towards your parents, is considered almost normal; people do not realize that it is a heavy sin.

"I have noticed that many of you often chat about unimportant things, but that you do not seem to be able to, or even want to, visit a sick person or a little old lady, perhaps to listen for the tenth time to that old person's complaint, to show your understanding, to say a good word. If you only knew the importance of your visit, the hope and joy you bring into their lives, that would mean that you understand the meaning of the words of our Savior, 'I was hungry and you gave me food, I was thirsty and you gave me to drink, I was a visitor and you let me in, I was naked and you clothed me, I was ill and you visited me, I was in prison and you came to visit me' (Mt 25:35–36). The totality of the meaning of God-inspired Christian love is expressed in the words of Jesus Christ in his commandment, 'Love your neighbor as yourself' (Mt 22:39)."

Reading the memoirs of many of his spiritual children as well as his own memoirs, I notice constant quotes about the commandments of God regarding love for God and people. On these commandments (Mt 22:37–40) he built the directing of his community until 1940 as well as his relations with the spiritual children who visited him in Rostov after 1958. The same element infuses the stories told by his camp friends about his relationship with those around him in those labor camps.

In his teachings and his talks, Father Arseny did not use many words; he tried to communicate his thoughts in a compact, clear way. Whatever the topic of conversation would be, whoever he would be talking to, he was always well-meaning and the person would feel the inner goodness and warmth of the words he heard. He did not permit gossip, the "washing of bones," accusations against anyone, especially priests, or any sort of disparaging words. He never allowed gossip among his spiritual children; he would try to make peace among them and clear up the reason for the conflict.

Father Arseny was a true erudite in the fields of theology, art, ancient architecture, and Russian history, but he never showed this off. If a complicated theological theme came up, he would always say, "The elders of Optino, Fathers Anatoly and Nektary and Bishop Ilarion, gave me their blessing to serve as a pastor. They said, 'This is your path. Remember the teachings of the Church. Let theologians discuss theology.'"

I have read all the memoirs written about Father Arseny and the lives of his spiritual children. I don't know why there is so little said about the person in whose house he lived for seventeen years in Rostov. He lived a calm life thanks to her. He was fed on time, he was surrounded by constant care. Even when up to fifteen persons would come they would also be fed and often given beds. All that was left to the concern of Nadezhda Petrovna, who refused no one and was always ready to serve, although even then she was then not so young herself.

She became exhausted to the limit, but she bore it all, never complaining to anybody. It was only at the beginning of 1960 that we realized that she needed help. She no longer had to cook meals and was not admitted to the kitchen: food was brought by those who came. Every woman helped with the cooking or cleaning. Each person would bring two sheets, a pillowcase and a towel and took them all home again when leaving. The only thing Nadezhda Petrovna did not want to give up was taking care of Father Arseny, preparing his breakfast, lunch, dinner and tea for him; when people tried to replace her, she got angry and upset.

The doctors (and there were many of them in the community) were not the only ones who helped Father Arseny to keep on living. It was only thanks to the patient care of Nadezhda Petrovna that our sick Father Arseny could have lived for seventeen years and have led such enormous numbers of people to God, direct them, teach them, and pray constantly for all his spiritual children. His *podvig*[79] was difficult for an old man, it was very heavy. When you begin to wonder where he could have found his strength, you realize that God gave it to him for the sake of us sinners.

---

[79]A *podvig* is a physical or spiritual task or a difficult way of life that is taken up by those on a spiritual journey. —Trans.

HEALINGS

I WILL TELL YOU NOW about real miracles that occurred as a result of Father Arseny's prayers. Marina Petrovna's granddaughter, Tania, who was twenty-five years old, got sick: she had pains around her stomach and liver. She was hospitalized for tests. They took x-rays, they performed a gastroscopy, and discovered a tumor. They decided to operate to remove part of her stomach. They placed Tania in the best surgical hospital, the one where Julia was the chief. When they opened her up, they discovered an enormous tumor in her stomach, a lesion on her pancreas, and metastasis even in her liver. It made no sense to operate, so they sewed her up and did not tell her anything.[80] Her whole family was devastated, and she had a little three-year-old daughter! Tania's husband, Evgeni, eight years older than Tania, almost lost his mind: he adored his wife. Marina and I decided to go see Father Arseny since Tania had been his spiritual daughter since 1959. She was a lovely person, always ready to help all those in need, always ready to console and assist, she always knew what words to use. I always thought that God had put on her His special seal of perfection. We came and told it all to Father Arseny. All his spiritual children were equal for him, but I knew he cared especially for Tania. "We will go see her tomorrow! O Lord, what grief!" Whenever Father Arseny wanted to go to Moscow, his doctors and Nadezhda Petrovna would be worried; they were all afraid for his health, but he was definite and said firmly, "I am going!"

We went directly to Marina's apartment. Marina was Tania's grandmother. Tania was in bed and gently moaning because of the pain. Father Arseny entered the room, prayed, blessed Tania and, to the surprise of all those in the room, said, "Tania, Tania, you are so young and have become sick with cancer. They opened you up and then sewed you back up. God is merciful. We will pray for his mercy and for the intercession of the Mother of God." He asked us to light the oil lamps. He put on his cassock and stole, asked us all to leave, and knelt next to her bed. He did not leave the room for four hours. He confessed Tania, anointed her and gave her Communion. He stayed in the apartment for

---

[80]In Russia they believe that a patient might lose the desire to live if he is told how serious his ailment is. The practice of medical disclosure is thus sharply limited. —Trans.

three days and prayed next to Tania's bed for a few hours each day. Then we all prayed together with him, asking for Tania's healing. He left on the fourth day to go back to Rostov.

A month went by. Tania had already been up and about for a while. The doctors examined her and could find no more tumor; all that remained was the scar on her abdomen from the operation. The doctors who had examined her were amazed and could not understand what had happened. Well, what happened was a miracle that followed Father Arseny's prayer to God and His Holy Mother. A big, real miracle.

There were many miracles of this sort, but I will only mention two. The husband of Valentina, Kirill Petrovich, had been a heavy smoker; he found out during a checkup at his workplace that he had cancer in his left lung. The operation would be complicated because he was fifty-five years old, had an arrhythmia, a bad heart, and had suffered a serious heart attack some time before. The doctors agreed not to operate since his probability of death on the operating table was a hundred percent. Kirill Petrovich understood the situation but remained calm. Understanding that he would never be in good health again, he decided to go to see Father Arseny for him to hear his confession. When Father Arseny saw him, he said, "God is merciful: it will all be all right. Stay here two days and we shall pray to God and the Holy Mother of God to have mercy on you and to heal you."

For two days we all gathered together and prayed almost constantly. Father Arseny and Kirill prayed even at night and, of course, Father Arseny confessed him and anointed him. At his next checkup at the clinic, Kirill amazed the doctors: his tumor had disappeared, but no one could explain it. It was a miracle obtained by the prayer of a righteous man; that could be understood only by people who believed in God.

Another healing happened to Maria Fedorovna's daughter, Eugenia. She was thirty years old when her diabetes took a serious turn for the worse. The newest medications were unable to help, insulin did not lower the sugar in her blood. She started losing her sight and became weaker and weaker. The doctors foretold her imminent death. I remember how we got together in Father Arseny's room and he asked us all to pray for Eugenia. He himself was on his knees and prayed, with tears, and did not get up again for at least three hours. Father Arseny seldom cried, but now while praying his tears were rolling down his face; at times he was unable to say the words of prayer. On that day Father Andrei arrived and was also praying on his knees with us, begging the Holy Mother of God to heal the servant of God, Eugenia.

Two months passed, Eugenia regained her sight and the sugar in her blood went to normal. She was completely cured and two years later gave birth to a healthy little boy with no complications. Father Arseny obtained this through his prayers.

I could tell more of such miraculous healing obtained through Father Arseny's prayers. Such stories tell us about his strong spirituality and the grace God gave him. God gave this to Father Arseny for his efforts in prayer and his love for other people.

ON PRAYER

MANY TIMES I WAS present at Father Arseny's talks with people who had come to visit him; sometimes the talks would be repeated if those who had arrived earlier had not heard what Father Arseny had said. Here are two of his talks on the subject of prayer:

"All the words of the Gospel are inspired by God. But it is with exceptional feeling that I hear the words of the Lord, 'Where two or three are gathered in my name, there I am in the midst of them' (Mt 18:20). There is an excellent and profound prayer, apparently composed in the sixteenth century, but never included in a single prayer book, it's called popularly, 'A Prayer in Accord.' There are many theories about its possible composer, but I believe it sprang from the souls of many Orthodox Christians since its main words are taken directly from the Gospel. As a rule, when tragedies or sorrows arise, several Orthodox Christians agree to read this prayer at the same time of day and ask God for the healing of the sick one, for mercy to the fallen one, for the salvation of a soldier or a captive. The people praying can be in different homes, or even in different towns, but they all read the prayer at the same time, whether in the morning, during the day, or in the evening. Many know this prayer, but I will read it now:

" 'Lord Jesus Christ, Son of God, Thou hast said by Thy pure lips that "if two or three agree on earth about anything they ask, it will be done for them by my Father in heaven. For where two or three are gathered in my name, there am I in the midst of them."

" 'Inscrutable are Thy words, O Lord. Thy love of mankind knows no limits. Thy mercy is without end. We, Thy servants (name those praying), pray in accord for Thy servants (mention the names and circumstances). Help us in all our works, today, tomorrow and on any day, that these may be to Thy glory. But not as we will, but as Thou dost will. Thy will be done. In the Name of the Father, and the Son, and the Holy Spirit. Amen.'

"All believers are members of the Church of Christ. Without the Church, it is difficult for one person alone to find the way of salvation, the right way to act in this earthly life. Outside the Church, a person ails: he easily gives in to temptation, to doubts, to confusion, to depression of the spirit. The Church spiritually nourishes every person who comes to it. We live amidst different people: bad, good, believers, nonbelievers. We meet with followers of teachings that are dangerous for the soul. Unaware of this, we strive to give them something of our own, but more often receive something that is bad for us, some unnecessary knowledge, some unhealthy information. Our faith in the Lord is gradually pushed out by foreign ideas and, although we consider ourselves to be Orthodox Christians, we in fact become a weak reflection of a Christian. Regular contact with the Church helps battle the evil that surrounds us and reestablishes in us the spirit of Christ, the spirit of faith.

"If a person prays by himself and does not live the life of the Church, the trials and worries of this age will carry him further and further from the way of faith. It is necessary to attend Church regularly, to pray with all who stand there, since 'where two or three are gathered in my name, there am I in the midst of them,' to go to confession, and to receive the Holy Mysteries. The prayer of one person alone can be compared to a lone candle burning, while prayer in church, hundreds of people praying together, unite the lights of their burning candles, and this produces an enormous pillar of light enlightening all those who stand there. And our prayers, united as one, will be carried to the House of the Lord, the Church, to the Creator. And He hears and receives our prayer. When in Church, pray for your friends, that the Lord will help them live, that they may keep and multiply their faith; pray also for your enemies and for those who have hurt you, in order to be reconciled with them; and never forget to pray for the dead: your prayer helps the souls of the departed. Remember that you must always help other people. On the tombstone of the merciful Dr. Haas[81] you can read these words, 'Make haste to do good!' Yes, yes, make haste; this is a Gospel truth. Kindness and prayer, that is what Jesus Christ teaches us."

I don't remember the exact date, but this talk was in 1969; eight people were present.

This second talk about prayer was given on the day of Saint Alexis, the Man of God, on March 30, 1973; nine or ten people were present. The conversation lasted a long time. People argued about the meaning of prayer, its influence on human soul, and the meaning of prayer at home versus prayer in church. Four people were talking. Father Arseny did not say anything, while the others, including myself, just listened and did not participate in their heated debates. When all were silent, Father Arseny said, "I am a hieromonk. My duty, with the blessing of the elders, is to help people, to bring peace and tranquillity, to bring love, to teach how to pray and how to love your neighbor and God with all your heart and all your mind. I believe in the Father, the Son and the Holy Spirit—the undivided Trinity. My faith is exactly the one professed in the creed that was established by the Ecumenical Councils. I have been ordered never to enter theological arguments, and I consider them useless.

"If I am not mistaken, if my memory does not fail me, almost every apologist and theologian, after he has written many good books, has always admitted to one or two inaccuracies for which he was criticized cruelly and was blamed by his opponents (but it is true that great theologians have sometimes been canonized for their work). I have accepted the obedience to serve people and what I am going to say about prayer comes only from the canons of the Church and from my own pastoral experience, experience which I have gathered during the

---

[81]We have no information on this person. —Trans.

many years I have been close to my spiritual children and to the other people who have come to see me.

"I have listened to you talking about prayer with great interest, and each one of you is right: prayer is varied and diverse and it does come out of the heart (the soul) of each person in its own way depending on his inner being, his spiritual experience, his knowing how to tune himself up for prayer, and his ability to lift up his heart.

"Almost everything I am going to say is well known, but I will repeat it for the sake of those who have just come and do not know it. All the Church Fathers have written about the importance of prayer for believers. In the nineteenth century, these included Metropolitan Philaret (Drozdov) of Moscow, Bishop Theophan (Vichenski), Bishop Ignaty (Brianchaninov), the elders of Optino (in their letters to their spiritual children) and other spiritual writers; recently even a classification of prayers has appeared. As far as I am concerned, I think what is most important in prayer is spiritual concentration, complete sincerity, a departure from all worldly bustle and temptations, and full immersion in the state of prayer. Only then can the soul really concentrate on God, but this ability is not given to everybody in the same degree.

"You could classify prayer this way:

"1. Intercessory prayer. The one praying asks God to help him in difficult times or in his grief, or he asks God to help his loved ones, heal their sickness, console them in their sadness, feed them, or forgive their transgressions; or he prays for the departed. For most people this prayer is the most important: even a person who does not feel God to be very close, will sometimes, in difficult circumstances, address Him with a request. When coming to church and praying, we always ask God for something.

"2. Prayer of thanksgiving. You thank God for the help you or loved ones have received from Him, or for the fulfillment of a request you made in your intercessory prayers. You also thank God for having given you life and His mercy. Many people only ask for things, just like people who only borrow from others and forget to repay what they owe. Prayers of thanksgiving are addressed to God, the Holy Mother of God and the saints. It is not sufficient to pray this way once only, but you must do it many times, it is as if you returning what you owe to God for His having listened to your prayers. But, as I have said before, not everyone addresses God in order to thank Him. The responsibility of the priest is to explain to those who come to him that they must thank God, His Holy Mother and the saints for all the help they have received.

"3. Prayer of Glorification. This is the highest prayer to God, the creator of heaven and earth, glorifying Him for everything and everyone. For calamities, for sadness, for being saved or for deliverance, for the fact that we live, for joys and for sorrow and, I repeat, for everything and for everyone. God is our Creator; everything comes from Him. He created us and He gives us the possibility, through His mercy, to attain the Kingdom of God by leading a pious life on earth. This is the great prayer of a perfect soul; each one of us, after having learned the prayer of thanksgiving, can enter the circle of glorifying prayer.

"The prayer of glorification can always be heard in church, and especially during the greatest of church services, the liturgy."

"I will say a few words on the subject of how we must pray. To separate yourself from the world around you and enter into the words and spirit of prayer is difficult for those who lack long prayer experience. You pray, trying to concentrate on your prayer, but the prayer comes absent-mindedly. In tandem with the prayer you have earthly thoughts and you are unable to let go of them. To overcome this, you must pray more and more often; it is important in the beginning to pray aloud, if this is possible.

"Often do priests say and write that absentminded and distracted prayer is unacceptable to God and is even sinful because the one who prays does not give his soul fully to God and in that way he sins. Of course, such prayer is not of full value. The one praying tries to gather his will and put the soul in a prayerful mode, but due to his weakness is unable to do it, but at least he did try to do it. Only God can decide on the sincerity and the spiritual value of such prayer. But, as far as I am concerned, I believe that, if the prayer was sincere but, due to reasons unknown to us, the person was unable to achieve a warm and sincere prayer, he did still pray. He did not forget to pray his rule of prayer at his regular time—that is already an offering, an effort held up to

God—and God will accept this prayer having weighed the spiritual state and the sincerity of the one praying. Many people, and even many priests will not agree with me, but this is what I think, and I have found some indirect confirmation of my words in spiritual literature and even in old 'Lives of the Fathers of the Church.'

"Whatever the level of prayer, be it a prayer of intercession, of thanksgiving or glorification, a person must aim to pray with his whole soul, trying to get away from all concerns of earthly life. If you absolutely cannot find the ability to pray sincerely, you must talk about that with your spiritual father and ask his advice.

"When people come to me I often pray with them for a long time aloud, articulating each word and every sentence, trying to put all my soul in each word. Later I explain the meaning and importance of prayer. Usually, the prayers of intercession are the most sincere ones, because the one who prays, even if he did not yet reach spiritual perfection, is entirely sincere in these prayers: he is asking for healing, mercy, help for those he loves, or he asks for the good things of life, for them to be saved from death, from illness; in short, he prays for what gives him pain and suffering."

I wrote down these conversations about prayer from memory. These two talks by Father Arseny about prayer were typical of the ones he gave to new visitors. Father Arseny always had a personal talk about prayer with each new person who came to him and became his spiritual child, and the conversation about prayer would be followed by a talk about how to relate to other people. He considered it important and requested that each person should have and follow without fail a rule of prayer. He first asked what the rule was that the person followed, listened carefully to the answer and then, depending on the spiritual state of the person, he would give his advice: which prayers to include, which to exclude. He recommended that you should look carefully at the previous day, at your actions, thoughts, conversations, you had to figure out what you had done wrong and pray to God to ask His forgiveness. You should try not to repeat those evil actions on subsequent days. Father Arseny did not approve of long rules of prayer; he used to say that, towards the end of them, the person praying would get tired and repeat the prayers without feeling, mechanically; however, he recommended to some people that they pray for an hour or more.

He advised people to pray morning and evening, always at a fixed time of day; to parents with children, he recommended that they pray as a family but, so that the children do not get tired, first you should have a short prayer with them and then continue the complete rule of prayer among adults. He suggested that you pray on the way to work or from work repeating the whole rule or part of it; he considered that this was a good way to prevent people from having empty and useless thoughts. He constantly reminded people, "Pray to God, but do not forget to pray for other people, and to do good deeds. Prayer to God and love for others must be united: the one without the other does not stay alive."

MEMOIRS OF FATHER ARSENY

YURI AND I WENT TO VISIT Father Arseny for the ten days of our Christmas holidays. We were staying at the Platonovs' where we rented a room every summer.

It was the third day of Christmas, January 9, 1975.[82] During these last days Father Arseny's health had taken a turn to the worse. Two doctors, Irina and Lyuda, had already been staying at Nadezhda Petrovna's for several days to watch him closely. This day the liturgy was celebrated by Father Nikolai along with Fathers Herman and Paul. Father Arseny was in bed. He was very weak, had great difficulty breathing, and suffered from arrhythmia to the point that he could not stand or even sit.

When the liturgy was finished and after we had had breakfast, Father Arseny invited all those who had come that day to his room: Lyuda, Irina, Yuri, Father Nikolai, Father Herman and Father Paul, Nadezhda Petrovna, Natasha and myself. We sat in silence in armchairs, chairs, or on a footrest. Father Arseny was pensive. Lying on his sofa he played absentmindedly with the fringe of his plaid blanket. Silence

---

[82]On the Old Calendar, Christmas falls on January 7th. —Trans.

reigned. Lifting his head he looked at his icons for a long time, crossed himself three times, and said in a quiet voice:

"My dear and beloved friends and spiritual children, life is slowly but surely leaving my body. This is the will of God. I want to tell you now about parts of my life which helped form my spiritual outlook on the world and showed me the path I was to take, a path that led me to knowing God and leading the people entrusted to me as well as others that I met during my life.

"I have lived a long life. For two-thirds of it I was surrounded by people who carried God's joy and light. The first such person was my mother, Maria Alexandrovna (I already spoke about her some time ago). She was a gifted person, a wise person imbued with a deep faith in God, a very deep faith. She looked at me not only as at her son but also as God's creation. She felt it was her obligation to keep me and raise me in a deep faith in the Creator. She felt responsible before Him who had entrusted her with a human soul. I was her third child: my brother died when he was two years old, my sister when she was four. When I was born my mother promised God she would keep in me faith, truthfulness and love for others, and that is how she raised me. When I was sixteen I became fascinated with ancient Russian art, but I had already thought about monastic life. Then I spent time in Optino where it was difficult to come under the tutelage of elders but, through the mercy of God, I was accepted and I was taught by Fathers Anatoly and Nektary. Why two elders? Many will be surprised at that, but it was probably part of their plan in training me. I lived under their authority for two years.

"Sometimes when I went to Father Nektary, I would have to wait for a long time. I would ask him something, and he would answer, 'Go see Father Anatoly! He will tell you.' I would go to Father Anatoly, who would answer, 'Go ask Father Nektary!' In the beginning I felt lost, and sometimes I would cry, feeling offended, but then I understood that 'that means that it just has to be like that!' and this formed the spiritual philosophy I lived by when Fathers Nektary and Anatoly gave me their blessing to become a hieromonk and serve 'in the world'[83] in a parish church.

---

[83]Instead of in the monastery. —Trans.

"When you are in a monastery, you are under the obedience of elders. It is not permitted for you to have your own will; you must behave in the way your spiritual adviser tells you. You must obey whether you like what he says or not, because, by accepting the will of the elder, the novice perfects himself, he cuts himself off from his own thoughts and sins, he lives by the will of the elder who has the grace of God, and who knows his soul and knows what is indispensable for him in attaining monastic perfection.

"The circle of contacts in a monastery is small—constantly the same people, the same monks whom you know and see every day, the same work, a constant prayer in church, in your cell and at work. You are not supposed to talk much, you listen to the teaching of your elders. You strive for submissiveness and humility in your contacts with other novices and monks. It would be wrong to think that the relationships with those around you in the monastery are cloudless; they were sometimes so painful that your soul ached—these were temptations tolerated by God. You would go to your elder crushed and upset, you would want to tell him everything but he knew it all already and from your reaction to what had happened he would gauge your own spiritual perfection or failing, and he would teach you how to accept what had happened with prayer and as the will of God.

"Your opinion, the offense you had experienced, your hurt were not taken into consideration—only humility before God was recommended. You had to understand that you were still so imperfect that what happened was just the result of your own sinfulness and therefore was fair. The elder in the monastery is your father, your teacher, your guide in everything. You no longer possess your own will; you must completely renounce your vain ego.

"When I received the blessing of Father Anatoly and Father Nektary to go serve in the world in a parish (in those days this was absolutely unusual for a monk) I was deeply surprised and lost. I do not know who spoke about me to Patriarch Tikhon, but he invited me, received me, and allowed me to serve in a parish church where Father Pavel was the senior priest. The Patriarch spoke with me for ten minutes, blessed me, and spoke some prophetic words about my priestly path; I will not repeat those words, they are too intimate. I will only say one thing:

when I was exiled, in labor camps, taken away to be shot, beaten during questioning, and near death on freezing treks, I trusted the words of the great saint of our Russian land, of Patriarch Tikhon who had said that I would come back to you, my spiritual children. I believed audaciously because they were the words of a patriarch.

"And now, I, the inexperienced hieromonk Arseny, went to the parish priest Pavel. He was tall and portly, on the heavy side but with a good and welcoming face. He looked at me skeptically and asked me to tell him about myself. I spoke for a long time, in detail about my life in the monastery, my childhood, my education, my love for ancient Russian art and architecture, my life in the Optino hermitage. Father Pavel asked me no questions, but said, 'You are from the intelligentsia. I have some parishioners that are also of this kind; even though they search and search, they cannot find themselves in the Faith—you will take care of them since I understand them very poorly. I never was in Optino; I have only heard a great deal about the elders Nektary, Anatoly, Nikon and Varsonofy. They say they are great elders, but Moscow is not Optino, it is a noisy and sinful city.

" 'From time immemorial my ancestors were priests, good priests, and I always wanted to be a priest myself. I finished the seminary and then the Academy but I never met any elders. There are priests in Moscow who have created communities, they want to have the Optino way in the world—God help them. You know, Father, it is difficult to be in the world, and especially to be a priest in Moscow—you cannot imagine how difficult! This is no monastery, where everything is on a schedule. I would be happy to join a monastery but I cannot leave my parishioners, my wife and my children—my children may be grown, but they still are my children.' Did Father Pavel foresee his future? He was arrested, sent to Arkhangelsk and died there of starvation six years after this conversation. He said, 'The authorities are destroying the Church. They are sending priests to labor camps; to whom will I leave the parish? Father Mikhail is a good person, but he loves to drink. You know what, Father Arseny, I will leave it all to you,' and he blessed me.

" 'You know what, Priest, everything you have learned in the monastery will stay with you, but for you to be able to serve in the city I will have to reeducate you. Don't be hurt: you are very strong in your education, but I have been a priest for thirty years and I will pass on to you everything I know.' "

Father Arseny continued, "You know, this heavy, portly Father Pavel—joyous, smiling, a lover of strong tea with sugar, which he liked to drink with black bread—possessed a spiritual perfection. I revered him. His spiritual world was in no way less than that of the Optino elders, but it was different, it was urban.

"And there I was, Hieromonk Arseny. I could feel and see two paths, each very different but leading to the same goal. I thought about it and asked God to show me which path I should choose to follow. I thought for a long time, I prayed, begging God to help me make the right choice. I went to Optino, to hear the advice of my elders. I stayed there for three days. Father Anatoly listened to me and said, 'I give you my blessing! God's grace be with you. Dare!'

"Father Nektary saw me only after three days, just before I was supposed to leave. He listened to me and was silent for a long time; he was probably praying. Then he said, 'There is a *starets* in Moscow who has been leading his parishioners the Optino way: he is the one you must follow. Visit churches, look around, ask for advice. God will help you make a decision. Go, you will find your way.'

"I left and I went to visit several Moscow priests who were leading communities. They each had their own opinion, they gave different advice, their opinions were sometimes contradictory, but the advice I had received from Father Anatoly was my guiding light. I saw that the authorities were doing all they could to destroy the Church and I understood that it would only get worse in the future: priests would be in labor camps, the churches would be closed and destroyed.

"My idea was to teach people to believe in God boundlessly and to love their neighbor. I thought then and I still think that faith in Christ is based on two commandments: love of God and love of one's neighbor. I have spoken to you about this many times.

"God was merciful to me and showed a great miracle to me—to me, unworthy as I am. At about two o'clock, after the end of a liturgy, I was walking along the streets deep in thought. I was thinking about my serving and suddenly I saw that I was on Goncharev Street near Tagas Square. I looked at my watch; it was already five o'clock, which meant that I had been walking for some three hours. What had brought me there? Was it memories of my childhood, or what? I realized that I was right next to the house of a friend whom I had not seen for a number of years. I knew nothing of his life now; I was tempted just to go on by, but some strong power pushed me to go into the house. I rang the bell. Kostya opened the door. He was very happy to see me, but said, 'Piotr! Wait in the next room. I have here Bishop Ilarion, the bishop of Verezh, we are about to have a long and important conversation.'

"I felt that I was interrupting and, having said a few words, was ready to leave. I opened the door onto the stairwell but heard a commanding voice saying, 'Hieromonk Arseny! I have been waiting for you!' This was a great miracle. I walked back in. Vladyko Ilarion blessed me and invited me to sit down. I was seeing him for the first time in my life, but I knew about him. People said that he was close to Patriarch Tikhon. I was in close contact with no bishops, so how could he know anything about me, me, the third priest in a small Moscow church, not far from Sadov Circle in the 'commercial' district?

" 'Tell me about your doubts.' How could Vladyko Ilarion know about my thoughts and doubts? Shyly, I started to tell him. He interrupted me and said, 'I have the time, so stop being timid. Talk as though I were hearing your confession.'

"I tried to put aside my shyness and not to be afraid to say something which did not follow established rules. I began my story. At times it was contradictory, full of doubt and of the search for a path in my priesthood. I spoke about my desire to create a community, about the way I wanted to lead my spiritual children, work with them, teach them. I spoke about many things. Vladyko listened to me carefully, never interrupting me. I quoted God's commandments. I said that I wanted to introduce into the souls of my parishioners a faith in God and a love for the other, so that they would be able to walk the way of faith and love among the sin, evil and violence that surrounded them during this cruel time of the persecution of Orthodoxy.

"I was raised in Optino. I belonged to them with all my soul and clearly understood the greatness of the Optino elders, their *podvig* and the way they were leading their spiritual children. I thought that theirs was the best way the Church had to offer for the salvation of the human soul. But could I, a parish priest, lead dozens and perhaps hundreds of spiritual children on this way, advising each of them and leading each of them individually? I could not do that. As I was serving in that church, as I talked to the people and heard their confessions, I could see people among the great crowd who would be able to accept the great path of Optino; but there were also the other ones, believers who had a life experience, a psychology, a character or environment which left them totally unable to accept it. So what was I to do? I had to teach them all to believe in God and I had to teach them to love their neighbor. Having introduced in their souls, hearts and minds a resistance to evil, violence, and atheism, I also had to 'force' those people to throw away all that was bad and to know how to orient themselves in life's chaos and evil. As to those who were able to accept it, I had to lead them in the special way of the Optino elders.

"The way Father Pavel was leading his parishioners was the traditional way for urban priests, but in my opinion it did not develop spiritual steadfastness.

"I daringly said everything I was thinking and was dreaming about to Bishop Ilarion. I felt shy and almost scared. Who was I, after all, to tell a bishop my particular thoughts about the way to lead spiritual children?

"After he had heard me out, Bishop Ilarion began to talk to me as if he knew my whole life. He talked about my mother, my love for art, my life at Optino; he spoke very warmly of Father Pavel. He stood up, went over to the icons and said, 'Let us pray!' He said several prayers and sat back down; I remained standing.

" 'You want to unite two paths into one, the Optino tradition and the one that resides in parishes like that of your Father Pavel?'

" 'Yes,' I answered.

" 'You want to introduce loving God as demanded in the Commandments and loving one's neighbor as oneself into the souls of your spiritual children. And doing this, you want to create in people's souls a resistance to sin, persecution, confusion, atheism, falling. Our meeting happened by the will of God and has been important for both of us. I, Bishop Ilarion, give you my blessing to go the path you have chosen—of uniting the two paths into one. I will report our conversation to Patriarch Tikhon. I give you my blessing to go your path. God will preserve you in all your difficulties and disasters.'

"I fell to my knees. Vladyko put his hand on my head and blessed me once again. All the while we were talking, he was focused and serious; only when he blessed me for the last time did a warm smile appear on his face. I am not sure now, but as far as I can remember he was then Patriarch Tikhon's secretary.[84]

"From that time on I lived as I had been blessed to do by this remarkable Church figure, later Archbishop of Vereev. He died in prison, he suffered in Solovki where he was mocked, abased and beaten along with Hieromonk Seraphim, where they were both ordered to clean the latrines (you know Father Seraphim, you remember his recollections about his meeting with Vladyko Ilarion).

"My meeting with Archbishop Ilarion was unusual. It was a miraculous manifestation of the grace of God toward me, me, an insignificant priest who had just started serving in a small Moscow church. In the life of a man a miracle does not happen just by chance. It is given depending on spiritual necessity and on the influence it will have on that man's inner world. God sent me one such miracle through Vladyko Ilarion, and I followed my path constantly remembering the blessing I had received.

"When I returned to my church I served a *moleben* of Thanksgiving and told everything to Father Pavel. He told me, 'If Vladyko Ilarion blessed you, go that way. He is a man of deep spirituality. As for me, I am an old man and it is not possible for me to change, but I will help you!'

"From that day on, I started to serve in church following the direc-

---

[84]Archbishop Ilarion (Troitsky) (1886–1929) worked closely with Patriarch (later Saint) Tikhon. He was a talented theologian and thinker, a church writer, a professor in the Moscow Religious Academy. During the Sobor of 1917–1918 he was an ardent defender of the idea of reestablishing the Patriarchate in Russia. In 1920 he fought ardently against the "Living Church." He was arrested many times and spent time in prison, labor camps, and exile. During 1924–1925 and again during 1926–1929 he was interned in the Solovki labor camp, and in 1925–1926 in Yaroslavl prison. In Church circles he was known as "Ilarion the Great" for his talent, his enormous church activity, his firmness on questions of faith and his devotion to the Church. He died of typhus in the hospital of Kresty prison in Leningrad. He was canonized on May 10, 1999.

tive I had received to go the way I had decided. I served an early liturgy every morning. I tried to make everything understandable and clear for the parishioners, to make them participants in the service. I agreed with deacon Lev (who later died in a labor camp in 1937) that every and each word of the litanies should be loud and clear. I talked in the same way to our choir, which was composed of three women. Some eight or ten people used to come to the early morning liturgy, they were those who lived near by, but no one came to me for confession. The later liturgy was attended by many people; Father Pavel served and I assisted. A long line of people used to wait to go to confession to Father Pavel; I would be standing next to my stand (my *analoy*) with the cross and the Gospel, but people did not come. Father Pavel began sending me some people. They came unwillingly, but once they did come I confessed them at length, explained the meaning of confession, told them of the necessity for praying daily and for reading a chapter of the Gospel every day. They would listen to me inattentively, sometimes they would even argue with me but, after a while some ten or fifteen people started coming to me. I organized evening talks and lessons.

"Father Pavel was happy for me and sent me many people, but Father Mikhail, the second priest, started hating me for no reason I knew of. He called me a heretic and a sectarian. He soon started to drink heavily and went to another parish. The community was growing. Gleb was ordained a priest and you all became my helpers. The blessing I had received from Bishop Ilarion, the knowledge I had acquired at Optino, the teachings of Father Nektary and Father Anatoly, the grace of God that Patriarch Tihon sent me to the church where Father Pavel was serving, were of enormous importance for me. Do you remember the lectures we used to have at our meetings? How useful they were for you (alas, many of you are not with us any more). The community grew, you grew, and I taught you and was taught by you."

We could see that Father Arseny was tired. Doctor Irina and Julia got up at the same time and said, "Father Arseny! We forbid you to talk any longer, you will continue tomorrow."

"I absolutely must finish saying this, it is important."

But Julia waved her hand at us and out we went.

On the fourth day of Christmas, January 10, 1975, Father Arseny asked us to come back into his room. Father Nikolai had left, for which he was very sorry, but Olga and Nadezhda (Yuri's sister, who had become a secret nun some time before) came. Our doctors were unhappy that Father Arseny had gathered us together again. We sat wherever we could. Father Arseny looked a little better than the day before: even his voice was stronger.

"I told you yesterday how I came to have a community, how it was created; you know the rest because you lived in it and knew its life. Now I will talk to you about the years which might have been physically difficult but which were spiritually full of light. Whether I was in exile or in labor camp, I always met people of very great spirit, utterly devoted to their faith, martyrs who helped the people around them. You know I met people whose faith was so perfect and so great that it seemed to me that should one bring a wax candle near them, it would burst into an unearthly flame. These are the people I will talk to you about because I was constantly learning from them.

"I will come back to my mother, Maria Alexandrovna. I have already said that my mother was an unusual person. She grew up cultured in a family of professors, where faith was considered to be one of the obligatory traditions of the Russian people, similar perhaps to popular folklore. In that environment she came to the faith and became a believer, and brought her own mother and father to the faith. Her faith in God was so colossal, and her knowledge of the Church Fathers and religious literature so great that she amazed religious philosophers who were her contemporaries. Why am I talking about this? Because my mother is the one who put the seeds of faith into my soul and cultivated them, and I entered life standing on a foundation so solid that nothing could push me off. Optino monastery, my ordination to the priesthood, my creation of the community, and my difficult life in camps and exile—all this was anchored by the faith which my mother had given me.

"I will now talk about the third of my life spent in exile and camps. I won't mention the physical difficulties, but will talk instead about the remarkable people I met there who taught me so much and who passed on to me their spiritual experience.

"The first such light was the priest Ilarion, who had been given the name Ioan when he became a monk. He served in the village Troitsk near Arkhangelsk. Xenia Vladimirovna wrote an interesting memoir about him. She tells of his influence on me. Then there was Hieromonk Seraphim from the Nilo-Stolobensk monastery; Alexander Sergeevich wrote about him. The third one, I met in my labor-camp barracks— the monk Mihail. Each one of them passed on to me, without knowing it, a deep spiritual wisdom which enriched me.

"The camp was beyond our strength and frightening, but the numerous encounters and confessions of the prisoners opened to me, a priest, people's immeasurably high spirituality. Don't think that all these people were bishops, priests, or monks; no, among those devoted heroes you could find simple laypeople who had found such a faith in Jesus Christ that I, a hieromonk, was far below them. Their confessions were God's revelations for me. I remember the simple peasant Ivan Sergeevich. Always quiet and calm, he came to confession three days before his death. He was crushed by a rock falling in a mine. I listened to his confession. As he was telling about his life, I heard these words, 'Father, in three days I will die, they are sending me to work in the mine.' He was talking as though he were speaking of someone else, with a deep faith in God. I listened and tears ran down my cheeks.

"I also remember a middle-aged engineer. I only remember his first name, Viacheslav, but I saw him in the barracks every day. One evening he came up to me. 'Father, I am a bad believer, but tomorrow they will be "cleansing" the camp and I will be shot. I want to confess, please forgive my sins.' This 'bad believer' was so highly spiritual that I listened to him in trembling. The next day he was shot. I had so many such encounters; they gave me so much.

"In the same camp I met Hierodeacon Ioan from the monastery of Pechor. He was not tall, he was shaven like all the prisoners, and always had a sad face. But when he spoke his voice resounded. The musicians among our prisoners said that he had that rare kind of bass, a *basso profundo*; with such a voice he should have been singing in the Italian opera at La Scala in Milan. Well, this Father Ioan came to me for confession in the barracks. He tried to whisper but each word he said could be heard five yards away. Such confession was impossible, so we agreed that we would meet in the forest where I was being sent that year to cut wood.

"It was impossible to confess for a long time; our conversation, with interruptions, lasted fifteen minutes. What I heard made me tremble spiritually. I had in front of me a great ascetic and, in confessing Father Ioan, I was myself spiritually enriched. Everything he said about his life and his behavior was a true revelation to me and a lesson for my entire life. I cannot name all the ascetics I met in labor camps."

"I want to stay a while on the topic of confession. If the one who comes to confession is full of a desire to open up his soul to God, to the works of the grace given to the priest, if he wants to clean his soul and ask forgiveness for what he has done, this would always fill me with joy and be a step toward perfection. If a person came with an enormous grief, the death of a child, of a wife or husband or any other grief, and who asked for prayers and spiritual support, I always welcomed him, prayed with him and took his grief as my own and suffered with him. I united myself with him in his pain, and if he or she left confession calmed and understanding that the will of God is in everything, I was spiritually joyous and continued praying with all my soul for those who had confessed.

"Once I told Bishop K. from Nizhni Novgorod about the way I see confession, and got the following answer. 'It is not right to take confession this way. You will burn out; your soul will run out of room for everybody's pain.' I did not agree. Perhaps I have told you already, but I want to repeat it: I have confessed hundreds, perhaps thousands of people and have received from each one of them a spark of spiritual light and goodness which has enriched me, and then I have been able to pass it on to other grieving and suffering people.

"While I was still parish priest, there would be parishioners who would come during Great Lent and ask me to 'give them absolution as usual.' They used to come once a year, it was a formal tradition, and whatever I would say to them fell flat, my words would not be accepted and I would be sincerely distressed."

Father Arseny was tired and fell silent. We wanted to leave. Lyuda walked over to him and took his blood pressure. She said, "Ninety over sixty; that is low."

When he saw that we had gotten up, Father Arseny said, "Do not leave. I will rest a little and then I will say more about the confessions of prisoners and criminals in the camps."

"In the course of the many years I spent in the 'death camp'—that is the way that we, the prisoners, used to call the camps of strict regime where you were not sent just to serve your time, but to die and only to die—I came to understand that a person living in such a camp had no hope. He was only waiting for death and that is why his concept of good and evil became completely distorted from when he had been a free man. This is why people's attitudes to each other, to their own life or to your life, were on a totally different scale: cruel, crude, uncompromising. The concepts of good and evil were changed to a demonic understanding: what was bad for someone else was good for you, and what was good for someone else was bad for you. That was what determined your actions and that was how you measured the actions of others.

"In the hell of camp, if a man did come to repent he would be under the weight of such heavy sins that a priest sometimes got lost and did not know whether he had the right to forgive. The person would not have time to change his way of life, to improve it. You might be killed tomorrow by the other criminals, the guards might shoot you, you might be killed by a falling rock, by a falling tree—and should I refuse to hear his confession, he would depart this life without repentance, without having made peace with God. He could have been the worst sinner, but he would come to bring his repentance and be forgiven according to his conscience. As I stood next to the one who confessed, as I listened to his sincere confession, I was sometimes horrified at what I heard, my soul would freeze, but I would listen, take it into myself and, if I could feel a sincere repentance, I would forgive his sins. It would also happen that after I had heard him, I would have to ask the person to wait for absolution until the next day—and I would spend the night praying to God begging Him to give me the strength to forgive these sins. It would sometimes happen that the next day the prisoner would die; that was God's will. If I saw a lack of sincerity in the person's repentance, I would tell him so and not forgive him. There were several prisoners who came to me whom I could not forgive; I did not feel the sincerity of their repentance, and their actions were so evil that my conscience did not allow me to do it. Two or three times they even tried to kill me for that, but this only confirmed that my decision had been the right one.

"I had read many excellent spiritual books on confession before, books written by the Holy Fathers of the Church and also by some contemporary authors and all that had entered into my soul and consciousness as absolute truth. They gave me a direction in my relations with my spiritual children; I also borrowed from the experiences of priests who were much higher than I in the spiritual sense and who had been enriched by long service in church. They are the ones who prepared me for the unexpected meetings I had in labor camps with people condemned to be annihilated, laden with the heaviest of sins, with multiple murders, rapes, thefts, violence.

"Doubt about the rightfulness of what I had done possessed me and, in 1961, when I met Bishop Athanassy in Petushki, I told him in detail about my experiences and asked him whether I had behaved correctly as a priest when I confessed criminals who were carrying the weight of terrible crimes on their souls. Vladyko answered that he, too, had had to confess such people and that, if he saw true repentance, he knew that God himself would decide their fate having weighed the sincerity of their repentance."

"You remember our church, it wasn't big, those who entered were seized with a feeling of peace and joy, it was not 'glorious' as in some other communities. The parishioners were mostly intellectuals, many young people between the ages of eighteen and twenty, but we also had some older people and there were also the local parishioners. The community had ninety to ninety-five members, many coming from different districts in Moscow. The church was always full.

"I created this community along with all of you sitting here; that is why I want to share my thoughts with you, my spiritual children.

"I have been here with you for sixteen years. In the course of the eighteen years of my stay in labor camps the world changed, the way people think changed and even you, my spiritual children, changed. In many of you the faith itself changed: your perception of God became tinted with 'secularity.' Of course God exists, the Holy Trinity, the Mother of God, the saints, the sacraments, the canons, tradition and even, and please note the 'even,' the Church exists, but everything became covered with a light mist of 'modern progress.' Of course God exists and there is no doubt about His existence, but I often hear things like, 'coming out of the cosmos, cosmic, from outer space,' and that I hear from believers. 'Of course, the Most Holy Mother of God and the saints are a nice tradition, and maintaining the Apostolic succession keeps the faith alive. This tradition adds color to its spiritual antiquity and adds to its general goodness. The Church is indispensable, but, just think,' say these believers, 'two thousand years separate us from its creation. During these two thousand years man has become different, "intellectual," he grew and everything around him lived and changed, whereas the Church remained "in its own circle." So let us "adjust" the Church to modern man, keeping everything that existed before, but changing it just a little to make it fit in with the ideas of the twentieth and twenty-first centuries.'

"And these words 'keeping everything that existed before, but changing it just a little to make it fit with the ideas of the twentieth and twenty-first centuries' are never defined and are ominous for the Church. Alas, it is not only laypeople who think this way. Some priests think this way and some of my spiritual children follow them. The word 'ecumenism' is, in itself, a good word, but it can be destructive for Orthodoxy.[85] That is what I think but I do not impose this opinion on

---

[85] The word "ecumenism" can refer either to an unOrthodox (and hence destructive) "Branch Theory of the Church," or simply to inter-Christian dialogue. This double meaning has led to much misunderstanding in the Church. —Ed.

anyone. The pure, primitive faith, a faith that is called 'like that of a child' and which used to exist within many Russian people, is now rare. The human soul is very conscious of its own 'intellectuality.' This is bitter and sad, but I do believe that, after all, the Lord our God will show His Wisdom to his people.

"I meet many people and each one of them opens his or her soul to me to a certain degree, but can I call them my spiritual children? Alas, not all of them. Within some of them has appeared rationalism, so for them I am not a spiritual father as I was in our community, a father who directs their life, but I am a priest who is only supposed to hear confession, give absolution, and give communion. They may listen to the advice I give, but they behave and live according to their own ideas, and while they may consider me their spiritual father, they are fooling themselves that they live under my spiritual tutelage. As I talk to the bishops and priests who come to visit me, I hear the same concerns from them. There are fewer and fewer spiritual sons, spiritual daughters and spiritual fathers in the true meaning of these words. This is the deep spiritual tragedy of the contemporary believer, but I trust that this too shall pass and that monasteries and communities will exist again. The Church will have a leading role in society."

This was Father Arseny's last talk. Each day he felt worse and worse.

Every year that passed saw the number of us, the members of the community, become smaller and smaller. Some time ago I became unable to remember the names of all the members, and by 1977 we were so few that a feeling of extreme sadness and grief seized one's soul. In the 1920s, we were all twenty or thirty years old, and now the youngest of us was at least seventy-five; others are already eighty.

Each one of us who was still alive and those who had already gone suffered an enormous number of deep wounds and scars. Many had lost relatives in the war, in labor camp, in exile, in prison, some died of starvation or some other tragedy—such was life of almost everyone in our generation.

But we had had what is most important in the existence of man: our faith in God, the Church, and our spiritual father, Father Arseny, who had put into our souls an understanding of spirituality and a love for our neighbor. Those who were dying, who left life, left it with faith in God and prayer to the Mother of God and the saints, with the hope of salvation of their soul by the mercy of God.

After 1958 Father Arseny gave the faith to many dozens or perhaps hundreds of people. He directed them to the knowledge of God's Church through his own praying to Him. Now the old members of the community, the members from the 1920s and those who joined after 1958 met as the closest of friends, united by the direction and teaching of Father Arseny as well as by love of Father Arseny. He loved us all, us, his spiritual children. Father Arseny may no longer be with us, but we are all ready to help one another in times of difficulty or pain because he taught us to do so.

Each one of us who is still on this earth asks Father Arseny to pray for him or her, to pray to God and His Holy Mother. We, your orphans, ask you, our dear Father Arseny, to pray for us sinners! Memory Eternal to you, our elder and spiritual father, Hieromonk Arseny!

These memoirs were recorded and written by Kyra Bakhmat,
who also used the memoirs of other spiritual children.
From the archives of V. V. Bykov

Afterword to the Memoirs of Father Arseny and His Spiritual Children

ON JUNE 21, 1999, the Dean of Saint Tikhon's Orthodox Theological Institute, Archpriest Vladimir Vorobiev, asked me to write some memoirs of my meetings with Father Arseny. I agreed without thinking. How do I mean "without thinking"? When I got home, I looked again at the book *Father Arseny*, which had been written by spiritual children of his who had known him long and closely, starting in 1920 and up to his death in 1975, and I realized that I could add only very little to what has already been so well written. I met Father Arseny for the first time in Moscow in 1961. After that I saw him only eleven or twelve times and then only in Moscow, where he was staying for two weeks or so at the house of one of his spiritual children after he had had to spend some time in a clinic. I always came with my wife Elizaveta, who already knew him well and visited him in "R." Now we can say that "R" is Rostov the Great.

My longest meeting with Father Arseny occurred in 1967 and lasted three hours. Part of our conversation was about my personal problems, but the main topic had to do with Father Arseny's wanting to know about the community created by Father Sergei Mechev (everybody knew this community under the name "Maroseika"), about the bishops and the priests we had met in the course of our life—I will talk about this later. In spite of the fact that our other meetings were shorter in duration, I have to say that I always entered Father Arseny's room one man and left it another, having received spiritually renewing instruction, advice, help or clarity about of doubts I might have had. My memory is less sharp after all these years, I forget much: but I gave my word to Father Vladimir and I must do what I gave my "yes" to.

Before I started writing I went to my bookshelf and looked to see how many printings of *Father Arseny* had seen the light and I discovered that starting in 1993 there have been six printings, with a total of

500,000 copies, two printings in Greece in Greek and two in the United States of America in English. There is also word that this book will appear in French in France. The number of printings in Russia and abroad and the great number of copies make this book one of the most popular among Orthodox Christians and this is to the credit of the brotherhood of Saint Tikhon's Theological Institute and the Brotherhood of the Merciful Savior, who started its publication and made it available to so many of the faithful.

I will have to tell a little about the community led by Father Sergei Mechev and about my own personal life because those are related to my hearing the name of Father Arseny in 1938–1939.

In 1920–1930 there had been some discussion with Father Sergei Mechev about the ordination, in secret, of nine members of the community to the holy priesthood by Bishop Afanassy (Sakharov). Three brothers had already been ordained: Fedor Semenenko, Herman and Georgy. But Vladyko was again arrested and detained in a labor camp, so Father Sergei said in sadness, "We did not have enough time, but Vladyko did have the time to ordain ten brothers from the community of Hieromonk Arseny. We are trying to arrange our ordinations through Bishop Manuil (Lemeshev); he is ready to perform it for the brothers of our community." Out of the nine, Bishop Manuil ordained five, Roman, Boris, Piotr, Konstantin and I cannot remember the name of the fifth. But soon after, all those he had ordained were summoned to the Lyubianka prison: three received prison terms, two denied having been ordained, were beaten heavily and let go, but they were watched carefully. It is surprising that Bishop Manuil visited those two who had denied ordination and asked them to admit to the authorities that they had indeed been ordained.

Bishop Manuil did not know that four more of the brothers were to be ordained. Three of them became priests under Patriarch Alexis I in different dioceses and served in different churches. I found out about everything that I am writing about here only the 1950s, because even those who were ordained did not know who the other brothers were who had received ordination. It was a dangerous time. A priest who had been ordained in secret celebrated liturgies in homes and could only have a few people present, people who were forbidden to tell anyone the names of the priests who had served. That is how we lived during these years!

The second time I heard the name of Father Arseny was in 1940, after the liturgy, during a meal in our own house. My wife Elena and I were living by ourselves in a two-room apartment on Kozinhinsky Street and that is why we were able to have the liturgy celebrated in our home twice a month. These liturgies were celebrated by priests who were trying to avoid being arrested, priests from churches that had been closed by the authorities, or priests that had been ordained in secret.

This liturgy that was celebrated in 1940, I remember vividly, as do all the people who were present. Usually we would invite only members of our own community, though sometimes we might also invite members of other communities we were absolutely sure about. So that you might understand, I want to explain that the choice of people invited was not up to the hosts, but up to people who had been especially selected for this role (in our case it was Seraphima Soloviev). We ourselves could invite only two of our closest friends. Seraphima organized a list of brothers and sisters and when it would be their turn to come. Father Sergei Mechev was the priest of the community. He was the son of the famous elder Father Alexei Mechev, whose spiritual son I became when I was twelve years old. In 1939, Father Sergei lived in Tver under the strict supervision of the NKVD. I visited him often: sometimes he would go unofficially to the Msiri railroad station where many could meet him in the forest and talk to him. Father Sergei was the spiritual father of my wife and myself, and he blessed our marriage.

Now I will return to the liturgy celebrated in our home. Father Alexander celebrated. We called him Hunchback Alexander, for he was not tall, but a little hunchbacked. I do not know his last name, but he had served in a church that had been closed by the authorities. He was living in hiding in different apartments or in Borovsk, where he died of pneumonia during the German occupation. He served in our apartment often. He was small, ever welcoming, smiling and light-giving; he reminded us of Father Alexei Mechev. Everyone who knew him loved him. When I went to him for confession I did not have to force myself to talk, I would tell him everything I had done as if I were talking to myself, and each word he said and each gesture he made expressed love and forgiveness. He was an amazing person.

The liturgy ended and we congratulated each other since all of us had taken Communion. We set the table, the cups and plates were ready, and my wife and I started serving everybody. We knew all the people present, except two. Their names were Kyra and Yuri, so Father Alexander asked them who their spiritual father was. "Our priest is Hieromonk Arseny. He was exiled and now he is in a labor camp."

Father Alexander asked them a few more questions, after which he said, "Oh yes, Hieromonk Arseny. I met him sometime between 1925 and 1927, but I was not yet a priest then. I know him!"

So you understand that I had heard his name only twice, but had not paid any serious attention to it. I did not know then that I would later meet Father Arseny myself.

In 1960, the first cousin of my second wife, Elizaveta, Lyudmila Diligensky (who later became a nun with the name of Seraphima) invited Liza (my wife) to go to Rostov to visit the elder, Hieromonk Arseny: this was the third time I heard his name. They went to Rostov with Kyra Bakhmat. When she got back home, she was very touched as she told me about him, because from 1941 to 1960 we had not had any real spiritual direction. From this time on, Liza visited Father Arseny twice a year, always either with Lyudmilla or Kyra, since I would not let her go alone. As for me, I did not visit Father Arseny. I was working two jobs. I used to get up at six in the morning, work until four-thirty, then rush to my second job and come home only at ten-fifteen, have dinner and go to bed. Liza did not work after we got married; she took care of the house and raised her son, Alexander.

The first time I met Father Arseny was in January 1961. At the time I had been offered a two-room apartment in an unpleasant district. We were living on the Arbat in a communal apartment.[86] Liza could not decide whether we should move or not—she really did not like the new

---

[86]An apartment where each room is occupied by a family. They share the bathroom and the kitchen—a difficult way to live. —Trans.

place's district. We went to see Father Arseny together, she and I; he listened to us and blessed us to move. We met in Kyra and Yuri's apartment, and from that time on nearly always met with Father Arseny at their place.

The second meeting was lengthy. "Tell me about yourself," he said to me and I told him everything in detail. I told him about the death of my first wife, Elena. From 1930 on she had been an invalid with a heart condition. She received a pension and worked a little, typing at home. I loved Lelia. She had not wanted to marry me, but after I had spent a long time convincing her, and after we were blessed by her spiritual father, Father Sergei Mechev, we were married on July 17, 1936. She was afraid that her illness would spoil my life, but that was her mistake.

She was a philologist by education. She could not work but she joined Father Sergei's community in 1924 together with some friends. That is where she found peace after the death of her mother. She received Father Sergei's spiritual direction and warmth from the friendship of other members of the community; they remained her friends up to her death.[87] Elena lived in and for the community. She was a loving person, prayerful and always ready to help others. From 1934 on she was very close friends with Elizaveta Zamiatin, a member of the community. Elizaveta was always present at the liturgies celebrated in our apartment. Three times a week we read vespers, matins and the akathist with our closest friends. I used to come home late and would only catch the end of the service.

I told Father Arseny about Elizaveta's last illness, in 1943 (every year from 1934 on she used to be very ill for three months and would be bedridden with pneumonia). I told him about Elena and Elizaveta's friendship; when my wife knew she was dying, she asked Elizaveta to be my wife. Elena told me, "I am going. You cannot stay alone, you need a spiritually strong person. I know I am dying, do not contradict me; I know. I am asking you to marry Elizaveta. She is strong and she is good-hearted, and she will help you. She is much better than I am in the spiritual sense, and she is more beautiful and more attractive. This is what I'm leaving you with. I also spoke to Liza and asked her to be your wife."

---

[87]Here followed a list of friends. —Trans.

But things were not so easy. Liza refused to be my wife. Since the age of eighteen she had wanted to be a nun, but that is not what I should talk about now. God did unite us in matrimony.

I told Father Arseny my whole life. He never interrupted me, never stopped me; he listened to me while looking at me attentively, and when I finished he said, "Let us pray to God and His Holy Mother as well as to the saints Elizaveta and Zachary, Prince Vladimir and saints Constantine and Helen to thank them for their great mercy to you."

After we had prayed, he spoke words by which he changed the meaning of what I had said. He opened it all up and reevaluated it from the point of view of faith. He put right in front of my eyes everything I had not said about Elena, Liza and myself. He said, "Vladimir, Vladimir! I am amazed at the mercy God has shown you. He sent you two strongly spiritual women, your wife Elena and your wife Elizaveta, who through their faith and their way of life have instilled into you the power of faith, and nourished you through this faith, saving you from all evil. When you were still a twelve-year-old boy, God in His mercy brought you to meet the very great elder Father Alexei Mechev and then his son Father Sergei Mechev (I knew him), and God allowed you to be his spiritual child almost up to the time he was shot. What you have told me about your wife Elena and about Elizaveta Alexandrovna makes me, Priest Arseny, joyous; how I wish that all the sisters of our community were like them. Thank God for all and everything. I have known Elizaveta Alexandrovna for two years now!" He told me much more, and my whole soul united itself with him. In the rare meetings that we had I always found spiritual joy and consolation.

I have read almost all the stories about Father Arseny. I remember that they were written by people who had gone to confession with him or who talked with him and were amazed by his capacity to see into their souls with his spiritual sight. I myself was shaken by the way that the whole story I had told him about myself suddenly appeared superficial and incomplete to me. When he talked to me, Father Arseny used each of his words to remove a layer from my soul (like the peel of an onion!) and show me my mistakes, my errors, my imperfections. When he spoke about Elizaveta, he underlined her high spirituality and faith and, smiling with his nice, warm smile, he pronounced, "In this life she is your spiritual leader and teacher. She is easily wounded. Being so perfect and pure, she takes everything to heart and this leaves deep scars. Take care of her: such people are rare."

Father Arseny had the gift of intuition, a gift which sometimes surprised and even scared some of the people who came to him. He was taller than average and had a handsome, elongated oval face, a little beard and thick hair which probably had been dark, but then was graying. With large brown eyes in an ever-welcoming face, he immediately set people at ease. On the left side of his face, starting almost at his eye, two scars stretched down his face to hid under his beard; on the right side of his forehead there was a whitish mark that ran to his temple and beyond his hairline. The memoirs of Father Arseny and of his spiritual children are full of the physical burdens and suffering he had to bear in camp, and yet he never hunched over. His back was straight and he never complained, even when he was very ill. He was always thanking God and the Mother of God for everything and constantly praying the Jesus prayer, "Lord Jesus Christ, Son of God, be merciful to me, a sinner!" He most especially venerated Saint Sergius of Radonezh, Saint Seraphim of Sarov, Saint Panteleimon the healer, Saint Mary of Egypt, Saint John the Theologian, the apostle of love and Saint Nicholas the Wonderworker.

In 1967 Father Arseny had a long talk with Liza, Kyra, Yuri, Lyuda and me. He asked us to tell him about Father Sergei Mechev's community in detail, about the elder Father Alexei Mechev and, for some reason unknown to me, wanted us to tell him about the priests we had met during our life. There were many of them; sometimes Father Arseny would say, "I know him, I met him Optino" or "he was the spiritual son of the elder Nektary" or " he died in camp" or "he was shot." He said about one of them, "He erred; he joined the Living Church." He was sad as he was listening to us: many of the names reminded him of people who had left this world long ago, people he had known or who had been his friends, though some of the names we mentioned were unknown to him. "Write down for me the names of the priests, those who had been shot, those who had died in labor camps on in exile, those who had died and I will pray for them," he said. We wrote down the names of the priests and deacons we had mentioned to him and added many more.

In 1971 I saw a notebook of memoirs about Father Arseny in the hands of some friends; I was struck by their relevance, their frankness and their spirituality in showing the lives of people in the difficult times we had between 1920 and 1960. I began to gather together the memoirs of his spiritual children. Some people gave them to me willingly; others I had to beg from; still others refused to give them to me. In 1975, Father Arseny died and many of his children began to write more and more about him. I had to collect these new writings.

In 1993 Saint Tikhon's Orthodox Theological Institute and the Brotherhood of the All-Merciful Savior "home-published" the book *Father Arseny.* The faithful loved it and the book sold out immediately. But I knew that many of Father Arseny's spiritual children had written many memoirs that weren't part of that book. Twenty years had passed since Father Arseny died. Our friends Kyra, Yuri, Natalia Petrovna, Julia, Lyuda had died (in 1995 they would have been ninety-two or ninety-three years old), but their children or grandchildren gave over their notes unwillingly or not at all. Why? It was hard to understand. Still, with the blessing of Father Vladimir Vorobiev we were able to add twelve more stories for the third edition (1998) and for the fourth edition sixteen more that had been obtained with great difficulty.

I am now over ninety years old. What Father Arseny said lives within me and reminds me of the importance of deep faith in God, constant prayer and faithfulness to the truth that is expressed in the words of the Gospel, "Love your neighbor as yourself."

Vladimir Vladimirovich Bykov